INTELLECTUAL ORIGINS
OF
AMERICAN RADICALISM

NEW EDITION

Now an established classic, *Intellectual Origins of American Radicalism* was the first book to explore this alternative current of American political thought. Stemming back to the seventeenth-century English Revolution, many questioned private property, the sovereignty of the nation-state, and slavery, and affirmed the common man's ability to govern. By the time of the American Revolution, Thomas Paine was the great exemplar of the alternative intellectual tradition. In the nineteenth century, the antislavery movement took hold of Thomas Paine's ideas and fashioned them into an ideology that ultimately justified civil war.

This updated edition contains a new preface by the author, which describes the inquiries that he undertook in his books of the 1960s and their conclusions. David Waldstreicher has contributed a new historiographical foreword that discusses the book's lasting importance and contrasts its ideas with the work of Bernard Bailyn and Gordon Wood.

Staughton Lynd received his BA from Harvard College and his MA and PhD from Columbia University. He taught at Spelman College and at Yale University. He is the author, editor, or co-editor of more than a dozen books and has published articles in journals including the *Journal of American History*, the *William and Mary Quarterly*, and the *Political Science Quarterly*.

David Waldstreicher is a professor of history at Temple University.

STAUGHTON LYND

INTELLECTUAL ORIGINS OF AMERICAN RADICALISM

NEW EDITION

CAMBRIDGE
UNIVERSITY PRESS

CAMBRIDGE
UNIVERSITY PRESS

32 Avenue of the Americas, New York NY 10013-2473, USA

Cambridge University Press is part of the University of Cambridge.

It furthers the University's mission by disseminating knowledge in the pursuit of education, learning and research at the highest international levels of excellence.

www.cambridge.org
Information on this title: www.cambridge.org/9780521134811

© Staughton Lynd 1968, 2009

First published by Pantheon Books 1968
New edition published by Cambridge University Press 2009

A catalogue record for this publication is available from the British Library

Library of Congress Cataloguing in Publication data

Lynd, Staughton.
Intellectual origins of American radicalism / Staughton Lynd – New ed.
p.   cm.
Includes bibliographical references and index.
ISBN 978-0-521-11929-0 (hardback) – ISBN 978-0-521-13481-1 (pbk.)
1. United States – Politics and government.   2. Radicalism – United States.   I. Title.
E183.L98   2009
320.530973–dc22   2009021694

ISBN 978-0-521-11929-0 Hardback
ISBN 978-0-521-13481-1 Paperback

For by naturall birth, all men are equally and alike borne to like propriety, liberty and freedome, and as we are delivered of God by the hand of nature into this world, every one with a naturall, innate, freedome and propriety (as it were writ in the table of every mans heart, never to be obliterated) even so are we to live, every one equally and alike to enjoy his Birthright and priviledge; even all whereof God by nature hath made him free.

> RICHARD OVERTON, *An Arrow Against All Tyrants and Tyranny, Shot from the Prison of New-Gate into the Prerogative Bowels of the Arbitrary House of Lords* (London, 1646)

There is a higher law than the law of government. That's the law of conscience.

> STOKELY CARMICHAEL, UPI dispatch October 28, 1966

Political freedom . . . is an elemental condition of the individual will.

> CARL OGLESBY, *Containment and Change* (New York, 1967)

CONTENTS

AFTER FORTY YEARS: A NEW PREFACE

I

I decided to study the period of the American Revolution in 1959. It seemed to me that if there was anything good in the past of the United States on which a hopeful and idealistic future could be built, it might be found in the period that produced the Declaration of Independence.

To be sure, the failings of the great white men who stood astride the events of the American Revolution were manifest. When I was a boy, the five-cent piece in the United States was the "Indian head" nickel. Anthropologist Gregory Bateson, a friend of the family, remarked that the history of the United States could be seen in this coin. On one side of the nickel was the head of a Native American and the word "Liberty." On the other side was the image of a bison and the words "E pluribus unum," or as Bateson translated them: "There used to be a lot of us and now there's only one."

Later, when I was in high school, my history teacher took me to
Monticello. What stayed in memory from that visit was the device
Jefferson used to make copies of his letters. Recently I returned
to Monticello with a ten-year-old grandson. This time I saw what
seemed like an oversized wooden deck, which turned out to be
the roof over a passageway. There slaves cooked Mr. Jefferson's
meals and carried them to a spot directly underneath the dining
room, whence they could ascend on a dumbwaiter and appear on
a "lazy Susan," both designed by the master. It struck me that in
this way the Sage of Monticello could entertain guests without the
troubling appearance of a black face.

And yet, what alternative do we have to the American Revolution as the archetype of our hopes and dreams? Surely it is
significant that when United States soldiers in Vietnam and Iraq
searched for a way that they could dissent profoundly and yet con-
tinue to think of themselves as patriotic Americans, they returned
in imagination to the citizen-soldiers of the American Revolution.
Remembering the words of Thomas Paine's first *Crisis* pamphlet
about sunshine patriots and summer soldiers, they called themselves "winter soldiers."[1]

II

I began my study of the American Revolution by setting out to
prove or disprove what other historians—especially Carl Becker
and Charles Beard—had to say about the political choices made
by poor and working people during the American Revolution. I
studied farm tenants in Dutchess County, New York, and artisans
in New York City.

What I learned about tenants was that in southern Dutchess
County and neighboring Westchester County tenant farmers supported the Revolution. I held in my hands the petitions that they
wrote to the Revolutionary New York legislature in which they
asked for confiscation of Loyalist estates.

Thus far, Becker's idea that the Revolution was a struggle over
who should rule at home, as well as a struggle for home rule,
worked well. While a coalition of classes struggled for independence, little people at the bottom demanded more: economic

independence in the form of freehold ownership of the land that they tilled.

But in northern Dutchess County the tenant farmers were Loyalists. They made their way out into the Hudson River, where the Continental Congress had strung nets to obstruct the junction of British forces from New York City and Albany, stole the lead used to weight the nets, and made bullets out of it. In 1777 they staged a tenant uprising on Livingston Manor in support of the King.

So what can explain this ideological diversity? Why were the tenants who rented from Beverly Robinson in southern Dutchess County ardent patriots, whereas the tenants on the land of Robert R. Livingston only a few miles away became Tories?

There is a simple answer, I suggest. It all depended on the politics of your landlord. If you rented from a Tory like Robinson, who sheltered Benedict Arnold when the latter fled across the Hudson, you supported the Revolution in the hope that if Robinson and his friends were defeated, you might get fee-simple ownership of your farm.

But if you rented from Livingston, an ardent Whig, your calculus was just the opposite. You sought victory for the King of England because if he won, Livingston might be deprived of his lands, and in this way you too might realize the American dream and become the owner of the land that you cultivated.

So it was not ideology that determined the political choices of Hudson Valley tenant farmers. It was economic interest.

While the politics of Hudson Valley tenants may be little known, it is otherwise with city artisans. These are the Sons of Liberty. These are the folks who erected liberty poles, enforced nonimportation agreements, dumped tea into Boston Harbor, and carried the news that the British were coming. These were Paul Revere and friends in Boston, who met at the Green Dragon tavern, and comparable groups in New York City, Philadelphia, and Charleston. Carl Becker said they were the heart and soul of both the struggle for home rule and the struggle over who should rule at home. And he was right.

There is only one problem. As Charles Beard noted in passing but did not explain, these same artisans enthusiastically supported

the Federalists' constitution in 1787. They did so not only at the
ballot box, but in elaborate parades in every major seacoast city.

So how did the artisan radicals of 1763–1776 become Hamilto-
nians in 1787? And what does this ideological transformation tell
us about the relationship of economic interest and ideology?

Again, there is a simple answer. What preoccupied these folks
before the Revolution was the danger that imported British manufactured goods might destroy their livelihoods. Hence they supported all things anti-British, especially nonimportation agreements.[2]

And what preoccupied them in the mid-1780s as British manufactures once again began to pour into American seaports
was . . . exactly the same thing. Hence they supported the project
of a strong national government that could impose an effective
tariff on imported manufactured goods.[3]

Artisans were altogether consistent. There only appears to have
been an inconsistency because we have supposed their politics to
be driven not by economic interest, but by ideology.

As I have reflected on these findings over the years, it seems
to me that historians of "the inarticulate" sometimes seek to discover among the poor the internally coherent discourse one might
expect at an Ivy League sherry party. I have not found such coher-
ence, either as a historian or as a lawyer for poor and working-class
clients in Youngstown, Ohio, for more than thirty years. When it
appeared that the automobile assembly plant in nearby Lords-
town, Ohio, might close, workers encouraged their children to
write postcards to General Motors' headquarters in Detroit, pleading with the powers-that-be to keep the plant open. But when
steel mills closed in Youngstown and Pittsburgh, workers seriously considered using the power of eminent domain to permit
worker-community–owned steel companies to acquire the mills
by compulsion.[4]

My tentative answer to questions about the political choices
of working people is, accordingly, as follows. Poor and working
people, unendingly pressed by economic necessity, will ordinarily
focus on personal, short-run, material gain: owning the land that
one tills, protecting the market for the goods produced in one's
shop. Extensive experience with other kinds of workers, common

oppression (as in a prison or in war), or a dramatic disruption of shared expectations (such as a plant closing), may give rise to a broader class point of view. But it will always be more difficult for lower-class protagonists to rise above the interests of the moment than it is for upper-class historical actors, who, then and now, have more money, more leisure, and a smaller number of persons to organize into a cohesive force, and who instinctively gravitate to the preservation of the system as a whole.

This conclusion should not be understood to devalue the aspirations of poor and working-class persons, then or now. It does not denigrate the lives of farm tenants to recognize that they wished to own the farms on which they toiled. Nor should urban laborers be faulted for overriding concern with economic survival.[5]

III

How then might we describe what the period of the American Revolution offers to latter-day efforts to create a more just society? This was the question I sought to answer in *Intellectual Origins of American Radicalism*. My answer, in a nutshell, is: certain ideas, presented to the world by particular persons who were marginal dissenters in their own time just as many of us are today.

Much as the same worker may view the world differently now than he did only a few weeks ago, so in any group, such as "tenants" or "artisans" or (more recently) "steelworkers," there are likely to be individuals whose outlook is quite different from that typical of the group as a whole. The great artisan radical Thomas Paine was also to some extent atypical and should not be understood merely as a spokesman for a group. Such atypical figures may be like mutations, prefiguring species changes still in the making.

In *Class Conflict, Slavery, and the United States Constitution*, published a year before *Intellectual Origins*, I suggested that the "artisan radicalism" of Thomas Paine might be a source for an American radical tradition distinct from the more familiar vision of Thomas Jefferson. I wrote that Paine's artisan radicalism affirmed that "strong central government accessible to the people was more democratic than decentralized rule by gentlemen; that common men, whether or not formally educated, had the capacity to govern; that slavery must stop."[6]

Some academic commentary has blurred the uniqueness of Paine's ideas and of the radical intellectual tradition that he originated. Edmund Morgan, for example, concedes that the best and brightest men who led the American independence movement "accepted the continuance of slavery," but argues that Paine, who harshly condemned slavery throughout his adult life, "was one of them."[7]

Soon after arriving in Philadelphia in 1774, Paine denounced slavery in two essays. These essays prefigured the moral urgency of nineteenth-century abolitionism, very much in contrast to the "deistic coolness of temper" of the Founding Fathers.[8]

In "African Slavery in America" the man later reviled as an atheist took his stand on "the time of reformation" and "gospel light":

> All distinctions of nations, and privileges of one above others, are ceased; Christians are taught to **account all men their neighbors; and love their neighbors as themselves; and do to all men as they would be done by; to do good to all men; and man-stealing is ranked with enormous crimes**. Is the barbarous enslaving our inoffensive neighbors, and treating them like wild beasts subdued by force, reconcilable with all these **divine precepts**? Is this doing to them as we would desire they should do to us? If they could carry off and enslave some thousands of us, would we think it just?—One would almost wish they could for once; it might convince more than reason, or the Bible.[9]

In the second essay, "A Serious Thought," Paine expressed the hope that the first legislative act of the colonies when they became independent of Great Britain would "put a stop to the importation of Negroes for sale, soften the hard fate of those already here, and in time procure their freedom."[10]

Paine tried to put into practice what he advocated. On March 1, 1780, the Revolutionary legislature of Pennsylvania passed the first law in the new United States for the emancipation of African American slaves. Paine was Clerk of the Assembly when the measure was introduced. It has been suggested that he wrote its preamble[11] or even "draft[ed] the legislation."[12] The preamble stated in part:

> we conceive that it is our duty, and we rejoice that it is in our power, to extend a portion of that freedom to others, which has been extended to us. . . .

Continuing, the preamble declared: "Weaned, by a long course of experience, from those narrow prejudices and partialities we had imbibed, we find our hearts enlarged with kindness and benevolence toward men of all conditions and nations." The condition of Negro and mulatto slaves, it concluded,

> not only deprived them of the common blessings that they were by nature entitled to, but has cast them into the deepest afflictions, by an unnatural separation and sale of husband and wife from each other and from their children, an injury, the greatness of which can only be conceived by supposing that we were in the same unhappy case.[13]

In the late 1780s Paine attended meetings of the Pennsylvania Society for Promoting the Abolition of Slavery and the Relief of Free Negroes Unlawfully Held in Bondage.[14] Paine's anti-slavery activities in the 1780s coincided with the work of his British contemporaries Granville Sharp and Thomas Clarkson, who founded the British antislavery movement in the same month (May 1787) that the Constitutional Convention assembled in Philadelphia.[15] Together these men refute the argument that it is "ahistorical" and anachronistic to insist that the Founding Fathers should have done more to abolish slavery at the Constitutional Convention in 1787.

During several tumultuous years in revolutionary France, Paine's closest associates "[a]ll were critics of slavery": one of them, J. P. Brissot de Warville, was "a leading figure in the French Society des Amis des Noirs."[16] Paine consistently expressed solidarity with the successful slave insurrection in Haiti. He wrote to William Short in 1791 that the Haitian revolution was "the natural consequence of Slavery," and to Jefferson in 1805: "All that Domingo wants of France, is, that France agree to let her alone, and withdraw her forces."[17]

Four years before his lonely death, Paine wrote a long letter to Jefferson in which he discussed the newly acquired Louisiana Purchase, believing (correctly) that whether it ultimately became slave or free would determine the future of the United States. Therein:

1. Paine advocated that Louisiana should be settled not by plantation owners with their slaves, but by indentured servants from Germany. He had gone so far as to discuss with a merchant in

Hamburg, Germany, the cost of shipping such laborers to the United States. Anticipating the Homestead Act and the Reconstruction demand for "forty acres and a mule," Paine urged that just as an indentured servant at the end of his time received some means of livelihood from his master, so Congress should give each of these German indentured servants twenty acres of land.

2. Referring to the city of Liverpool as the center of the slave trade in Great Britain, Paine wrote: "Had I the command of the elements I would blast Liverpool with fire and brimstone. It is the Sodom and Gomorrah of brutality."

3. Paine recalled that when they were together in France, Jefferson had spoken of a plan to "allot to each Negro family a quantity of land for which they were to pay to the owner a certain quantity of produce" (in other words, sharecropping). Paine urged that free Negroes be provided for in this way in Louisiana. Congress should pay their passage to New Orleans; they should hire themselves out for a year or two to learn the business; thereafter they should be placed on tracts of land.

4. Finally, as in previous correspondence with Jefferson, Paine urged mediation between the French Emperor and the Emperor of the new African American state Haiti.[18]

Perhaps Paine's lifelong condemnation of slavery helps to explain why, when he died, certain free African Americans are said to have been among the handful of mourners.[19]

Eric Foner, in his study of Paine's life and thought, explored other aspects of my suggestion that Paine's "artisan radicalism" differed from the "agrarian radicalism" of Thomas Jefferson. He found the difference between Jefferson and Paine primarily in their "differing conceptions of the nation's future." Foner agrees with me that Jefferson was deeply pessimistic about the long-run future, believing that when the West had been settled "America would come to resemble Europe, with its crowded cities, landless lower classes, social conflict and governmental corruption." Paine was more optimistic, even naive, about the predictable impact of commerce on democratic self-government.[20]

When I revisited Paine in the first edition of this book, I argued that the American radical tradition originating with Paine contemplated the use of centralized *means* to achieve the *goal* of a decentralized good society.[21] It now appears to me that Paine had an experimental attitude about what kinds of governmental institutions could best address the needs of poor and working people. The very years in which Paine first experienced America were the years in which the extra-legal committees of the American Revolution reached fullest expression. He wrote about these committees:

> For upward of two years from the commencement of the American War, and to a longer period in several of the American states, there were no established forms of government. The old governments had been abolished, and the country was too much occupied in defense, to employ its attention in establishing new governments; yet during this interval, order and harmony were preserved as inviolate as in any country in Europe.[22]

Hannah Arendt offers similar reflections on committees like those that Paine celebrated. She compares the "sections" of the French Revolution, the Paris Commune of 1871, the Russian soviets in 1905 and 1917, the workers' and soldiers' councils of post–World War I Germany, and the council system that sprang into existence in Hungary in 1956. What happened in each case, Arendt writes, was "the amazing formation of a new power structure which owed its existence to nothing but the organizational impulses of the people themselves."[23]

During the course of the Revolutionary War, however, Paine became disillusioned with the efforts of popular committees to regulate prices. He entered into an unpublicized agreement with Philadelphia financier Robert Morris, New York aristocrat Robert R. Livingston, and George Washington, who paid Paine to write public letters and pamphlets in support of a stronger national government.[24]

Later still, in his *Rights of Man*, Paine put forward what Eric Foner terms a "new vision . . . of the republican state as an agent of social welfare."[25] Yet the actual administration of the fund (drawn from "surplus taxes") to assist every poor family in the education of its children was to be in the hands of "the ministers of every parish."[26]

In his last major writing, *Agrarian Justice*, Paine held up the decentralized society of North American Indians as a model for what "the state of society ought to be."[27] He proposed that the "primary assemblies" of every "canton" (he was writing for revolutionary France) elect commissioners who would administer an inheritance tax intended to compensate each member of society for that member's original right to a portion of the value of the land once held by society in common. But a national bank— a principal object of Paine's American writings on behalf of a stronger national government—also had a role to play in Paine's European Utopia. Each inheritor would give bond to the canton commissioners to pay one-tenth of the value of his inheritance into the local compensation fund within the space of one year or sooner. One half of the inheritance was to serve as security for payment of the bond. The bonds themselves would be held by a national bank, which would issue bank notes, to be used by the canton commissioners to pay the appropriate sums in compensation.[28]

I look back on Paine's proposals now with the benefit of eighteen years' experience in one of the few enduring institutions created by the 1960s, National Legal Services:

> It is the conviction, or alleged conviction, of many Americans that anything funded by the government must be centralized, bureaucratic, and wasteful.... Legal Services workers are in an opportune position to rebut this nonsense. We know, from experience, that money can be appropriated by Congress, allocated to offices in the field on the basis of objective criteria, administered in communities by more-or-less democratic boards of directors, monitored to assure compliance with national statutes and regulations, and spent to provide a needed service free of charge.[29]

The intertwining of local and national administration in National Legal Services is effective. And it works in a fashion remarkably similar to what Thomas Paine proposed in *The Rights of Man* and *Agrarian Justice*.

Paine's radical views about society and government cannot be separated from his marginal position in Revolutionary high society. A great social gulf separated Paine from the well-to-do leaders of the Revolution. Paine was imprisoned and very nearly executed in revolutionary France after he passionately opposed the execution of the King. Gouverneur Morris, the United

States ambassador to France at the time, considered Paine "a mere adventurer . . . without fortune, without family or connexions, ignorant even of grammar" and did nothing to obtain his release.[30]

IV

One final aspect of Paine's thought deserves respectful attention. Paine, and after him, Garrison, Frederick Douglass, Albert Parsons, and Eugene Debs, transcended any form of nationalism with the words "My country is the world."[31] This was and is an astonishingly radical idea. It is the thesis that dissenters in the United States cannot be content with *any* interpretation of the American experience confined within national boundaries. So long as we limit ourselves to that which has occurred within the framework of a single nation, we will always arrive at a place that is parochial and chauvinistic. A merely American set of values will always be Athenian in the sense that whatever equality it extends to those who are considered "citizens," even if that designation is extended to, say, women, people of color, and Native Americans, there will always be those not included, whom the Greeks called "barbarians." A society that affirms anything less than the belief that every human being on the face of the earth is equally entitled to the good things that the earth provides will in the end find some group of enemy combatants to hate.

I conclude that the American Revolution most deserving to be remembered is not a tradition associated with any of the better-known Founding Fathers. Rather, what is most enduring from this period is the set of ideas promulgated by Paine, and by other self-taught workingmen in the succeeding 125 years.

In recent judgments, the Supreme Court of the United States offered impressive support for the concept that there are universal human rights, the existence of which arises not from the laws of any nation but from human nature itself. In their decisions about the rights of prisoners at the Guantánamo detention facility, the justices turned historian and cited such precedents as the case in which Lord Mansfield set free an African slave purchased in Virginia, bound for Jamaica but temporarily detained on a ship docked in England.[32] In another decision about a Mexican doctor kidnapped by drug enforcement agents, the Court continued to probe the "ambient law" of the Revolutionary era, concluding that courts of that period were open to claims based on "the law of nations" and that a court today should likewise entertain a claim that rests "on a norm of international character accepted by the civilized world."[33]

These decisions affirm the tradition that "my country is the world." The most riveting expressions of that tradition come from Henry David Thoreau. In Thoreau's essay on "Civil Disobedience," he famously observed that "the fugitive slave, and the Mexican prisoner on parole, and the Indian come to plead the wrongs of his race" should find good citizens in "the only house in a slave State in which a free man can abide with honor," namely, prison.[34] Less well-known is another comment that just as he who would save his life must be prepared to lose it, so it is more important for the American people to abolish slavery and to give up war on Mexico than that the United States should survive as a nation.

> If I have unjustly wrested a plank from a drowning man, I must restore it to him though I drown myself. This, according to Paley [a writer on moral questions], would be inconvenient. But he that would save his life, in such a case, shall lose it. This people must cease to hold slaves, and to make war on Mexico, though it cost them their existence as a people.[35]

In "Slavery in Massachusetts," written after the abduction of a fugitive slave from Boston, Thoreau called on his countrymen to be "men first, and Americans only at a late and convenient hour."[36]

Here is an American revolutionary tradition on which scholars, activists, and even courts of law can take a stand together.

NOTES

1. Richard Moser, *The New Winter Soldiers: GI and Veteran Dissent during the Vietnam Era* (New Brunswick: Rutgers University Press, 1996). The words with which Paine began the pamphlet were: "These are the times that try men's souls. The summer soldier and the sunshine patriot will, in this crisis, shrink from the service of their country; but he that stands it **now**, deserves the love and thanks of man and woman." *The Complete Writings of Thomas Paine*, ed. Philip S. Foner (New York: The Citadel Press, 1945), v. 1, p. 50. Testifying before the Senate Committee

on Foreign Relations, April 22, 1971, John Kerry began by summarizing an occasion "several months ago in Detroit [when] over 150 honorably discharged and many very highly decorated veterans testified to war crimes committed in Southeast Asia, not isolated incidents but crimes committed on a day-to-day basis with the full awareness of officers at all levels of command." Kerry explained to the Committee: "We call this investigation the 'Winter Soldier Investigation.' The term 'Winter Soldier' is a play on words of Thomas Paine in 1776 when he spoke of the sunshine patriot and summertime soldiers who deserted . . . because the going was rough." "Legislative Proposals Relating to the War in Southeast Asia," http://www.truthout.org/article/transcript-john-kerrys-1971-senate-testimony, last visited Mar. 20, 2009.

2. See on this point Gordon S. Wood, review of T. H. Breen, *The Marketplace of Revolution: How Consumer Politics Shaped American Independence*, in *The New York Review of Books*, June 10, 2004, p. 29:

> The one major middling group that actively participated in the boycott movements did so not as consumers but as producers. Artisans and mechanics who wanted to manufacture some of the goods that Americans were importing naturally had a vested interest in stopping imports of British goods. . . . [W]hat evidence we have suggests that artisans and mechanics were major participants both in the anti-British "Sons of Liberty" organizations and in the enforcement of the boycotts.
>
> . . . By 1768 colonial manufacturers were supplying Pennsylvania with eight thousand pairs of shoes a year. . . . In 1767 the town of Haverhill, Massachusetts, with fewer than three hundred residents, had forty-four workshops and nineteen mills. By the 1760s the growing number of immigrants and ex-soldiers who were becoming mechanics and craftsmen in Philadelphia alarmed British authorities worried about American manufacturing competition.

3. I wrote in *Class Conflict, Slavery, and the United States Constitution*, new edition (New York: Cambridge University Press, 2009), p. 125: "Imported manufactures brought the menace of British economic power directly home to the New York City artisans. . . . [A]fter, as before, the Revolution, the encouragement of native manufactures seemed a part of the struggle for independence."

This would appear to be the conclusion of every student of artisan politics in the 1780s. In Philadelphia, for example, at the end of the Revolutionary War "Great Britain flooded American markets with manufactured goods." Billy G. Smith, *The "Lower Sort": Philadelphia's Laboring People, 1750–1800* (Ithaca: Cornell University Press, 1990), p. 75. The state tariff enacted by the Pennsylvania legislature in the mid-1780s "did not solve the problem of English competition for Philadelphia's laboring classes. By 1787 they would follow their collective interests and support the federal Constitution, which promised full and effective tariffs on a national level." Ronald Schultz, *The Republic of Labor: Philadelphia Artisans and the Politics of Class, 1720–1830* (New York: Oxford University Press, 1993),

p. 99. "From the mechanics' point of view, everything hung on the single question of a tariff. . . . Ratification of the 1787 Constitution was considered by mechanics to be a logical and satisfying culmination of the Revolutionary movement, not a thermidorian reaction." Charles S. Olton, *Artisans for Independence: Philadelphia Mechanics and the American Revolution* (Syracuse: Syracuse University Press, 1975), pp. 101, 117–18.

4. Lynd, "The Genesis of the Idea of a Community Right to Industrial Property in Youngstown and Pittsburgh, 1977–1987," *Journal of American History*, v. 74, no. 3 (Dec. 1987), pp. 926–58.

5. See James C. Scott, *Weapons of the Weak: Everyday Forms of Peasant Resistance* (New Haven: Yale University Press, 1985), pp. 295–96: "[T]o require of lower-class resistance that it somehow be 'principled' or 'selfless' is not only utopian and a slander on the moral status of fundamental material needs; it is, more fundamentally, a misconstruction of the basis of class struggle. . . . 'Bread-and-butter' issues are the essence of lower-class politics and resistance."

6. Lynd, *Class Conflict*, p. 267.

7. Edmund S. Morgan, "The Other Founders," *The New York Review of Books*, Sept. 22, 2005, p. 43, and "History from Below," *The New York Review of Books*, Dec. 1, 2005, p. 69.

8. Lynd, *Class Conflict*, p. 183.

9. *Complete Writings*, ed. Philip Foner, v. 2, p. 17 (emphasis in original).

10. *Ibid.*, p. 20.

11. *Complete Writings*, ed. Philip Foner, v. 1, p. xix.

12. Isaac Kramnick, *Republicanism and Bourgeois Radicalism: Political Ideology in Late Eighteenth Century England and America* (Ithaca: Cornell University Press, 1990), p. 139.

13. *Complete Writings*, ed. Philip Foner, v. 2, pp. 21–22.

14. James V. Lynch, "The Limits of Revolutionary Radicalism: Tom Paine and Slavery," *Pennsylvania Magazine of History and Biography*, v. 123 (July 1999), pp. 181–82.

15. See Adam Hochschild, *Bury the Chains: Prophets and Rebels in the Fight to Free an Empire's Slaves* (Boston: Houghton Mifflin, 2005), pp. 95–96, 106–8.

16. Eric Foner, *Tom Paine and Revolutionary America*, updated and with a new preface (New York: Oxford University Press, 2005), pp. 235–36.

17. *Complete Writings*, ed. Philip Foner, v. 2, pp. 1321, 1453–55.

18. Paine to Jefferson, Jan. 25, 1805, *Complete Writings*, ed. Philip Foner, v. 2, pp. 1456–64.

19. Two Negroes were reported to be among the six persons who accompanied Paine's body from Madame Bonneville's home in Greenwich, near New York City, the twenty-two miles to his farm in New Rochelle for burial. London *Packet*, Aug. 7, 1809, quoted in Moncure Conway, *The Life of Thomas Paine*, v. II (New York: G.P. Putnam's Sons, 1893), p. 417; Eric Foner, *Tom Paine*, p. 261.

20. Eric Foner, *Tom Paine*, pp. 100–6.

21. See pp. 162, 165, 170.

22. "The Rights of Man, Part II," in *Complete Writings*, ed. Philip Foner, v. 1, p. 358.
23. Hannah Arendt, *On Revolution* (New York: Viking Press, 1963), p. 260 and chapter 6.
24. Eric Foner, *Tom Paine*, p. 189.
25. *Ibid.*, p. 217.
26. "Rights of Man, Part II," in *Complete Writings*, ed. Philip Foner, v. 1, p. 425.
27. "Agrarian Justice," in *Complete Writings*, ed. Philip Foner, v. 1, p. 610.
28. *Ibid.*, pp. 622–23.
29. "Toward a Program for Publicly-Financed Jobs," in Lynd, *Living Inside Our Hope: A Steadfast Radical's Thoughts on Rebuilding the Movement* (Ithaca: Cornell University Press, 1997), pp. 137–38.
30. *Complete Writings*, ed. Philip Foner, p. xxxv; Eric Foner, *Tom Paine*, pp. 85, 244.
31. "Rights of Man, Part II," in *Complete Writings*, ed. Philip Foner, v. 1, p. 414 ("my country is the world, and my religion is to do good"); for Garrison and Debs, see pp. 9 (Debs) and 131–38 (Garrison). For additional instances of the same working-class rhetorical tradition, see, for Frederick Douglass in the 1840s, Simon Schama, *Rough Crossings: Britain, the Slaves and the American Revolution* (New York: HarperCollins Publishers, 2006), pp. 416–18; and, for Albert Parsons, speaking to his jury before being sentenced to death in 1886, James Green, *Death in the Haymarket: A Story of Chicago, the First Labor Movement and the Bombing That Divided Gilded Age America* (New York: Pantheon Books, 2006), p. 237 ("Opening his arms wide, he declared: 'The world is my country, all mankind my countrymen'").
32. *Somersett v. Stewart*, 20 How. St. Tr. 1, 79–82 (K.B. 1772), cited in *Rasul, et al. v. Bush, et al.*, 542 U.S. 466, 481 n.11 (2004), and again—this time in the text, not in a footnote—in *Boumediene, et al. v. Bush, et al.*, 128 S.Ct. 2229, 2248 (2008) ("a petitioner's status as an alien was not a categorical bar to habeas corpus relief").
33. *Sosa v. Alvarez-Machain, et al.*, 542 U.S. 692, 714–25 (2004).
34. Henry David Thoreau, "Civil Disobedience," in *Nonviolence in America: A Documentary History*, ed. Staughton Lynd and Alice Lynd (revised edition; Maryknoll, N.Y.: Orbis Books, 1995), p. 29.
35. *Id.*, p. 25.
36. Henry David Thoreau, "Slavery in Massachusetts," in *Anti-Slavery and Reform Papers* (Montreal: Harvest House, 1963), p. 35.

PREFACE TO THE FIRST EDITION

No one could be more aware than I that the following pages present an exploratory sketch rather than a definitive analysis. But as C. Wright Mills once said in a similar connection, I had a choice between conclusively demonstrating something trivial (such as who influenced whom in the genesis of the concept that the earth belongs to the living generation) or being provocative about a matter of importance—whether, and if so in what sense, one can speak of an American radicalism before the Civil War— and, naturally, I chose the latter.

Any critic of the American present must have profoundly mixed feelings about our country's past. On the one hand, he will feel shame and distrust toward Founding Fathers who tolerated slavery, exterminated Indians, and blandly assumed that a good society must be based on private property. On the other hand, he is likely to find himself articulating his own demands in the Revolutionary language of inalienable rights, a natural higher law, and the right to revolution.

The tradition I have attempted to describe made the following affirmations: that the proper foundation for government is a universal law of right and wrong self-evident to the intuitive common sense of every man; that freedom is a power of personal self-direction which no man can delegate to another; that the purpose of society is not the protection of property but fulfillment of the needs of living human beings; that good citizens have the right and duty, not only to overthrow incurably oppressive governments, but before that point is reached to break particular oppressive laws; and that we owe our ultimate allegiance, not to this or that nation, but to the whole family of man.

This tradition is both English and American. One of my principal conclusions is that its theoretical axioms were first clearly articulated by a group of English radicals in the quarter-century preceding the Declaration of Independence. The reader may find the first two chapters, dealing with these axioms, hard going. I can only plead that the Declaration itself emerged in part from the polemics of Price and Priestley, Sharp, Cartwright, and Paine; and further, that as radical abolitionists used the Declaration to justify nonvoting, tax refusal, and other extreme tactics, they repeatedly drew directly on the same English theorists. Radical American "praxis" (the word Marx used to describe practical-critical activity) derived from radical English theory.

This Anglo-American tradition was linked, in turn, both to Rousseau, who influenced America by way of England, and to Marx, whose concepts of alienation and fetishism can be paralleled in the pages of *Walden*. David Herreshoff writes in his *American Disciples of Marx* that "the socialist and individualist movements of the nineteenth century had common intellectual origins." I agree; and this book seeks to explore certain intellectual themes which Marxism and native American radicalism share.

Hopefully it will also be clear that there are a number of things worth doing which the present study does *not* attempt. Ideas do not exist *in vacuo*; and it goes without saying that impinging social pressures in England were connected with Price's clarification of the theory of ethics and Priestley's of political philosophy. Those connections have begun to be assessed by scholars such as George Rudé and E. P. Thompson. But they did not seem essential to the argument here, for which it is enough to say that, by whatever processes, a certain complex of ideas appeared in England which became available to Americans as an intellectual resource.

Nor have I felt obligated to demonstrate in detail the impact of the ideas of English radicals on their American readers. Every student of the ideas of the American Revolution has recognized that impact (see pages 25–26). The phenomenon of Thomas Paine should be demonstration enough that the transmission of English radical ideas to the American resistance movement is no mere scholar's invention.

But let me put the baldest face on my intention. In one sense the concern of the following chapters is ahistorical. I am less interested in eighteenth-century radicalism than in twentieth-century radicalism. Accordingly, the process of historical causation—how certain ideas came into being, what influence they subsequently had—matters less to me than the fact that those ideas existed. I want to show, simply, that we are not the first to have found an inherited deterministic radicalism inhibiting, nor is ours the first attempt to make an opportunity of that dilemma. The characteristic concepts of the existential radicalism of today have a long and honorable history. Acquaintance with that history may help in sharpening intellectual tools for the work of tomorrow.

As to acknowledgments, Kenneth Rosenthal not only checked and rechecked footnotes and quotations, but he did significant independent research on the themes of the book. Jim Bond performed similar services at a later stage. I am deeply grateful.

S. L. 1968

FOREWORD TO THE NEW EDITION

DAVID WALDSTREICHER

For the generation that came of age intellectually during the 1970s and 1980s, this book was one you could find in any good used bookstore because it had been widely read. I acquired my tattered Vintage paperback while trolling for cheap course books during my freshman or sophomore year in college. I devoured it and it has ever since had a place of honor on my shelf. Its most important lesson had a great impact on me and perhaps still does. A dissenting tradition informed the American Revolution. It survived the capture of the Revolution and its legacy by conservative nationalists, not least because it was older, broader, and altogether truer to ideals than the Revolution itself. Only years later did I learn how true to those ideals Staughton Lynd himself has been.

Intellectual Origins of American Radicalism came out a year after Bernard Bailyn's *The Ideological Origins of the American Revolution* and issued a potent challenge to that book's interpretation of Revolutionary-era political thought.[1] Radicalism, bourgeois or otherwise, could not be conceived of as merely a "contagion of

liberty" resulting from the Revolution, much less from the Revolution's motivating, anticonspiratorial ideology derived from early-
eighteenth-century "real whig" opposition writings. There was an
earlier radical tradition, Lynd insisted, religious but no less radical for being so, that trusted in ordinary people's consciences. It
was not so much American as Anglo (but not only that), in some
iterations explicitly internationalist, and dissenting with respect to
both church and state depending on the time and place. We see
echoes of it in many different sorts of attacks on wealth and power
throughout U.S. history. This tradition included Garrisonian abolitionism, native socialisms, aspects of Jefferson and Lincoln as
well as Thomas Paine. Radicals could claim a true and thought-
ful, not merely rhetorical or mythical, connection to the American
past—as some of them have done ever since.

   That this view was ever controversial, or that it raised some
hackles in 1968, perhaps requires some explanatory history as well
as historiography. Between 1961 and 1968 Staughton Lynd published a body of work—articles and anthologies as well as the two
books now being republished by Cambridge University Press—
that was remarkable for its breadth and vision.[2] Indeed, the rapid
publication of his essay collection *Class Conflict, Slavery, and
the United States Constitution* (1967) and *Intellectual Origins of
American Radicalism* by trade presses reflected the demand for
his research and teaching, as well as the recognition he had already
achieved among historians during the same years and, to a significant extent, *before* he became famous as an antiwar activist. He
certainly had every reason, while working on *Intellectual Origins*,
to believe that he'd earned the right, and perhaps even had the
responsibility, to creatively combine his political work and his historical writing—and that there would be a ready crossover audience for such an effort. He had been hired by Yale because of his
standing, in the public eye and in the profession, as perhaps the
best "New Left" historian yet to emerge.[3]

   Lynd's writings on the possible confluences of history and
activism were also widely admired and anthologized. Being at
Yale, in turn, made it even more likely that he would be turned
to as a leader and speaker by the movement, whether at demonstrations against the war or at meetings of the American Historical

Association. Lynd emphasized, in the conclusion of *Intellectual Origins*, that the book was written for "radicals." While writing it, he described himself as "more and more committed to the thesis that the professor of history should also be a historical protagonist." He was also trying to "save the Movement of the Sixties" as he put it recently, from bad ideas and their effects. If there was a usable, vital radical tradition, a historian could play an extremely important role as "the custodian of such memories and dreams."[4]

Despite what might seem like a privileging of political over scholarly concerns, the book was in fact well received in the mainstream press and by respected historians.[5] Given its subject (ambitious intellectual history by its very nature rarely commands universal assent), its broad ambitions (more than a century of thought and politics), and its brevity, it is hard to imagine much better reviews. Yet it is now an established fact that the Yale history department, with the assent of the liberal historians who had hired him, had decided to get rid of Lynd for political reasons and chose to construe *Intellectual Origins* as an excuse, with an assist from Eugene D. Genovese, a critic from the left whose objections had little to do with the merits of Lynd's account of ideas in the seventeenth, eighteenth, and nineteenth centuries.[6]

Lynd's neo-Marxism clashed with Genovese's more orthodox variety; his emphasis on abolitionists and founding fathers clashed with Genovese's exclusive interest in the old South. Genovese had also publicly attacked Lynd's brand of New Left politics before he reviewed Lynd's two books in the *New York Review of Books*. The review deliberately conflated the issues, calling Lynd a "demagogue" and wielding its title, "Abolitionist," as a slur. For Genovese, Lynd's insistence on slavery as an issue during the Revolutionary era, and on the abolitionists as carrying on a broader tradition, was simply ahistorical. Real abolitionism had to mean support of slavery's dialectical opposite, wage labor, which was unthinkable in this precapitalist era or among slaveholders who were not capitalists—a position that, it subsequently became clearer, undergirded Genovese's own work. Genovese went further in denouncing Lynd's elaboration and celebration of rights, natural law doctrines, and conscience as politically irresponsible. In a subsequent exchange of letters to the editor that Gary B.

Nash remembers as deeply influential (though disturbing for Genovese's vitriol), Lynd insisted that "the Founding Fathers morally condemned slavery." Other countries abolished slavery between the Revolution and the 1820s: "it is not in the least anachronistic to ask why the United States failed to do likewise."[7]

Understandably, Staughton Lynd has continued to raise tough questions about the academic life and its limits, urging radical historians to cast their net wider. He also wonders why historians have stopped proposing "big ideas that could be tested."[8] What is striking in retrospect about *Intellectual Origins* is that Lynd did not claim more for the traditions he investigated than he could plausibly demonstrate. For the variety of intellectual history Lynd practiced here, it was not necessary that ideas traced be mainstream or become "ideology"; what mattered was that they survived and grew and came to inspire some effective actors in American life, in this case progressives of various sorts.

In a sense, this was an older and still venerable kind of intellectual history, more catholic in its interest in multiple traditions or strands of thought than a new variety of intellectual and cultural history that was gaining adherents in the profession at the time. The new trend was intellectual history as the study of ideologies that expressed the mythic imaginations of large groups of people and motivated major movements or political parties. On the basis of his study of the pamphlet literature of the coming of the Revolution, Bailyn argued for a revolutionary mindset that added up to a consensus with perhaps radical implications for the future but not radical in terms of advocating fundamental social change. His claim was to have figured out the mind of the Revolutionary mainstream; hence the emphasis on *the* ideological origins of the Revolution.[9] As Lynd realized—and strongly refuted—Bailyn's revolutionary consensus marginalized both John Locke and Thomas Paine, even while citing them, and neglected natural rights as a source of radicalism.[10]

One reason for this neglect in Bailyn lay in Bailyn's privileging of the "real whig" opposition sources of republican ideology at the expense of its earlier origins in seventeenth-century English dissent. Lynd's sensitivity to the politics of religion has received ample reinforcement from the subsequent literature on the English Civil War and its legacies. Indeed, recent work finds the late seventeenth century to have been a time of "troubles" that sparked an "extraordinary intellectual fertility" that was international in nature and productive of precisely the radicalizing questions of conscience that Lynd highlights.[11] Lynd, unlike Bailyn and the republican "school," puts us in a position to understand the turmoil of the late provincial period in the mainland colonies without excessively localizing or provincializing that politics. In his hands, wars—and, in America, the unavoidable turmoil that war provokes in the politics of slavery and race—generate moral and political crises that spur creative reassessments of social relations. People entered or re-entered politics to "cast their whole vote," regardless of the previous rules of the political game. In these ways, Lynd's account of the sources of radicalism in America before and after 1776 is more in tune with recent and emerging scholarship than it was with the mainstream scholarship being published in 1968.

Lynd takes issue with Bailyn again in the third chapter, noting Bailyn's insistence on separating dissenters from any concern with society and property. He insists, instead, that dissenters and leading writers who followed in their footsteps, including especially Paine and Jefferson, did at least begin the process of questioning the inalienability of private property—the bedrock of government for Locke, but also the source of a potent critique of slavery (as a violation of inalienable property in one's own person). In the United States, the property question could never be divorced from the slavery question. In *Class Conflict, Slavery, and the United States Constitution*, Lynd constructed an interpretation of why the Revolutionaries ultimately compromised on the slavery question. Here he tells the sunnier side of the story: an important strain of thinking survived the compromises that secured northern (mercantile) private property by solidifying southern (slave) property. If certain strands of the Revolution "demythologized" private property, then the Revolution could still be a resource for those who argued against slavery, despite the Constitution's turn toward the safeguarding of property as a greater good.

And, indeed, the struggle against racial slavery could be about more than that: more even than a defense of a free labor system construed as the opposite of chattel slavery. It could become, like the ideology of the Revolution itself, a site of internationalism in a nationalist age and of a critique of capitalism insofar as contemporary capitalism relied on slave labor. While the mainstreaming of antislavery in the north may have had much to do with its compatibility with wage labor, there were other aspects of abolitionism, especially in its more radical versions, that existed in tension with the status quo antebellum and pointed toward radical expansions of the political landscape. It was these aspects, including the right of free speech, perhaps as much as the insistence on free labor in the territories, that upset the political compromises over slavery. In many ways, recent treatments of the abolitionists can be read as an extended footnote to Lynd; the key departure is in the importance now given to African American activists and thinkers. The irreverent populists, influential Quakers, working-class William Lloyd Garrison, and anticapitalist Henry David Thoreau we meet in *Intellectual Origins*, all of whom thought long and hard but still emphasized action, are familiar figures in recent scholarship.[12]

The revival of the abolitionists' fortunes in the historiography was of course already beginning in the 1960s: Lynd had contributed his essay on antislavery constitutionalism to *The Antislavery Vanguard*, an influential 1965 collection of essays. Lynd was unusual, however, in emphasizing the connection of abolitionism to the Revolutionary generation, though these connections have become much more prominent in recent accounts of black and white abolitionists. Revealingly, though, Lynd also refused to choose between a Revolutionary and a cosmopolitan internationalist tradition, finding ample precedent for both in radical and antislavery figures like Thomas Paine and Wendell Phillips. What Lynd portrayed in terms of thought and activism has become a major theme in recent cultural studies of nineteenth-century America, in which black and white internationalists like David Walker and Frederick Douglass, who riffed on the Revolution and its limits, have become heroes of a "post-nationalist" and post-imperial American studies.[13]

All of which suggests that the book Staughton Lynd published in 1968 is good history even after forty years.

Notes

1. As David Donald noted in his appreciative review in *Commentary* (Aug. 1968, excerpted on the back cover of the Vintage paperback edition), the challenge was also to Progressive historians' denigration of ideas as propaganda: "Though brief, this is a major work in American intellectual history.... The great contribution of [Lynd's] book is to demonstrate that there has been a strong and continuous stream of Anglo-American radical thought down to the Civil War era. Boldly challenging the views of Carl L. Becker, Bernard Bailyn, and Clinton Rossiter, he shows that spokesmen of this dissenting tradition from the very beginning raised fundamental questions 'which threatened private property and the authority of the state.' Persuasively he puts this radicalism into a broader perspective." Donald was no pushover or even a fellow traveler: that same year he was very critical of Barton J. Bernstein, ed., *Towards a New Past: Dissenting Essays in American History* (New York, 1968), which included Lynd's "Beyond Beard" (*American Historical Review* 74 [Dec. 1968], pp. 531–33).

2. Staughton Lynd, *Antifederalism in Dutchess County, New York: A Study of Democracy and Class Conflict in the American Revolutionary Era* (Chicago, 1962); Lynd, *Class Conflict, Slavery, and the United States Constitution: Ten Essays* (Indianapolis, 1967); Lynd, *Intellectual Origins of American Radicalism* (New York, 1968); Lynd, ed., *Nonviolence in America: A Documentary History* (Indianapolis, 1966); Lynd, ed., *Reconstruction* (New York, 1967). Some of the essays in *Class Conflict, Slavery, and the United States Constitution* had appeared in major journals like *Political Science Quarterly*, the *William and Mary Quarterly*, and the *Journal of Negro History*. They were also anthologized in widely read collections like Martin Duberman, ed., *The Antislavery Vanguard* (Princeton, N.J., 1965); Barton Bernstein, ed., *Towards a New Past*; Melvin Drimmer, ed., *Black History: A Reappraisal* (New York, 1968); Alfred F. Young, ed., *Dissent: Explorations in the History of American Radicalism* (DeKalb, Ill., 1968); Allen Davis and Harold Woodman, eds., *Conflict and Consensus in Early American History* (Lexington, Mass., 1976).

3. This theme appears repeatedly in reviews. See, for example, Irwin Unger, "The 'New Left' and American History: Some Recent Trends in United States Historiography," *American Historical Review* 72 (Jul. 1967), 1243, 1258; David Donald, review of *Towards a New Past* ed. Bernstein, *American Historical Review* 74 Dec. 1968), 533; E. P. Thompson, "Preface" in Lynd, *Class Conflict, Slavery, and the United States Constitution*, ix–xiii.

4. Staughton Lynd, "A Profession of History," *The New Journal* I (Nov. 12, 1967), reprinted as "The Historian as Participant" in Robert Allen Skotheim, ed., *The Historian and the Climate of Opinion* (Reading, Mass., 1969), 111, 118; Lynd, "Historical Past and Existential Present" in Theodore Roszak, ed., *The Dissenting Academy* (New York, 1968),

92–109; Staughton Lynd to author, email correspondence, Sept. 28, 2008.

5. Charles Barker pronounced the book "strong" in the *Journal of American History* 55 (Dec. 1968), 633–34; see also "For the Gentleman Rebel," *Time* (Jul. 5, 1968); Robert Middlekauff, "Reconstructing Society From Below," *The New Republic* (Jul. 20, 1968), 39–40; Jon Wiener, "Radical Historians and the Crisis in American History, 1959–1980," *Journal of American History* 76 (Sept. 1989), 417–18.

6. Wittingly or not, Genovese seems to have functioned as something of a hired gun. C. Vann Woodward was showing his review around the history department before it appeared in print, and Genovese was invited to teach at Yale for a year soon afterward. The story of Lynd and Yale has been well told by Carl Mirra, "Radical Historians and the Liberal Establishment: Staughton Lynd's Life with History," *Left History* 11 (Spring 2006), 69–101. See also Geoffrey Kabaservice, *The Guardians: Kingman Brewster, His Circle, and the Rise of the Liberal Establishment* (New York, 2004), 221–22, 243, 328; Jim O'Brien, "'Be Realistic, Demand the Impossible': Staughton Lynd, Jesse Lemisch, and a Committed History," *Radical History Review* 82 (Winter 2002), 65–90; and Staughton Lynd and Alice Lynd, *Stepping Stones: Memoir of a Life Together* (Lanham, Md., 2009), 82–84. For Lynd's commitment to scholarly objectivity see Peter Novick, *That Noble Dream: The "Objectivity Question" and the American Historical Profession* (Cambridge, UK, 1988), 423, 427.

7. Eugene D. Genovese, "Abolitionist," *New York Review of Books* (Sept. 26, 1968), reprinted in Genovese, *In Red and Black: Marxian Explorations in Southern and Afro-American History* (New York, 1972), 354–67; Staughton Lynd, "Self-Evident Truths?" and response by Eugene D. Genovese, in *New York Review of Books* (Dec. 19, 1968); Staughton Lynd, "High Noon," *New York Review of Books* (Feb. 27, 1969); Gary B. Nash, "Class in Early American History: A Personal Journey," *Labor* 1 (Winter 2004), 20–22.

If one ignores the part about capitalism and antislavery, Genovese's argument that talk about slavery's relationship to the Revolution and the founding of the republic is anachronism or presentism is basically the same as that still being made by Gordon S. Wood, who also used the term "anachronistic" with respect to Lynd in 1969. Compare Wood, *The Creation of the American Republic, 1776–1787* (Chapel Hill, 1969), 626, and Wood, *The Presence of the Past: Reflections on the Uses of History* (New York, 2008), 291, 293–308. But even Genovese has admitted, recently, that slavery "loomed over the Constitutional Convention." To preserve his "honorable" planter class who "defended principles," Genovese, however, has elaborated their defense of "slavery in the abstract," ignoring the rise of racial defenses of slavery to answer the natural rights tradition. Genovese and Elizabeth Fox-Genovese, *The Mind of the Master Class: History and Faith in the Southern Slaveholders' Worldview* (New York, 2005), 72; Fox-Genovese and Genovese, *Slavery in Black and White: Class and Race in the Southern Slaveholders' New World Order* (New York, 2008).

8. Nasty reviews of the sort perfected by Genovese and controversial tenure cases like Lynd's are surely one reason. Staughton Lynd, "Intellectuals, the University, and the Movement" (1968) in *Journal of American History* 76 (Sept. 1989), 479–86; "Staughton Lynd" in Henry Abelove et al., eds., *Visions of History* (New York, 1983), 147–66; Lynd, "Father and Son: Intellectual Life Outside the University," *Living Inside Our Hope* (Ithaca, N.Y., 1998), 19–27; Lynd, "Revisiting Class in Early America: Personal Reflections," *Labor* 1 (Winter 2004), 31; Staughton Lynd and Andrej Grubacic, *Wobblies and Zapatistas: Conversations on Anarchism, Marxism, and Radical History* (Oakland, Calif., 2008).

9. For a reassertion of the method see Bernard Bailyn, "The Central Themes of the American Revolution" in Stephen G. Kurtz and James H. Hutson, eds., *The Era of the American Revolution* (New York, 1973), 3–31, revised in Bailyn, *Faces of Revolution* (New York, 1990), 200–24; Gordon S. Wood, "Intellectual History and the Social Sciences" in John Higham and Paul K. Conkin, eds., *New Directions in American Intellectual History* (Baltimore, 1979), 27–41. For Bailyn's "neo-whig" intellectual histories as a continuation of the "consensus" interpretation characteristic of Daniel Boorstin and Clinton Rossiter, see Colin Gordon, "Crafting a Usable Past: Consensus, Ideology, and Historians of the American Revolution," *William and Mary Quarterly* 46 (1989), 675–95.

10. For subsequent reassertions (and appreciations) of the need to figure out, as Lynd sought to do, the nature of American appropriations and revisions of Locke, particularly of natural rights, see Daniel W. Howe, "European Sources of Political Ideas in Jeffersonian America," *Reviews in American History* 10 (Dec. 1982), 28–44; Daniel T. Rodgers, *Contested Truths: Keywords in American Politics Since Independence* (New York, 1987), 45–79, 231n3; Isaac Kramnick, *Republicanism and Bourgeois Radicalism: Political Ideology in Late Eighteenth-Century England and America* (Ithaca, N.Y., 1990); Joyce Appleby, *Liberalism and Republicanism in the Historical Imagination* (Cambridge, Mass, 1992); Richard J. Ellis, *American Political Cultures* (New York, 1993), 28–42; T. H. Breen, "Subjecthood and Citizenship: The Context of James Otis's Radical Critique of John Locke," *New England Quarterly* 71 (Sept. 1998), 378–403; Michael P. Zuckert, *The Natural Rights Republic* (Notre Dame, Ind., 1996); Seth Cotlar, *Making Democracy Safe for America: The Rise and Demise of Trans-Atlantic Radicalism, 1789–1804* (Charlottesville, Va., forthcoming).

11. Jonathan Scott, *England's Troubles: Seventeenth Century English Political Instability in European Context* (Cambridge, UK, 2000), 33 and passim; Philip Baker, "Rhetoric, Reality, and the Varieties of Civil-War Radicalism" in John Adamson, ed., *The English Civil War: Conflict and Contexts, 1640–49* (New York, 2009), 202–24. See also Peter Linebaugh and Marcus Rediker, *The Many Headed Hydra* (Boston, 2000); Carla Gardina Pestana, *The English Atlantic in an Age of Revolution, 1640–1661* (Cambridge, Mass., 2004).

12. Jane E. Calvert, *Quaker Constitutionalism and the Political Thought of John Dickinson* (New York, 2009); Thomas P. Slaughter, *The Beautiful*

Soul of John Woolman, Apostle of Abolition (New York, 2009); Linebaugh
and Rediker, *The Many Headed Hydra*; Paul Goodman, *Of One Blood:
Abolitionism and the Origins of Racial Equality* (Berkeley, 1998); Timothy
Patrick McCarthy and John Stauffer, eds., *Prophets of Protest: Reconsider-
ing the History of American Abolitionism* (New York, 2006); James Oakes,
*The Radical and the Republican: Frederick Douglass, Abraham Lincoln,
and the Triumph of Antislavery* (New York, 2007); Manisha Sinha, "An
Alternative Tradition of Radicalism: African American Abolitionists and
the Metaphor of Revolution" in Manisha Sinha and Penny Von Eschen,
eds., *Contested Democracy: Freedom, Race and Power in American His-
tory* (New York, 2007), 9–30; Terry Bouton, *Taming Democracy: "The
People"*, *The Founders, and the Troubled Ending of the American Revolution* (New York, 2007); Ronald P. Formisano, *For the People: American
Populist Movements from the Revolution to the 1850s* (Chapel Hill, 2008);
Larry Kramer, *The People Themselves: Popular Constitutionalism and
Judicial Review* (New York, 2006); David Waldstreicher, *Slavery's Con-
stitution: From Revolution to Ratification* (New York, 2009), chapter 3;
Elizabeth B. Clark, "'The Sacred Rights of the Weak': Pain, Sympathy,
and the Culture of Individual Rights in Antebellum America," *Journal
of American History* 82 (Sept. 1995), 463–93; Charles Capper, "'A Little
Beyond': The Problem of the Transcendentalist Movement in American
History," *Journal of American History* 85 (Sept. 1998), 528; Kimberly K.
Smith, *The Dominion of Voice: Riot, Reason, and Romance in Antebellum
Politics* (Lawrence, Kans., 1999).

13. John Carlos Rowe, ed., *Post-Nationalist American Studies* (Berkeley,
2000); Michael Bennett, *Democratic Discourses: The Radical Abolition
Movement and Antebellum American Literature* (New Brunswick, N.J.,
2005); Robert Fanuzzi, *Abolition's Public Sphere* (Minneapolis, 2003).
This new American studies has proven less interested in tracing the roots
of the dissenting tradition back to the seventeenth or eighteenth century.
In this regard, contemporary academic radicalism seems all too invested
in the myth of early American consensus, perhaps as a foil for stories of
politicization, if not progress. Or to put it a different way: they have read
too much Bailyn and not enough Lynd.

For Lynd's version of radical history as a progenitor of Cultural Studies
and as inspired in part by his parents, the sociologists Robert S. Lynd and
Helen Merrell Lynd, see Joel Pfister, *Critique for What? Cultural Studies,
American Studies, Left Studies* (Boulder, Colo., 2007), 4–6, 103–8.

INTELLECTUAL ORIGINS
OF
AMERICAN RADICALISM

NEW EDITION

INTRODUCTION:

THE
RIGHT
OF
REVOLUTION

Americans have made two revolutions, in 1776–1783 and in 1861–1865. They were "bourgeois" revolutions: the first preserved inherited property as it destroyed inherited government, the second enhanced property in factories and railroads as it abolished property in man.[1] Nevertheless, it is untrue that the American Revolution and the Civil War had no "ideology . . . capable of being made universal."[2] To energize and explain these upheavals, the men who made them created a revolutionary intellectual tradition. They addressed to the opinion of mankind the dramatic proposition that all men are created equal with natural liberties which, if taken away at all, cannot be justly taken without consent. As Thomas Paine observed, the American Revolution was unique precisely in being "a revolution in the principles and practise of governments" and not "merely a separation from England."[3] That is why those principles have been echoed by revolutionaries the world over from that day to this (most recently by the Vietnamese, whose

1945 declaration of independence begins with the words, "all men are created equal").

Because they expressed the aspirations of different social groups united only on behalf of independence, the ideas of the American Revolution meant many things to many men. Abolitionists, as they built a new revolutionary movement against chattel slavery, drew selectively on the intellectual resources of the past, clarifying and interpreting to suit their own needs. The American revolutionary tradition described in this book is the tradition which culminated in abolitionism: a tradition based on the more radical readings of the Declaration of Independence, which traced its intellectual ancestry more to Paine than to Locke.

Of necessity, however, all variants of the revolutionary tradition defended the right of revolution. During the century between 1760 and 1860 the right of revolution was justified by presidents as well as prophets, by politicians in power as well as by radicals out of it. "Revolutionary ground should be occupied," stated the Address of the Executive Committee of the American Anti-Slavery Society in 1844, which continued: "Up, then, with the banner of revolution!"[4] But this was only to rephrase more flamboyantly what the Declaration of Independence termed the people's right "to alter or to abolish" the governments that they created. And Abraham Lincoln's First Inaugural Address asserted: "This country, with its institutions, belongs to the people who inhabit it. Whenever they shall grow weary of the existing government, they can exercise their constitutional right of amending it, or their revolutionary right to dismember or overthrow it."

I

For all its ambiguities, the preamble to the Declaration of Independence is the single most concentrated expression of the revolutionary intellectual tradition. Without significant exception, subsequent variants of American radicalism have taken the Declaration of Independence as their point of departure and claimed to be the true heirs of the spirit of '76. Jefferson developed the philosophy of the document he had drafted in the direction of states' rights and the defense of Southern sectionalism. But in doing so Jefferson continued to invoke the Declaration of Independence, as did the very language of the South Carolina Declaration of the Causes of Secession in 1860. Northern radicalism also traced its lineage to Independence Hall. On July 4, 1826, the day Jefferson and John Adams died, Robert Owen delivered a declaration of "mental independence" comprising secularism, equality of the sexes, and common ownership. These ideas inspired one current of Jacksonian dissent. But William Lloyd Garrison, anything but secular and intensely anti-Jacksonian, also adopted the rhetoric of the Declaration in drafting the manifestos of the American Anti-Slavery Society in 1833 and the New England Non-Resistance Society in 1838. Lincoln referred to the Declaration of Independence as the "standard maxim for a free society" and compared its role as a spiritual regulator to that of the Biblical injunction, "Be ye perfect."[5] The Radical Republicans, Charles Sumner for example, maintained that the Declaration was part of the United States Constitution, or if it was not should at once be made so.

After the Civil War the glittering generalities of the Declaration retained their potency, and American radicalism continued to present itself as their fulfillment. "The reform I have proposed," wrote Henry George in *Progress and Poverty*,

> . . . is . . . but the carrying out in letter and spirit of the truth enunciated in the Declaration of Independence. . . . They who look upon Liberty as having accomplished her mission, when she has abolished hereditary privileges and given men the ballot, . . . have not seen her real grandeur. . . . We cannot go on prating of the inalienable rights of man and then denying the inalienable right to the bounty of the Creator.[6]

Edward Bellamy, in *Looking Backward*, had Doctor Leete explain the new society to Julian West in similar terms. "In a word," he said, "the people of the United States concluded to assume the conduct of their own business, just as one hundred odd years before they had assumed the conduct of their own government, organizing now for industrial purposes on precisely the same grounds that they had then organized for political purposes."[7] Henry Demarest Lloyd invoked the analogy of the American Revolution in *Wealth Against Commonwealth*, declaring:

> Myriads of experiments to get the substance of liberty out of the forms of tyranny, to believe in princes, to trust good men to do good as kings, have taught the inexorable truth that, in the economy of nature, form and substance must move together. . . . Identical is the lesson we are learning with regard to industrial power and property. . . .

"Liberty recast the old forms of government into the Republic," Lloyd concluded, "and it must remould our institutions of wealth into the Commonwealth."[8] For Eugene Debs, Patrick Henry was "one of my first heroes; and my passion for his eloquent and burning defiance of King George inspired the first speech I ever attempted in public." Among the French and American revolutionaries who inspired Debs, Tom Paine "towered above them all."[9]

During the New Deal and World War II, it was voguish among radicals to identify their various causes with the alleged tradition of "Jefferson, Jackson, and Lincoln." The New Left of the 1960s, despite its oft-described sense of alienation and its quarrel with the intellectual habits of the previous generation, also uses the Revolution as a touchstone. Thus in November 1965 Carl Oglesby, then president of Students for a Democratic Society, asked an antiwar demonstration gathered at the Washington Monument to imagine what Thomas Jefferson or Thomas Paine would say to President Johnson and McGeorge Bundy about the war in Vietnam. And in August 1966, when the House Un-American Activities Committee subpoenaed antiwar activists, the head of the Free University of New York issued a statement invoking the Green Mountain Boys, and the chairman of the Berkeley Vietnam Day Committee appeared in the hearing chamber in the uniform of an officer of George Washington's army.

American Revolutionary rhetoric has been as popular with uneducated poor men as with articulate spokesmen, with Marxists as with non-Marxists, with Negroes as with whites. All, in the words of rebellious New York tenants in the 1840s,

have sought to "take up the ball of the Revolution where our
fathers stopped it and roll it to the final consummation of
freedom and independence of the Masses." Thus American
Marxists, except for a short period under the influence of
Friedrich Sorge, have "viewed labor radicalism as a movement
to redeem the promise of the American Revolution." For instance, Daniel De Leon's rigidly doctrinaire Socialist Labor
Party asserted in its 1889 program that "the inalienable right
of all men to life, liberty and the pursuit of happiness" was its
objective, too.[10] The same generalization holds for the history
of black radicalism in America. The first major slave insurrection following the Revolution planned to march under a flag
reading "Death or Liberty." One of the most celebrated fugitive slaves of the nineteenth century declared he was inspired
by "that law which God wrote on the table of my heart, in-
spiring the love of freedom, and impelling me to seek it at
every hazard." Both the NAACP and SNCC derive from
W. E. B. Du Bois's seminal essay "Of Mr. Booker T. Washington
and Others" that ended with an appeal to "those great words
which the sons of the Fathers would fain forget": the preamble
to the Declaration of Independence. The most militant Afro-
Americans in the 1960s, similarly, still refer to a "higher law
than the law of government" and to the conflict between
"property rights" and "human rights," as did earlier American
revolutionaries, white and black.[11]

For almost two hundred years all kinds of American radicals
have traced their intellectual origins to the Declaration of
Independence and to the Revolution it justified. They have
stubbornly refused to surrender the memory of the American
Revolution to liberalism or reaction, insisting that only radicalism could make real the rhetoric of 1776.

II

This process of looking backward has its perils. In its un-
critical historiography of Jefferson, Jackson, and Lincoln, the
Old Left mirrored its overcommitment to Franklin Roosevelt.
Just as they failed to maintain sufficient political distance from
F.D.R.'s coalition, so in rewriting American history radicals

of the New Deal era maintained too little intellectual distance between themselves and reform leaders of the past. In fact, it was no more accurate to characterize Jefferson, Jackson, and Lincoln as "friends of the common man" than it was to term Franklin Roosevelt "progressive" and leave the matter there. By defending states' rights and Southern sectional interests, Jefferson by implication protected slavery; by defending the Union and Northern sectional interests, Lincoln by implication promoted capitalism. It would be more accurate to say that at certain periods of their lives Jefferson and Lincoln expressed a revolutionary tradition, than to say that they created it. Six months before the Declaration of Independence a republican theory of natural rights was articulated by Paine and Richard Price. Long before Lincoln quoted the Declaration of Independence against slavery, abolitionists had roughhewed a revolutionary theory from the Declaration and the Bible. The characteristic exponents of the revolutionary tradition were poor workingmen who did not go to college and rarely held public office, such as Paine, Garrison, George, and Debs.

But if there is danger in romanticizing the past by fabricating a radicalism which was not there, it is equally misleading to suppose that there was no American radicalism prior to the formation of an industrial proletariat or the advent of Marxist theory. A continuous radical tradition existed. Ambiguous ideological axioms evolved, under the pressure of events, into radical corollaries which threatened private property and the authority of the state. These pages dwell on that unfolding clarification of abstract ideas. But it must not be forgotten that behind the words, constantly translating the printed pamphlet into the sermon or stump speech, and speeches into the whispers of conspiracy, stood men. When one asserts the reality of an unbroken continuity between the revolutionaries of 1776 and twentieth-century radicals, one refers not only to the intellectual fact that, for example, early nineteenth-century American socialists built on Jefferson's dictum that "the earth belongs to the living";[12] but also to the human fact that a son of utopian socialist Robert Owen was the principal draftsman of the Fourteenth Amendment, and a son of John

Brown sent grapes to the Haymarket anarchists as they awaited execution.[13]

The prophets of twentieth-century American radicalism, Debs and Du Bois, viewed themselves as executors of an American tradition which they were proud to inherit. Thus both men reverenced John Brown, whom Du Bois praised for (among other things) his "inchoate but growing belief in a more just and a more equal distribution of property," and Debs called "History's Greatest Hero."[14] Debs's best-remembered speech, to the jury on the occasion of his conviction for sedition in World War I, was a miniature history of the United States for radicals. He reminded his listeners that Samuel Adams had been condemned as an incendiary and Patrick Henry as a traitor, that Washington, Adams, and Paine "were the rebels of their day." Then the abolitionists began "another mighty agitation." Elijah Lovejoy, "opposed to chattel slavery —just as I am opposed to wage slavery," was "despised in his day as are the leaders of the I.W.W. in our day." It was my good fortune, Debs continued, to know Wendell Phillips personally; Garrison, Gerrit Smith, Thaddeus Stevens were once "regarded as monsters of depravity" but "you are teaching your children to revere their memories."

Then Debs turned to the theme of internationalism, quoting Paine's and Garrison's words, "My country is the world." He referred to Lincoln's opposition to the war with Mexico, and maintained that he himself did not go so far as Phillips, who had said that "the glory of free men is that they trample unjust laws under their feet." He ended, as his biographer notes, by paraphrasing, perhaps unconsciously, John Brown's last words to his jury in 1859.[15]

Politically as personally, recourse to the past can be a means of retrogression and escape; but it can also be the first step in a process of liberation. With or without the help of therapists all of us occasionally look back to our individual pasts to find strength for new beginnings. With or without the help of historians, similarly, Americans concerned to change the society around them have made appropriate use of the past as a source for forgotten alternatives, for encouragement to

endure. The Revolution-cum-Declaration can legitimately provide that "frequent recurrence to fundamental principles" which
the Virginia Bill of Rights advised.

III

Distant and archaic as it may often appear, the language
of the Declaration of Independence remains relevant as an instrument for social transformation. What pre-Civil War radicals
meant by these old words has much in common with what the
modern radical movement means by its own characteristic
phrases. Men should be free, according to the revolutionary
tradition, because on joining society they do not surrender their
essential natural powers. If existing society abuses those powers,
men should demand their restoration at once: "immediate
emancipation," or as Garrison sometimes put it, "freedom
now."[16]

Existential radicals of the mid-twentieth century have re-
discovered the central affirmations of the older tradition. They
have learned in the concentration camp or the American South
that no external circumstances can deprive man of his capacity
to be a free moral agent. At the Nuremburg Tribunal and elsewhere, they began to talk once more about the attributes of
man as man: to use Jefferson's language, about "the common
rights of mankind," "the rights of human nature," the "sacred"
laws of nations "which even savage nations observe."[17]

For us, then, it is no longer satisfactory to dismiss the
eighteenth-century rhetoric as mere myth. Even Carl Becker,
author of an excellent study on the Declaration, discounted its
philosophy as "a humane and engaging faith" which, however,
was founded not on fact but on "a superficial knowledge of
history" and a "naive faith in the instinctive virtues of human
kind."[18] The young Karl Marx found the meaning of the Declaration equally transparent. The liberty protected by the
French and American bills and declarations of rights was, for
Marx, "the right to do everything which does not harm others."
It rested, not on a communal relation between men, "but rather
upon the separation of man from man." It was "the right of the
circumscribed individual, withdrawn into himself," "the right

of self-interest." Citing the bills of rights of Revolutionary Pennsylvania and New Hampshire (the texts of which he found in Beaumont's *Marie*), Marx analyzed the "imprescriptible" and "inalienable" right of religious liberty as simply the reflection in the superstructure of bourgeois society of the absolute right of private property which was its economic base. Thus religion in capitalist society "is no longer the essence of *community*, but . . . an expression of the fact that man is *separated* from *community*." Like the economy, bourgeois ideology is fragmented, privatized: "only the abstract avowal of an individual folly, a private whim or caprice."[19]

Marx's analysis of the eighteenth century's "rights of man" was brilliant but one-sided. He exaggerated his own intellectual distance from the French and American manifestos, for he too built his intellectual system on the concept of "alienation" (*Entfremdung*) which he took from Hegel. Alienated man, as Marx portrayed him, was man "corrupted, lost to himself, . . . subjected to the rule of inhuman conditions":[20] one who had transformed his own energies into things and institutions outside himself which returned to oppress him. "Alienation" as described by Marx has a good deal in common with the Declaration's description of government as a creation of men designed to secure their "inalienable" rights, which on occasion becomes destructive of the ends for which it was designed.

Marx was right, of course, in perceiving a capitalist component in the American Revolution. The ambiguity of the Revolution's philosophy lay in affirming personal liberty while at the same time linking it to private property and economic self-interest. As Richard Hofstadter observes, the Founding Fathers "thought man was a creature of rapacious self-interest, and yet they wanted him to be free—free, in essence, to contend, to engage in an umpired strife, to use property to get property. . . . They had no hope and they offered none for any ultimate organic change in the way men conduct themselves."[21] Hofstadter's generalization is as applicable to James Madison or to John Adams as it is to Alexander Hamilton. Hamilton wrote in 1775 that "in contriving any system of government . . . *every man* ought to be supposed a *knave;*

and to have no other end in all his actions, but *private interest*" (a saying of Machiavelli's which Hamilton found in Hume).[22] But Madison, too, believed that freedom was inconceivable without greed and competition:

> Liberty is to faction what air is to fire, an aliment without which it instantly expires. But it could not be less folly to abolish liberty, which is essential to political life, because it nourishes faction, than it would be to wish the annihilation of air, which is essential to animal life, because it imparts to fire its destructive agency.[23]

The result was in significant respects a closed society, which held the meagerest hopes for human nature and foreclosed in advance the possibility that a community might be both free and fraternal.

Both American abolitionism and Marxism rebelled against the results of the eighteenth-century revolutions. To a significant extent the two movements shared a common vocabulary, desiring the "transcendence" (*Aufhebung*) of man's alienated condition and the reconstruction of society as a voluntary association of free moral agents: in the words of the *Communist Manifesto*, an association in which the free development of each is the condition for the free development of all. But despite these similarities between the American revolutionary tradition and Marxism,[24] Marx's American contemporaries laid more stress than he did on the experienced reality of conscience and the need for personal commitment. For Marx, responsible social action presupposed a rational survey of the economic situation in which one planned to act. Inevitably the required analysis fell to an elite which had the leisure and training to make it. Despite his emphasis on the dependence of theory upon practice, Marx felt considerable distrust for workingmen who sought to change society on the basis of their own experience and perceptions.[25] In this he somewhat resembled those American Founding Fathers who considered moral outrage against slavery premature and utopian, and placed their hope for its eventual abolition in long-run economic trends.

Abolitionist activism therefore has something to say to Marx's dialectical materialism just as it spoke tellingly to the materialism of the Founding Fathers. What it has to say is this: One cannot entrust men with a collective right to revolution unless one is prepared for them to revolutionize their lives from day to day; one should not invoke the ultimate act of revolution without willingness to see new institutions perpetually improvised from below; the withering away of the state must begin in the process of changing the state; freedom must mean freedom now.

NOTES

1. The relation between the American Revolution and the Civil War is explored in my *Class Conflict, Slavery, and the United States Constitution: Ten Essays* (New York and Indianapolis, 1967). It was Charles Beard who suggested that the Civil War was the "Second American Revolution."

2. Carl Degler, "The American Past: An Unsuspected Obstacle in Foreign Affairs," *American Scholar*, XXXII (1962–1963), 207.

3. "Rights of Man, Part Second," *The Complete Writings of Thomas Paine*, ed. Philip Foner (New York, 1945), I, 354.

4. *Liberator*, May 31, 1844.

5. Speeches of June 26, 1857, and July 10, 1858, quoted in Harry Jaffa, *Crisis of the House Divided* (Garden City, N.Y., 1959), p. 316.

6. Henry George, *Progress and Poverty* (San Francisco, 1879), pp. 490–96.

7. Edward Bellamy, *Looking Backward, 2000–1887* (Boston, 1888), p. 78.

8. Henry Demarest Lloyd, *Wealth Against Commonwealth* (New York, 1894), p. 517.

9. *Labor and Freedom: The Voice and Pen of Eugene V. Debs* (St. Louis, Mo., 1916), pp. 16–17.

10. David Herreshoff, *American Disciples of Marx: From the Age of Jackson to the Progressive Era* (Detroit, Mich., 1967), pp. 14, 174.

11. Testimony of Prosser's Ben at the trial of Gabriel and Anthony Burns to the Baptist Church of Fauquier County, Virginia, *A Documentary History of the Negro People in the United States*, ed. Herbert Aptheker (New York, 1962), I, 46, 371; W. E. B. Du Bois, "Of Mr. Booker T. Washington and Others," *The Souls of Black Folk* (Chicago, 1903), p. 59; Stokely Carmichael, "You Better Come On Home," *The Movement*, June 1967.

12. See David Harris, *Socialist Origins in the United States: American Forerunners of Marx, 1817–1832* (Assen, 1966), and Chapter 3, below.

13. "John Brown, Jr., and the Haymarket Martyrs," ed. Louis Ruchames, *Massachusetts Review*, V (1964), 765.

14. W. E. B. Du Bois, *John Brown* (Philadelphia, 1909), p. 375, also pp. 61–71, 165; *Debs: His Life, Writings and Speeches* (Chicago, 1908), p. 271.

15. Speech of September 11, 1916, in David Karsner, *Debs: His authorized Life and Letters from Woodstock Prison to Atlanta* (New York, 1919), pp. 23–44; Ray Ginger, *The Bending Cross: A Biography of Eugene Victor Debs* (New Brunswick, N.J., 1949), p. 373.

16. William Lloyd Garrison, *An Address on the Progress of the Abolition Cause* (Boston, 1832), p. 15; *Liberator*, July 13, 1838.

17. *The Papers of Thomas Jefferson*, ed. Julian Boyd (Princeton, 1950–), I, 119, 130, 196.

18. Carl Becker, *The Declaration of Independence* (New York, 1922), p. 278.

19. "On the Jewish Question," *Karl Marx: Early Writings*, tr. and ed. T. B. Bottomore (New York, 1964), pp. 22–25, 15.

20. *Ibid.*, p. 20.

21. Richard Hofstadter, *The American Political Tradition and the Men Who Made It* (New York, 1948), p. 16.

22. "The Farmer Refuted," *The Papers of Alexander Hamilton*, ed. Harold C. Syrett (New York, 1961–), I, 95, quoting David Hume, "Of the Independency of Parliament," *Essays, Moral and Political*, 3d. ed. (London, 1748), I, 63, who was quoting Machiavelli's *Discourses on Livy*, Book I, Ch. 3.

23. This passage from Madison's Tenth Federalist Paper was anticipated twenty-two years earlier by John Adams. In the first draft of his first published essay, "A Dissertation on Canon and Feudal Law" (1765), Adams wrote: "The Desire of Dominion, that encroaching, grasping, restless, and ungovernable Principle in human Nature, that principle which has made so much Havock and Desolation. . . ." (*Diary and Autobiography of John Adams*, ed. L. H. Butterfield [Cambridge, Mass., 1961], I, 255). But by the time he published the essay Adams had decided: "the love of power which has been so often the cause of slavery—has, whenever freedom has existed, been the cause of freedom. If it is this principle that has always prompted the princes and nobles of the earth by every species of fraud and violence to shake off all the limitations of their power, it is the same that has always stimulated the common people to aspire at independence. . . ." (*The Political Writings of John Adams: Representative Selections*, ed. George Peek, Jr. [New York, 1954], p. 4).

24. For an extended discussion of Marx and Thoreau, see Chapter 3, below.

25. Marx's dealings with real workingmen are examined in P. H. Noyes, *Organization and Revolution: Working-Class Associations in the German Revolutions of 1848–1849* (Princeton, 1966), and in Henry Collins and Chimen Abramsky, *Karl Marx and the British Labour Movement: Years of the First International* (London and New York, 1965).

I

THEORY

CHAPTER 1

TRUTHS
SELF-EVIDENT

The Declaration of Independence is so familiar that, to use its own language, its propositions seem "self-evident." But the Declaration's assertions were not commonplace and inevitable at the time they were written, nor are they so now. In the mid-eighteenth century (as in the mid-twentieth) a sophisticated social science viewed with amused contempt any argument which failed to recognize that what is held good in one culture may be considered bad by another: that ethics are determined by environment. The "best minds" of the Enlightenment came to believe that the state of nature, the social contract, and the rights of man—in short, the apparatus of John Locke's political philosophy—were human inventions. To grasp the significance of the Declaration as a source of revolutionary ideas one must first grasp equally firmly that from the standpoint of the ethical relativism of a Montesquieu, Voltaire, or Hume it seemed a piece of provincial propaganda, charming perhaps, but founded on fiction and unworthy of serious intellectual attention. It is not untrue to say that the language of the Declaration is the language of Locke; but to say no more than that ignores the fact that by the third quarter of the eighteenth century the natural rights philosophy had been seriously called into question, and required to be restated in a way that incorporated the insights of its critics. The distinctive qualities of the Declaration are the product of that struggle.

The preamble to the Declaration of Independence makes its case in universal terms. It appeals not to the British constitution but to nature and nature's God. It speaks not of the rights of Englishmen known to lawyers but of rights of man self-evident to all. These qualities led an earlier generation of historians to assume that the Declaration had been influenced by Rousseau.

Since the publication in 1922 of Becker's *Declaration of Independence,* historians have been content to ascribe its intellectual origins to John Locke. As Becker put it, "Jefferson copied Locke."[1] The recent scholarship of Bernard Bailyn and others adds the corollary that Americans often copied, not Locke himself, but English publicists of the early eighteenth century who made Locke accessible in popularized form. Among these publicists the names most often mentioned are John Trenchard and Thomas Gordon, joint authors of *Cato's Letters,* most of which appeared in the English press during the years 1720–1723.[2]

The trend of recent interpretation has more and more diluted the Declaration's revolutionary content. When Becker referred to Jefferson's use of Locke, he did so in the context of his thesis that the colonists turned to Locke's natural rights philosophy only when reasoning based on "positive law and custom" had failed. According to Becker, "step by step, from 1764 to 1776, the colonists modified their theory to suit their needs." If in the end Americans resorted to a theory which was not original, still it was a theory sharply distinct from the appeal to precedents and charters with which they began the dispute.[3]

Bernard Bailyn's modification of Becker's thesis stresses the continuity between the thought of the American Revolution and English Opposition thought of the early eighteenth century. "The configuration of ideas and attitudes" which made up the Revolutionary ideology appeared "intact—completely formed—as far back as the 1730's." In Bailyn's treatment the drama and daring of the appeal to nature against established authority fade from sight. Having observed at the outset of his discussion that "most commonly the thought of the Revolution has been seen simply as an expression of the natural rights philosophy," Bailyn ends with an interpretation in which the natural rights philosophy hardly figures at all.[4]

The argument presented in this and the next chapter challenges the conclusions of both Becker and Bailyn. Its contention is not only that an appeal to natural rights meant something quite different than an appeal to constitutional law, but also that the words of Locke's natural rights philosophy meant something quite different to Anglo-American radicals in the 1770s than they had signified a century before to Locke himself.

Consider Locke and Paine. It can be argued that, at least up to the publication of his *Rights of Man, Part Second,* Paine's political thought merely echoed Locke's theory of natural rights and social contract. But this observation looks only to the bare surface of their language, not to the context in which the language was used. Locke, who blamed poverty on the poor, sought to protect all forms of property including chattel slavery, and took it for granted that government must be the business of educated gentlemen, would have been horrified to find his doctrine turned toward the advocacy of common sense, government by common men, finally even common property.[5]

What needs clarification is the intellectual background to the new modeling of Locke's old meanings by Revolutionary radicals. We shall find that the preparatory steps took place largely in England, among a group of radical Englishmen associated with non-Anglican (Nonconformist or Dissenting) Protestant denominations such as the Quakers to whom Paine's father belonged. These men transferred to secular political discourse that reliance on the individual conscience of uneducated men for which they had contended in religion. Above all they broke with the Lockean thesis that man is the passive product of circumstance, and affirmed what they liked to call "the dignity of human nature."

I

Roughly halfway through the eighteenth century, as Becker himself emphasized, there took place a pervasive intellectual crisis based on the perception that Locke's environmental psychology contradicted his political philosophy.[6] In the preamble to the Declaration, those phrases justifying revolution taken from Locke's *Second Treatise of Government* logically depended on the prior statement which held it to be "self-evident" (or in the language of an earlier draft, "sacred and undeniable") that men were born equally possessed of inalienable natural rights. And although in the *Second Treatise* Locke referred to a law of nature "writ in the hearts of mankind" and natural rights which "cease not" in society, in the *Essay Concerning Human Understanding* he maintained, as Becker paraphrased him, that "God has not . . . stamped upon the minds of all men certain intuitively perceived intellectual and moral ideas."[7] Locke simultaneously advocated a political philosophy of liberation and a psychology that seemed to deny the reality of ethical judgment.

According to Locke's theory of psychology, ideas derived from experience as man was stimulated by pain and pleasure to repeat some actions and to eschew others. But if man was endowed by his Creator only with a mind which was a blank page, then what happened to self-evident inalienable rights? and to a theory of revolution which presumed those rights to exist? Impressions written by past experience upon the *tabula rasa* of the mind could presumably be erased by new experience in the future. Convictions shaped by a particular environment would change if the environment were altered. Reformers required, in Becker's words, "a fulcrum in Nature for moving the existing order": "they had to demonstrate that 'life, liberty, and the pursuit of happiness' were according to Nature and the will of God, whereas tyranny and cruelty and the taking of property without consent were not."[8] But Locke's environmental psychology appeared to demonstrate that ideas of right and wrong merely reflected existing society.

The dilemma which Locke thus bequeathed to his disciples may be compared to twentieth-century discussion of "what Marx really meant." Locke then like Marx now provided the most vigorous available rationale for social change, which no reformer wished altogether to discard. But Locke then like Marx now also brilliantly explained how circumstances created the convictions in the name of which change was demanded. A twentieth-century version of the resulting impasse, by Edward Thompson of the English New Left, runs as follows:

> . . . men had abandoned human agency. They could not hold back change; but change went with the shuffling gait of circumstance. It did not stem from the operation of human consciousness and will upon circumstance. Events seemed to will men, not men events. For meaning can be given to history only in the quarrel between "ought" and "is." . . .[9]

Eighteenth-century materialism led to the identical dead end. As Basil Willey paraphrased Holbach: "Our errors *cannot* be 'natural,' are not what Nature intended; yet there is nothing which Nature has not produced, nothing which does not fall within the 'domain of causality'."[10] Or as Ernst Cassirer put the problem: "How does the necessity and immutability of the concept of law agree with the proposition that every idea is derived from the senses and that, accordingly, it can possess no other and no higher significance than the various sense experiences on which it is based?"[11]

Stimulated by Locke's environmental psychology as by the economic determinism of James Harrington, English political philosophy in the eighteenth century turned away from natural rights toward a social science characterized by ethical relativism and pragmatic accommodation to existing reality. This generalization may hold most true of conservatives such as David Hume, but it also applies to Opposition ideologues such as Trenchard and Gordon. In the belief (following Harrington) that "the first Principle of all Power is Property; and every Man will have his Share of it in proportion as he enjoys

Property," the authors of *Cato's Letters* concluded that "the great Secret in Politicks is nicely to watch and observe this Fluctuation and Change of Natural Power, and to adjust the Political to it." Since property in England was unequally distributed, a republic was impossible: "the Phantome of a Commonwealth must vanish, and never appear again but in disordered Brains."[12]

Such sophisticated skepticism was no doubt less characteristic of the American colonies, a young and hopeful society. But as Alan Heimert maintains, in America too the rationalist "Liberal" clergy tended toward "restricting the Christian pilgrimage to a methodical adjustment to the given norms of existence." "The starting point of Liberal doctrine was the objective 'realities' of the 'present state' of human existence," Heimert continues; for the Liberal, according to Heimert, happiness "came through accommodation to the environment in which man had been placed."[13]

In the more secular discourse of the Revolutionary era, a persistent strain of American thinking continued to restrict the vision of the possible to what existing economic realities appeared to permit. All the Founding Fathers—Jefferson as well as Hamilton, Madison along with John Adams—shared a deep-seated fatalism about the ultimate instability of republican government. In Douglass Adair's words, "the Fathers' scientific reading of history committed them and their contemporaries in varying degrees of rigidity to a species of *political determinism.*"[14] In fact, as Adair adds, their determinism was fundamentally economic, for it followed from Harringtonian assumptions about the relation of property and power. Moreover, Jefferson and others of his generation tended to fall back on the argument from economic realism to explain their inability to put an end to chattel slavery. Abolitionism was in part an insistence that active human will might overcome the objective conditions which to the Fathers appeared inalterable.[15]

Up to this point in the discussion the relativism and fatalism of Locke's psychology have been counterposed to the natural rights philosophy of the *Second Treatise*. But a careful reading of the *Second Treatise* shows that Locke's environmental psychology seriously weakened his apologia for revolt. Thus the law which God has written on men's hearts turns out to mean, for Locke, Hobbes's instinct of self-preservation: "that great law of nature, 'Whoso sheddeth man's blood, by man shall his blood be shed'." Quoting Locke's subsequent assertion that "however strange it may seem, the law-maker hath nothing to do with moral virtues and vices," Leo Strauss concludes that even in the *Second Treatise* Locke did not subscribe to a law of nature in the traditional normative sense.[16]

Throughout his writings Locke systematically segregated things sacred from things secular, allowing freedom of conscience to religion only after carefully barring it from all interference in secular society. In his *Letter Concerning Toleration* Locke asserted that while liberty of conscience "is every man's natural Right," he esteemed it "above all things necessary to distinguish exactly the Business of Civil Government from that of Religion, and to settle the just Bounds that lie between the one and the other."[17] Locke either invoked the traditional morality to win acceptance for a theory based upon hard self-interest, or ignored the traditional morality entirely. The former is exemplified by the chapter on property in the *Second Treatise*, which begins with the observation that God has given the earth to "mankind in common" and ends by rationalizing the unlimited accumulation of wealth. An illustration of the latter is the society envisioned by the Fundamental Constitutions of South Carolina (drafted or at least transcribed by Locke), which gave its citizens broad religious liberty together with "absolute power and authority" over their Negro slaves.

Property rather than conscience was the basis of Locke's whole system. The *Second Treatise* declares that a man can justly kill a thief who threatens only his property, and that an officer who may not take a penny from a soldier's pocket can order the soldier's execution.[18] As Sheldon Wolin remarks, Locke made conscience into a safeguard for property by conceptualizing it as "an internalized expression of external rules rather than the externalized expression of internal convictions." Locke, in Wolin's words, "ushered in a new social world where men, no longer able to communicate on the basis of a common interior life, were reduced to knowing each other solely from the outside." Thus "man had become estranged from man, which corresponds exactly with Locke's terse description of the human condition where individual consciences are strangers to each other: 'no particular man can know the existence of any other being, but only when, by actual operating upon him, it makes itself perceived by him.' Man becomes conscious of his fellows only when he and they collide; conflict and friction are thus the sources of man's awareness of man."[19]

Therefore the neo-Lockeans of the eighteenth century, like the neo-Marxists of the twentieth, were obliged to reintroduce the ethical dimension. They insisted on the reality of the good and on man's ability to recognize it, defended the intuitions of the heart against the paralyzing analyses of the head. "It was necessary," Becker wrote,

> to execute a strategic retreat from the advanced position occupied by abstract reason, from the notion that nature has "no more regard to good above ill than to heat above cold." . . . The innate ideas which Locke had so politely dismissed by way of the hall door had to be surreptitiously brought back again through the kitchen window.[20]

The image is an apt one, for the energizing of Locke's doctrines in the third quarter of the eighteenth century was closely connected with a new emphasis on the political capacity of the common man.

II

James Burgh, Richard Price, Joseph Priestley, John Wilkes, John Cartwright, Granville Sharp, Catharine Macaulay, and Thomas Paine were the principal members of a group of English publicists whose writing cleared the ground for revolution. We shall term them Dissenters. Not all were Nonconformists to the established Anglican Church; Sharp, for instance, belonged to it, and Wilkes was scarcely religious at all. Yet their characteristic figure was, like Price, a preacher in Nonconformist chapels, or, like Burgh, a teacher in a Non-

conformist private school. Participation in radical Protestant
church life critically influenced the Dissenters' ideas. Further,
their refusal to swear prescribed religious oaths excluded them
from political office and university employment and meant
that, middle-class though most of them were, the Dissenters
had some personal experience of oppression. Their polemics
breathed a more-than-academic passion: as Morley says of
Rousseau, they "converted the blank practice of the *philosophes*
into a deadly affair of ball and shell."[21]

From 1750 through the American Revolution the Dissenters
poured forth books and pamphlets which cited one another
profusely (thus Paine refers to Burgh in *Common Sense,* and
to Price in the sixth *Crisis* and *The Crisis Extraordinary*) and
cumulatively expounded a common doctrine. This was the
doctrine of a natural law, made by God, evident to every man,
consonant with the best parts of the traditional law of England
but superior to any law or government which was arbitrary or
unjust. When, on the brink of open rebellion, Americans needed
an intellectual resource more potent than the rights of Englishmen to justify actions so obviously seditious as the Boston
Tea Party, they turned to the rights-of-man teaching of their
staunchest English supporters. "Not until the argument shifted
substantially away from English rights and over to natural
justice did Price and Priestley influence American minds."[22]
When that happened, after 1774, the Dissenters' works "appeared everywhere in the colonies"; their pamphlets and letters
"were read avidly, circulated, published and republished"; it
was they, rather than British Whigs like Burke, whose thought
corresponded to the thought of those called Whigs in America;
the exchange of materials between colonists and Dissenters
"gave both parties . . . a feeling of strength and pushed them
toward an ever more radical view of existing authority."[23]

Common Sense is the most spectacular exemplar of Dissenting influence, but it was only one work among many. The
subscription list for James Burgh's *Political Disquisitions,* published in London in 1774 and in Philadelphia the next year,
"reads like a 'Who's Who in the American Revolution'," but,
like *Common Sense,* Burgh's three-volume work is said to have

had "a widespread influence . . . upon the common folk," for example in the town meetings of western Massachusetts.[24] Very likely even more influential was Richard Price's *Observations on the Nature of Civil Liberty*, published early in 1776 in London at about the same time *Common Sense* appeared in Philadelphia, and reprinted the same year in Boston, New York, Charleston, and (two printings) Philadelphia, as well as in the Hartford and Boston newspapers.[25]

As if to make sure that the gist of Dissenting doctrine reached the common man, John Wilkes had earlier acted out before a transatlantic audience the core idea that conscience, not constituted authority, must be the ultimate arbiter of political good and evil. Writings of Wilkes's were reprinted in New York, Philadelphia, and Boston in 1763, and his complete works in New York in 1768; but it was of course his actions—his arrest for seditious libel, his flight to France, his return and successive re-elections by Middlesex County in the face of Parliament's refusal to seat him—which captured popular attention.[26] The press in America was so "full of his trials, tribulations, and speeches . . . that one may go to almost any issue of any newspaper between 1763–1775 and read of John Wilkes."[27]

A web of personal relations between English Dissenters and American radicals undergirded the written word. Catharine Macaulay sent her "more ardent pamphlets" to John Dickinson, Priestley forwarded to Franklin *Observations on Civil Liberty* by Price, Granville Sharp and Anthony Benezet exchanged pamphlets on slavery. When, after the outbreak of hostilities, Price's position in England became difficult, the American commissioners in Paris invited him to become a United States citizen; he later became a member of the American Academy of Arts and Sciences and the American Philosophical Society. Reciprocally, Benjamin Franklin, no doubt the American leader most influenced by the Dissenters, was closely associated with Price, Burgh, and Priestley in the "Honest Whig" club of London which met regularly from at least as early as 1764 until after the Revolutionary War and in which, according to James Boswell, "much was said . . . against Parliament."[28] Benjamin Rush was another American in constant touch with Dissenters throughout his life. As a student in Great Britain during the 1760s Rush attended Catharine Macaulay's salon, where he met James Burgh, dined with John Wilkes in King's Bench prison, and was converted to republicanism. Back in America Rush corresponded with Mrs. Macaulay, her brother Alderman Sawbridge, Granville Sharp, and Price. Paine, arriving in Pennsylvania with a letter of recommendation from Franklin, read the draft of *Common Sense* to Rush who (so Rush later claimed) suggested the title and found him a publisher. When Priestley was hounded out of England in the 1790s, he and Rush at once sought each other out.[29]

Far from simply elaborating the characteristic themes of Opposition ideologues of the 1720s, Dissenting radicalism reached back over the heads of Trenchard and Gordon, back even beyond Locke, to John Lilburne, Gerrard Winstanley, Richard Overton, and other religious republicans of the 1640s and 1650s. This meant, in part, that whereas the early eighteenth-century commonwealthmen explicitly disavowed republicanism, the Dissenters inclined toward it: Catharine Macaulay praised Lilburne's republican draft constitution for England, the "Agreement of the People,"[30] and Paine called George III a royal brute. More broadly, the ascendancy of Dissenting radicalism represented a return to an essentially religious outlook. Locke, Harrington, and their popularizers wrote as rational analysts, almost as social scientists, whose vision of what might be was "sensibly" limited by recognition of what was. The standpoint of the Dissenters was the experienced reality of conscience; their tone tended to be personal and prophetic; for them the great secular truths were "self-evident" in the same sense as the truth of religion, which is to say intuitively accessible to average men.

The Dissenters made clear their quarrel with an environmental psychology in their first major works. James Burgh's *The Dignity of Human Nature* was published in 1754, and well enough known in America eighty years later for Thoreau to borrow it from the Harvard library. The thesis was that a "self-evident truth is not collected, or deduced, but intuitively perceived." This proposition held equally for truth of all kinds, since "moral truth is in no respect naturally more vague or precarious than mathematical."[31]

Richard Price's *A Review of the Principal Questions and Difficulties in Morals,* published in 1758, was a more substantial book than Burgh's. William Ellery Channing credited to it his lifelong emancipation from Locke's psychology, and in the twentieth century it has enjoyed a revival among philosophers of the school of G. E. Moore. But Price posed the same problem as Burgh, whether *"right* and *wrong,* or *moral good* and *evil,* signify somewhat *really true* of actions, and not merely *sensations,"* and gave the same answer, that a man can intuitively tell of an action that it is good "in much the same sense [that he can say] of an object of sight, that it is *coloured,* or of an object of taste, that it is *sweet."*[32]

Price preferred not to repudiate Locke directly. Much as he admired Locke's excellent essay on understanding, said Price, he found it not "sufficiently clear or explicit." If Locke meant merely that sensation and reflection furnished all the "subjects, materials, and occasions of knowledge," that was well enough, but if he meant them to be "the sources of all our ideas, as he so often calls them," then he was in error. For the mind had a faculty of perception which could give rise to new ideas, "not received immediately from the aforesaid springs": "the power within us that *understands;* the *Intuition* of the mind."[33]

Price was in fact talking about a faculty very much akin to the Quaker inner light. This faculty was not a "moral sense," for Price rejected the theories associated with that term as variants of the environmentalism which reduced man to a machinelike recorder of pains and pleasures. Price conceived the perception of moral truth as an intellectual function. To describe its operation he resorted to some remarkable metaphors: it is the "eye of the mind," the "innate light," to which we owe "our belief of all self-evident truths, . . . our moral ideas, and whatsoever else we discover without making use of any process of reasoning." Sense "lies prostrate under its object" and "must therefore remain a stranger to the objects": it "sees only the *outside* of things." Reason, however, "looks *downwards* upon things" and "acquaints itself with their *natures.*" Failing to make this distinction, Locke offered a definition of the good as action in conformity to some rule or law which (said Price) cannot discriminate between a thing which is right because it is the will of God and a thing which is "right" because it conforms to "the *decrees of the magistrate, or the fashion of the country.*" Not that Locke admitted this: Price remarked that Locke "was strangely embarrassed, and inconsistent in his notions on this, as well as some other subjects." But Price himself was in search of a ground for moral truth which—he used the word—"transcends" the sense impressions man derives from the particular society in which he happens to be born.[34]

Confident intuition of a universal moral order made by nature's God was thus the preamble to the political faith of the Dissenter, as of the subsequent Declaration of Independence. It has been said of Paine that his radicalism was "an attempt to re-establish in politics and religion a lost harmony with this uniform, immutable, universal, and eternal law and order, and to modify or overthrow whatever traditional institutions have obscured this order."[35] For Trenchard and Gordon, as for Locke, the threat of Papism was so vivid that they sought to place limits on the pretensions of men who spoke in the name of religion to interfere with the affairs of secular society. The radical Dissenters, on the other hand, reverted to what Professors Haller and Woodhouse term the "confusion" between the law of nature and the law of God characteristic of the commonwealthmen of the 1640s: a belief better understood as the conviction that nature and nature's God speak with a single voice.[36] Just as John Lilburne in one of his pamphlets cited in the space of two pages the English Chronicles, the Petition of Right, half a dozen medieval statutes, Coke's *Institutes*, various speeches in the Long Parliament, Psalms, Romans, and Deuteronomy as equally appropriate authorities for a political argument (the footnote, "See the 36 Edw. 3, 15, and 1 Cor. 14. 7, 11, 16, 19, 23" suggests the tone of the whole) or Gerrard Winstanley, urging common ownership of land, argued suc-

cessively from "natural experience," "the old Scriptures," and
"the practice of Kings," so John Cartwright asserted that
"the law of God and the law of the land *are all one*" and
Granville Sharp maintained in tract after tract that statute
law must conform to the "eternal Laws of God (which the
Baron [Pufendorf] and other Civilians commonly call 'the
Laws of Nature')."[37]

In order to recover faith in some of Locke's own words
Dissenting radicals were driven back to sources older than
the *Second Treatise*. Their key tenets, the existence of a
higher law and the capacity to perceive it of that inner light
or intuition which all men shared, were religious in origin.
Locke's teaching left men isolated from each other and
passive recipients of sensory experience. The search to overcome that outer and inner alienation discovered no solid
resting-place until it reached theorists inspired by the Radical
Reformation who had shifted "the locus of fundamental value
from external authority to internal impulse."[38] The deep con-
gruity between that older existential orientation and the
approach of the Dissenters explains why Priestley turned
back to the sixteenth-century Unitarian Faustus Socinus;
why the most frequently quoted authority in the moral
philosophy of Price was the seventeenth-century Platonist
Ralph Cudworth; why Benjamin Rush, when he became convinced of universal salvation, found sustenance in the writings of Oliver Cromwell's chaplain; or why when the American
Quaker John Woolman decided not to pay taxes for war, he
remembered John Huss.[39] According to Anthony Lincoln, the
most searching analyst of the Dissenters,

> one great principle . . . lay at the center of all that the Dissenters
> thought and wrote, linking them spiritually with the storms and
> stress of the seventeenth century. That principle was the natu-
> ral right to freedom of conscience. . . .[40]

But what made the thought of the Dissenters politically
revolutionary was that, having restored conscience to the
center of man's experience, they generalized and secularized
it. Synthesizing secular and sacred, natural and divine, they
insisted that all forms of traditional authority should submit

to the judgment of a conscience concerned with both God and politics. Again in the words of Anthony Lincoln, Dissenting radicalism "was a vital movement in the history of political philosophy because it revealed the process by which Christian liberties could be transformed into the Rights of Man. The process was psychological. . . . Once men have taken the short step of investigation from the spiritual privileges of the Christian to the spiritual composition of the understanding, the transformation into Natural Rights is achieved."[41]

This forward step was at the same time a step backward to the un-Lockean thesis of the sixteenth-century treatise *Doctor and Student*, "a favorite of Jefferson's"[42] as of Lilburne, Cartwright, and Sharp, that there is a law

> written in the heart of everie man, teaching him what is to bee done, and what is to be fled: and because it is written in the heart, therefore it may not bee put away . . . and therefore against this law, prescription, statute, nor custome may not prevaile.[43]

Commenting on the tendency of Locke and those who came after him to let nature come between themselves and God, Becker alludes to the seventeenth-century English sectaries who justified resistance by "natural law, which was that right reason or inner light of conscience which God had given to men for their guidance."[44] It was precisely that inner light to which the Dissenters recurred. Its reliability in all things was their essential teaching. Conscience, relegated by Locke to the periphery of a society based on property, became the critic of all social orders.

III

Now if the past generation of scholarship on the American Revolution has considered any one thing to be finally settled it is that Rousseau had nothing to do with it. And despite the significant exception of James Otis' reference to "the celebrated *Rousseau*" in the first major colonial exposition of the doctrine that positive law is void if contradictory to the law of nature, Becker seems to have been right in his assertion that few Revolutionary Americans read French books.[45]

The possibility suggests itself, however, that Rousseau influenced the English Dissenters who in turn concededly influenced the natural rights philosophy of the Declaration. Such indirect transmission of ideas is evident in the case of the Levellers, who, despite what Rossiter terms their "complete boycott" by colonial Americans,[46] were well known to the English radicals whom colonial Americans read. Similarly, although Rossiter finds "precious few traces" of Rousseau in the colonies,

> in no country was Rousseau more highly esteemed than in England. The most favourable reviews both of his *Nouvelle Héloïse* and of his *Emile* had appeared in the English newspapers and periodicals. . . . The hearts of Puritans had been won by the *Letter to D'Alembert.* . . .[47]

One of those Puritans was Burgh, whose 1764 Utopia, *An Account of the Cessares,* idealized Rousseau's account in the *Letter* "of a people near Neuschâtel in Switzerland" who "live free from taxes, imposts and oppressions," whose "chief amusement is to sing Psalms with their wives and children," and who "have also useful books, and are tolerably well instructed, and reason sensibly upon most subjects."[48]

Burgh was not the only Dissenter to read Rousseau, and the case has been made that Dissenters were among all Englishmen particularly receptive to the libertarian asceticism of Rousseau's teachings on education, on luxury, on natural piety and the wisdom of the heart.[49] Illustrative of Rousseau's influence on English Dissenting radicals are Wilkes's reference, when himself in exile, to "the great philosopher, though *in these times* no longer the citizen of *Geneva*"; Priestley's *Essay on the First Principles of Government* (1768), perhaps the more insistent on civil liberties because it recognized "with *Rousseau*" that all representation involves a loss of freedom; Paine's tribute in the *Rights of Man* to Rousseau's "loveliness of sentiment in favor of liberty, that excites respect, and elevates the human faculties"; and

William Godwin's acknowledgment in *Political Justice* that Rousseau had been a principal source of his own thought.[50]

But such influence-hunting is always dubious. Imagine the scholar of the future who attempts to sort out the mutual interaction of Heidegger, Sartre, Camus, Buber, Adam Schaff, Castro, Robert Parris, Bonhoeffer, and Fanon! The important point is: just as all these twentieth-century men combined to create a new atmosphere of existential radicalism, so in the third quarter of the eighteenth century the English Dissenters transformed the Lockean tradition in much the same way that Rousseau did in France. Rossiter is quite mistaken when he says that "Rousseau's whole approach to man, society, and government ran counter to the basic principles of American Revolutionary thought."[51] This may be true of *The Social Contract* (although it was *The Social Contract* which Otis cited in his pamphlet of 1764) but it was not true of the five earlier works—the discourses on the arts and sciences and the origins of inequality, the *Letter to D'Alembert, the Émile,* the *Nouvelle Héloïse*—translated into English almost as soon as they were published during the critical years of the 1750s and early 1760s when English political philosophy began to take a new direction.

Rousseau turned away from the psychology of Locke just in the way that Richard Price did. In the words of Ernst Cassirer: "All ethical thought of the eighteenth century showed, despite deviations in detail, a common direction insofar as it understood the quest for the origin of morality as a psychological problem and as it believed that this problem could be solved only by penetrating the nature of moral feeling. . . . The philosophical ethics of Shaftesbury and Hutcheson, Hume and Adam Smith, were built upon the doctrine of the feelings of sympathy, the doctrine of the 'moral sentiment'." Rousseau like Price, on the other hand, regarded ethical truth as self-evidently apparent to reason, but to reason operating not by logic but by intuition. What was it in the mind that made possible "the self-evidence of ethical insight"? Rousseau, Cassirer says, groped for the right word, referring variously to "reason," "instinct," "divine voice," "inner light," "feeling," "conscience."[52]

Both Price and Rousseau counterpose the spontaneously ethical will to that lesser self determined from without by pain and pleasure. Rousseau, according to Cassirer, "transcends the limitations of the sensationalistic psychology. The self is not a datum of sense and can never be understood as the mere product of sense data. It is an original activity. . . ." An inquiry in psychology ends in a "religion of freedom," and returns in the case of Rousseau as in the case of Price to what Cassirer terms "the actual central principle of Protestantism": the affirmation that "no one can believe for another"; that not only in religion, but in the whole circle of life as well, "everyone must stand on his own and dare to wager his entire self"; that there exists "no kind of inspiration outside the sphere of personal experience," that "the deepest, indeed the only form of self-experience was the experience of the conscience."

Thus, if one cannot return to the older historical view that Rousseau influenced the Declaration of Independence, one can rephrase that proposition in this way: that the natural rights theorizing of Anglo-American radicals in the months and years immediately preceding the drafting of the Declaration made the same key affirmations that Rousseau did. Man was understood to be concerned with more than pain, pleasure, and material self-interest. Moral truth was rescued from environmentalism and once again perceived as an experienced fact. Hume, Voltaire, and Montesquieu notwithstanding, it again became possible to say, as Jefferson wrote in 1774: "the great principles of right and wrong are legible to every reader."[53]

IV

The difference between Locke's conception of the law of nature and that of his Dissenting quasi-disciples appears most clearly in response to the question: To whom is natural law "self-evident"? As Sheldon Wolin says, "the roots of the divergence between the liberal and the radical democratic traditions lie in their contrasting faiths concerning the ability of the human mind to fathom reality and to translate the results into practical actions."[54]

Locke believed that knowledge of the law of nature was accessible only to a minority of gentlemen, and that "the greatest part of mankind want leisure or capacity" for it.[55] Similarly Harrington expressed the opinion that "your mechanics, till they have first feathered their nests, like the fowls of the air whose whole employment is to seek their food, are so busied in their private concernments that they have neither leisure to study the public nor are safely to be trusted with it because a man is not faithfully embarked in this kind of ship if he have no share in the freight."[56]

Locke sought to make sure that, if political participation presupposed leisure, the poor would be kept at work. In 1697, in conformity with his view that unemployment was caused by "nothing else but the relaxation of discipline and corruption of manners," Locke recommended a poor law which among other things deplored the fact that the labor of the children of the laboring poor "is generally lost to the public till they are twelve or fourteen years old" and so provided that all children over three of families on relief should attend "working schools" which would ensure that they would be "from infancy . . . inured to work." Bread, he continued, should be given to the children at their "school" so that their parents would not waste a monetary stipend on drink. "And to this may be also added, without any trouble, in cold weather, if it be thought needful, a little warm water-gruel; for the same fire that warms the room may be made use of to boil a pot of it."[57] Here Locke anticipated the view of his popularizers, Trenchard and Gordon, who "in their vehement and repeated objections to Church of England charity schools, . . . want the children of the poor left in the servant class where they belong."[58]

The Dissenting radicals found their way slowly to faith in the common man's ability to know. Burgh, in his *Dignity of Human Nature*, observed that while all truths were "alike certain" they were not all "alike obvious," moral truth being as clear as mathematical truth only to "superior minds" that were "fitted for receiving and examining it."[59] In his essay "on liberal education" in 1765, Priestley disclaimed any wish of "teaching politics to low mechanics and manufacturers," a remark which his subsequent editor regretted.[60]

But as the American Revolution drew near, the Dissenters' faith in the capacity of the poor for knowledge grew together with their insistence that the poor should vote. Thus Wilkes told Parliament in 1775 that "the meanest mechanic, the poorest peasant and day-labourer" had rights affected by the laws, which, accordingly, "the mass of the people" should have some share in making.[61] Thus Burgh, in his *Political Disquisitions* republished that same year in Philadelphia, rejected "the commonly received doctrine, that servants, and those who receive alms, have no right to vote for members of parliament, [because thereby] an immense multitude of the people are utterly deprived of all power in determining who shall be the protectors of their lives, their personal liberty, their little property."[62] And in keeping with this political doctrine, John Cartwright's *Legislative Rights of the Commonalty Vindicated* of 1776 espoused the epistemological theory that "*common sense*" brought natural law within the reach of the "laboring mechanic and the peasant."[63]

It was an enduring controversy. Later Burke would denounce Price for his "mechanic philosophy" and maintain that the state suffers oppression if hairdressers or working tallow chandlers "either individually or collectively, are permitted to rule."[64] By then the friends of Franklin, whose father *was* a working tallow chandler, and Paine, whose father made corsets, were committed to Paine's great affirmation that

> there is existing in man, a mass of sense lying in a dormant state, and which, unless something excites it to action, will descend with him, in that condition, to the grave. . . . The construction of government ought to be such as to bring forward, by a quiet and regular operation, all that extent of capacity which never fails to appear in revolutions.[65]

In this way a belief in intuitively self-evident moral truth became associated with a belief in equality. All men came to be considered capable of perfection because every man was born predisposed to a correct intuitive knowledge of the essential truths.[66] The words with which Rousseau began his *Émile*—"All is well when it leaves the hands of the Creator of things"—were echoed during the American Revolution by Price, who affirmed that equality was a right with which men came "from the hands of their Maker," as by Paine, who said that the revolutionary constitution of Pennsylvania considered men "as they came from their maker's hands."[67] In 1787 Price, in a sermon on "The Evidence for a Future Period of Improvement in the State of Mankind," quoted the words of Condorcet: "Let us be cautious not to despair of the human race."[68]

So it happened that by the time the Declaration was drafted the belief was once more current that natural rights depend neither on past precedent nor on rational demonstration, but are (as Jefferson put it) "rights of human nature" evident to every man. Perhaps the most striking formulation of this thought before the preamble to the Declaration was in Cartwright's *American Independence*, printed in 1774 in London and republished in Philadelphia in 1776. "It is a capital error in the reasonings of several writers on this subject," Cartwright said,

> that they consider the liberty of mankind in the same light as an estate or chattel, and go about to prove or disprove their right to it by the letter of grants and charters, by custom and usage, and by municipal statutes. Hence too we are told, that these men have a right to more, those to less, and some to none at all. But a title to the liberty of mankind is not established on such rotten foundations: 'tis not among mouldy parchments, nor in the cobwebs of a casuist's brain we are to look for it; it is the immediate, the universal gift of God. . . .[69]

Thus was the way opened for reinterpreting John Locke in the spirit of Tom Paine.

NOTES

1. *Declaration of Independence*, pp. 27–28, 79.
2. The three most important books are Clinton G. Rossiter, *Seedtime of the Republic* (New York, 1953), which first made the point that

the colonists read "Cato" more than Locke; Caroline Robbins, *The Eighteenth Century Commonwealthman* (Cambridge, Mass., 1959), which portrayed "Cato's" predecessors and successors in England; and Bernard Bailyn, *The Ideological Origins of the American Revolution* (Cambridge, Mass., 1967).

3. *Declaration of Independence*, pp. 133–34.

4. The quoted phrases are from *Ideological Origins*, pp. vii, xi. Contrast Rossiter, *Seedtime*, p. 141: "*So long as* [my italics] Americans were more concerned with English rights than natural rights, Gordon and Trenchard were the witnesses most repeatedly called to support their pretensions to liberty."

5. Alan Heimert observes that nearly every Protestant minister in colonial America who commented on civil affairs used Locke's vocabulary, but some used it "almost as a justification of the *status quo*." "Echoes and expositions of Lockean theory" did not always "have the same meanings as those attached to the concepts by the authors of the Declaration of Independence." To understand the Declaration one must identify the influences which "infused the Lockean vocabulary with a moral significance, a severity and an urgency, and thereby translated the ideas of social contract and natural law into a spur to popular activity." Alan Heimert, *Religion and the American Mind from the Great Awakening to the Revolution* (Cambridge, Mass., 1966), p. 17.

6. Glanced at in his *Declaration of Independence*, pp. 57–61, this internal contradiction in the thought of Locke and the entire Enlightenment became the central theme of Becker's *The Heavenly City of the Eighteenth-Century Philosophers* (New Haven and London, 1932), pp. 66–70 *et passim*.

7. *Second Treatise of Government*, Sections 11, 135; *Declaration of Independence*, p. 56.

8. *Declaration of Independence*, p. 60.

9. E. P. Thompson, "Outside the Whale," *Out of Apathy* (London, 1960), p. 184.

10. Basil Willey, *The Eighteenth Century Background* (London, 1940), p. 157.

11. Ernst Cassirer, *The Philosophy of the Enlightenment*, tr. Fritz Koelin and James Pettegrove (Princeton, 1951), p. 244.

12. *Cato's Letters; Or, Essays on Liberty, Civil and Religious, and Other Important Subjects*, 3d ed. (London, 1733), III, 151, 154, 162. H. F. Russell Smith commented in *Harrington and His Oceana* (Cambridge, 1914), p. 146: "they concluded (with a sentiment typical of the age) 'we can preserve Liberty by no other establishment than what we have'." See for such sentiments, e.g., *Cato's Letters*, I, liii–liv.

13. *Religion and the American Mind*, p. 46.

14. Douglass Adair, "The Use of History by the Founding Fathers," a paper read before the American Historical Association in 1955. See also on the Fathers' fatalism my *Class Conflict, Slavery, and the United States Constitution*, essays 7 and 10.

15. See especially David B. Davis, "The Emergence of Immediatism in British and American Antislavery Thought," *Mississippi Valley Historical Review*, XLIX (1962), 209–30.

16. *Second Treatise*, Section 11; Leo Strauss, *Natural Right and History* (Chicago, 1953), pp. 212 n. *et seq.*

17. John Locke, *A Letter Concerning Toleration* (London, 1689), pp. 48, 6.

18. *Second Treatise*, Sections 18, 139.

19. Sheldon Wolin, *Politics and Vision* (Boston, 1960), pp. 338, 340.

20. *Heavenly City*, pp. 86–87.

21. Quoted in Willey, *Eighteenth Century Background*, p. 208.

22. Rossiter, *Seedtime*, p. 360.

23. *Idem;* Bailyn, *Ideological Origins*, p. 133; Robert R. Palmer, *The Age of the Democratic Revolution: A Political History of Europe and America, 1760–1800* (Princeton, 1959), I, 179; Oscar and Mary Handlin, "James Burgh and American Revolutionary Theory," *Massachusetts Historical Society Proceedings*, LXXIII (1961), 52.

24. H. Trevor Colbourn, "John Dickinson, Historical Revolutionary," *Pennsylvania Magazine of History and Biography*, LXXXIII (1959), 285 and n.; Handlins, "James Burgh," p. 38.

25. Kenneth Roberts has the protagonist in his *Rabble in Arms* carry a dog-eared copy of Price's pamphlet, not Paine's.

26. See particularly Pauline Maier, "John Wilkes and American Disillusionment with Britain," *William and Mary Quarterly*, 3rd ser., XX (1963), 373–95.

27. Rossiter, *Seedtime*, p. 527. As to the close relation between Wilkes and the Nonconformists, Anthony Lincoln quotes the contemporary comment: "Round the standard of 'Wilkes and Liberty' the nonconformists flocked in crowds. . . . A Dissenter and a Wilkite were synonymous terms" (*Some Political and Social Ideas of English Dissent 1763–1800* [Cambridge, 1938], p. 26).

28. Nicholas Hans, "Franklin, Jefferson, and the English Radicals at the End of the Eighteenth Century," *Proceedings of the American Philosophical Society*, XCVIII (1954), 407, 410, 416, 418–21; Verner Crane, "The Club of Honest Whigs: Friends of Science and Liberty," *William and Mary Quarterly*, 3rd ser., XXIII (1966), 210–33. Franklin wrote from England in 1770 and again in 1773 that "all" the Dissenters supported the American colonists (Franklin to an unknown correspondent in America, March 8, 1780, and to Thomas Cushing, July 7, 1773, *The Writings of Benjamin Franklin*, ed. Albert H. Smyth [New York, 1905–1907], V, 253, and VI, 78).

29. *The Autobiography of Benjamin Rush*, ed. George Corner (Princeton, 1948), pp. 60–62, 229–31; see, similarly, *Memoir of the Life of Josiah Quincy Jr.* (Boston, 1825), e.g., pp. 241, 339, 341–42.

30. *The History of England from the Accession of James I to the Elevation of the House of Hanover* (London, 1769–1772), V, 7–9.

31. James Burgh, *The Dignity of Human Nature* (London, 1754), pp. 171, 178. For Thoreau and Burgh, see Kenneth Cameron, *Emerson the Essayist* (Raleigh, N.C., 1945), II, 193.

32. Richard Price, *A Review of the Principal Questions and Difficulties in Morals* (London, 1758), pp. v. 13. Regarding Price and Channing, see Chapter 2, below.

33. *A Review*, pp. 18–19.

34. *Ibid.*, pp. 23, 53, 63–64, 169, 466; see Priestley's summary in *The Theological and Miscellaneous Works of Joseph Priestley*, ed. J. T. Rutt (London, 1817–1832), III, 146–51.

35. Harry Hayden Clark, "An Historical Interpretation of Thomas Paine's Religion," *University of California Chronicle*, XXXV (1933), 60; and in agreement, Robert R. Palmer, "Tom Paine: Victim of the Rights of Man," *Pennsylvania Magazine of History and Biography*, LXVI (1942), 164: "He believed in a fundamental natural harmony, an underlying peaceableness of society which the interference of governments disrupted."

36. *The Leveller Tracts*, ed. William Haller and Godfried Davies (New York, 1944), pp. 3, 43, 45; A. S. P. Woodhouse, *Puritanism and Liberty* (London, 1938), p. [93].

37. "The earnest Petition of many Free-born People of This Nation," *Tracts*, ed. Haller and Davies, pp. 108–9; "The Law of Freedom in a Platform," *The Works of Gerrard Winstanley*, ed. George H. Sabine (New York, 1941), pp. 520 ff.; John Cartwright, *The Legislative Rights of the Commonalty Vindicated; Or, Take Your Choice!* 2d ed. (London, 1777), p. 65 n.; Granville Sharp, *A Declaration of The People's Natural Right to a Share in the Legislature* . . . (London, 1774), p. xxiii.

38. David B. Davis, *The Problem of Slavery in Western Culture* (Ithaca, N.Y., 1966), p. 299. Woodhouse observes that the Leveller Agreements of the People derived from the concept of the church as a voluntary covenant "first found among the Anabaptists of Germany" (*Puritanism and Liberty*, p. [72]; see also George H. Williams, *The Radical Reformation* [London, 1962]), p. xxviii); more broadly, Ernst Troeltsch called the Anabaptists the "fathers of the rights of man" (Gustav Salander, *Vom Werden der Menschenrechte* [Leipzig, 1926], p. 84). The passage of Continental Anabaptist ideas to England is described by Rufus M. Jones, *Studies in Mystical Religion* (London, 1909), Chs. 17–20, and stressed by Roland H. Bainton, "The Left Wing of the Reformation," *Journal of Religion*, XXI (1941), 134. Lilburne believed himself to be in the tradition of "John Hus in Bohemia, Jerom of Prague, John Wickliff in England, the Martyrs in Queen Maryes dayes, the Hugonots or Protestants in France, the Gues in the Low-Countrys: all not only esteemed Hereticks by the Church, but rebels and traytors to their several States and Princes" ("The Just Defence of John Lilburn," *Tracts*, ed. Haller and Davies, p. 452). Lilburne, like Fox, "began as a proselyte of the Baptists" (*ibid.*, p. 40, and *Leveller Manifestoes of the Puritan Revolution*, ed. Don M. Wolfe [New York and London, 1944], p. 3; *George Fox, an Autobiography*, ed. Rufus M. Jones [Philadelphia, 1903–1906], I, 18).

39. The role of Cudworth and other Platonists in handing on, through Shaftesbury, an outlook on the world antagonistic to Locke's environmentalism, is described by Davis in *Problem of Slavery*, pp. 348 ff., and by Ernst Cassirer, *The Platonic Renaissance in England*, tr. James Pettegrove (Austin, Tex., 1953), especially pp. 191–95. For Rush and Jeremiah White, see the former's *Autobiography*, pp. 163–64; for Woolman and Huss, *The Journal and Essays of John Woolman*, ed. Amelia M. Gummere (New York, 1922), pp. 204–5.

40. Lincoln, *English Dissent*, p. 10.

41. *Ibid.*, p. 269. The thesis that the rights of man represented a secularization of religious rights of conscience is also argued in an almost forgotten little book, Georg Jellinek's *The Declaration of the Rights of Man and of Citizens*, tr. Max Farrand (New York, 1901).

42. Rossiter, *Seedtime*, p. 357.

43. Quoted in *Tracts*, ed. Haller and Davies, p. 42. See also Woodhouse, *Puritanism and Liberty*, pp. [71] n., [89].

44. *Declaration of Independence*, p. 34.

45. James Otis, "The Rights of the British Colonies Asserted and Proved," *Pamphlets of the American Revolution*, ed. Bernard Bailyn, (Cambridge, Mass., 1965), I, 436; Becker, *Declaration of Independence*, p. 27.

46. Rossiter, *Seedtime*, p. 357.

47. *Ibid.*, p. 359; J. Churton Collins, *Voltaire, Montesquieu and Rousseau in England* (London, 1908), p. 194.

48. [James Burgh], *An Account of the . . . Cessares* (London, 1764), p. 112 n.

49. Henri Roddier, *J-J. Rousseau en Angleterre au XVIIIe Siècle* (Paris, 1950), especially Ch. 7.

50. *A Complete Collection of the Genuine Papers, Letters, Etc. in the Case of John Wilkes, Esq.* (Berlin, 1769), p. 74; "Essay on Government," *Works of Priestley*, XXII, 10; "Rights of Man," *Complete Writings of Paine*, I, 299; William Godwin, *Enquiry Concerning Political Justice*, ed. F. E. L. Priestley (Toronto, 1946), I, ix, 4 n., etc.

51. Rossiter, *Seedtime*, p. 359.

52. This and the subsequent quotations are from Cassirer's *The Question of Jean-Jacques Rousseau*, tr. and ed. Peter Gay (New York, 1954), pp. 99–118, and *Rousseau, Kant, Goethe: Two Essays* (Hamden, Conn., 1961), pp. 45–47. On the essentially religious character of Rousseau's social philosophy, see also the summary of Lester G. Crocker: "Both his unshakable religious emotions and his increasing opposition to the entire direction of the philosophy of the encyclopedists led Rousseau to a firm belief in God's direct, continuing providence" (*An Age of Crisis: Man and World in Eighteenth Century French Thought* [Baltimore, 1959], p. 32).

53. *Papers*, ed. Boyd, I, 134.

54. Wolin, *Politics and Vision*, p. 297.

55. "The Reasonableness of Christianity," quoted in Strauss, *Natural Right and History*, p. 225.

56. "The Commonwealth of Oceana," *The Political Writings of James Harrington*, ed. Charles Blitzer (New York, 1955), p. 135.

57. Quoted in H. R. Fox Bourne, *The Life of John Locke* (London, 1876), II, 378, 383, 384. See also Locke's "Some Considerations of the Consequences of the Lowering of Interest . . ." (1691): "the labourers, living generally but from hand to mouth . . . may well enough carry on their part, if they have but money enough to buy victuals, cloaths, and tools" (*The Works of John Locke in Four Volumes* [London, 1768], II, 16).

58. J. G. A. Pocock, "Machiavelli, Harrington, and English Political Ideologies in the Eighteenth Century," *William and Mary Quarterly*, 3rd ser., XXII (1965), 575.

59. Burgh, *Dignity of Human Nature*, p. 178.

60. "Lectures on History and General Policy," *Works*, XXIV, 23 and n.

61. *The Speeches of John Wilkes* (London, 1777), I, 107.

62. James Burgh, *Political Disquisitions* (London, 1774), I, 37.

63. Cartwright, *Legislative Rights*, pp. 67–68.

64. Edmund Burke, *Reflections on the Revolution in France* (London, 1790), pp. 115, 72–73.

65. "Rights of Man, Part Second," *Complete Writings*, I, 368.

66. Priestley's assertion in 1768 that "the human species . . . is capable of . . . unbounded improvement" and that the "progress of the species [is] towards perfection" ("Essay on Government," *Works*, XXII, 8) has often been considered the first expression of perfectionism in Anglo-American political philosophy.

67. Price, *Additional Observations on the Nature and Value of Civil Liberty*, 3d ed. (London, 1777), p. 22; "A Serious Address to the People of Pennsylvania on the Present Situation of Their Affairs," *Complete Writings of Paine*, II, 285.

68. Price, *The Evidence for a Future Period of Improvement in the State of Mankind* (London, 1787), p. 51 n.

69. John Cartwright, *American Independence the Interest and Glory of Great Britain* (Philadelphia, 1776 [1st ed. London, 1774]), pp. 32–33.

CHAPTER 2

CERTAIN
INALIENABLE
RIGHTS

After asserting the self-evident truth that all men are created equal, the preamble to the Declaration added that they have certain inalienable rights that governments are created "to secure." What was striking about this formulation was its failure to mention rights given up in the process.

Traditional formulations of the social contract, such as Locke's, described a bargain: the exchange of certain rights fully enjoyed by individuals in the state of nature (such as the right to punish criminals) for the more secure protection by society of other rights (such as the right to private property). Thus Locke distinguished natural rights which a man "wholly gives up" in entering society from those which "cease not" after the social contract. Moreover, Locke failed to make it clear whether those rights which "cease not" even in society may be exercised by individuals at their discretion, or merely constitute (as it were) the moral stock on behalf of which authorized representatives act by proxy.[1]

In contrast, the rights enumerated by the Declaration are termed "inalienable." Nothing is said about other, alienable rights. Although linguistic details in a hastily drafted revolutionary manifesto should not be pushed too far, at first glance the adjective "inalienable" suggests a conflict between the social contract theory of the Declaration of Independence and that of Locke's *Second Treatise*.

My intention in saying this is not to revive the simplistic belief that the men who wrote the Declaration were "radical" in contrast to the "conservative" drafters of the United States Constitution. Many men were in both bodies. Among those most urgent for independence in 1776 who were not members of the Constitutional Convention in 1787, some (such as Patrick Henry and Richard Henry Lee) opposed the Constitution but others (such as Jefferson, Paine, and Sam Adams) supported it. The drafters of 1776 were the same sort of propertied gentlemen as the drafters of 1787.

What was different in 1776 was not the men but the situation. The drafters of 1776 did not yet feel the need to protect themselves against unpropertied majorities. As Lefebvre says of those who wrote the French Declaration of the Rights of Man and Citizen:

> The bourgeoisie had no doubts of itself, nor did it doubt that the new order it had conceived, in accord with the laws of nature and the divine will, was destined forever to assure the welfare and progress of the human race. . . . The bourgeoisie expressed its thought in less measured and prudent language than it used later, since it did not foresee that its own political ascendancy would ever be questioned. . . . Thanks to the superb confidence of the bourgeoisie, its Declaration could become a charter of political and even social democracy.[2]

Within ten years of 1776, as will appear in the next chapter, men like James Madison and John Adams made exactly the same analysis of their failure to include in the Declaration of Independence explicit protection for property rights. The importance of their failure to do so was that it left the Declaration sufficiently ambiguous that, once the coalition which produced it had disintegrated, the more radical elements in that coalition could still stretch Jefferson's language to cover their new needs. Becker is misleading when he states that the Declaration exhibited "simplicity, clarity, logical order" because the age which wrote it did not doubt that the universe itself was "simply constructed, open and visible."[3] Owing to its failure to qualify or explain the adjective "inalienable" the Declaration could be interpreted in two quite different ways.

If rights were viewed as property, then inalienability might mean only that a man must consent to what is done with them. Pitt used the term in this sense when, moving the withdrawal of British troops from Boston in 1775, he asserted that a British subject's property was "invariably inalienable, without his own consent."[4] Inalienability thus defined did not exclude the permanent transfer of a right from original owner to a delegated purchaser or donee. David Brion Davis comments that

> as Rousseau shrewdly observed, Pufendorf had argued that a man might alienate his liberty just as he transferred his property by contract; and Grotius had said that since individuals could alienate their liberty by becoming slaves, a whole people could do the same, and become the subjects of a king.

"Here, then," Davis concludes, "was the fatal flaw in the traditional theories of natural rights."[5]

The consequences were quite different if inalienability was defined by analogy to conscience. Liberty of conscience, wrote Francis Hutcheson in his *System of Moral Philosophy*, "is not only an essential but an unalienable branch" of natural liberty. "This right appears from the very constitution of the rational mind which can assent or dissent solely according to the evidence presented, and naturally desires knowledge. The same considerations shew this right to be unalienable: it cannot be subject to the will of another. . . ."[6] When rights were termed "unalienable" in this sense, it did not mean that they could not be transferred without consent, but that their nature made them untransferrable.

This was a proposition peculiarly congenial to Dissenting radicalism. For it freedom of conscience was inseparable from moral agency. When this conception was transferred to the secular sphere, conflict was inevitable between inalienability thus defined and any understanding of rights which stressed their surrender when men joined society or which regarded them as powers not personally exercised but delegated to trustees.

The institutional foundations of bourgeois society—representative government and the market economy—were at stake in this debate. Radicalism thrust toward the conclusions that true freedom was incapable of delegation, and that what was inalienable was what could not become a commodity. At heart the controversy was between two definitions of freedom: on the one hand, freedom defined as control over the finished products of human activity; on the other hand, freedom defined as self-determining human activity itself.

I

As in the 1960s, radical definitions of "inalienability" evolved from polemics concerning the corruptions of an affluent society. Similar, too, was the fact that discussion at first focused upon the connection between the loss of public spirit believed to follow from excessive preoccupation with material goals, and the institution of education. Then as now, some favored using the schools to indoctrinate prescribed nonmaterialist values. Others, in the one situation as in the other, considered this remedy a symptom of the underlying problem, and in the ensuing controversy first clearly defined what they meant by freedom.

Even before 1750, for example, James Burgh was warning England against "LUXURY and IRRELIGION" in a volume entitled *Britain's Remembrancer*. Burgh predicted that these "characteristic Vices of the Age" would bring Great Britain to the same melancholy end as Rome.[7] Manners, he repeated in his *Political Disquisitions* on the eve of the American Revolution, were more important than laws in determining a people's fate. When commerce had led to luxury, and luxury to bribery and dissipation, the best of lawgivers could not long preserve freedom.[8]

What then was to be done? Burgh's *An Account of the Cessares* sketched a society every feature of which was designed to forestall the prophecy of *Britain's Remembrancer*. Drawing lessons from Harrington and Plato, the Cessareans (Dutch settlers somewhere in South America) divided their land equally so as to "banish riches as well as poverty," and deliberately chose for settlement "a distant and retired country, out of the common course of trade"; for

> though some commerce with other nations would be attended with several advantages to us, yet we were afraid it would be productive of some unhappy consequences, and bring in luxury, and customs injurious to the welfare of our state.[9]

Lest iniquity creep in regardless, the Cessarean senate was enjoined "to establish sumptuary laws, and carefully to guard against the first introduction of all sorts of luxury: and to prohibit all those arts and trades, which minister only to idleness and pride, and the unnecessary refinements and embellishments of life, which are the certain fore-runners of the ruin of every state."[10]

The overall tone of this first Dissenting remedy for the ills of an affluent society is authoritarian and Calvinist. Although "all men are here considered as brethren, united together in one band, to promote the common good," the Cessareans preferred the "mixt form" of government to "the anarchy, licentiousness, and wild tumults of a democracy." Geneva is repeatedly praised, as are Sparta and the empire of the Incas. The hereditary governor and senate for life of the Cessareans are associated with a species of official called "inspectors," who oversee morals. Horse racing and cockfighting are forbidden, as are usury and interest (except by permission of the senate); honest debtors have their debts "discharged out of the public stock"; dueling is punished by a year's imprisonment and temporary loss of citizenship; also—a radical proposal in eighteenth-century England—all are free to hunt wild animals, birds, and fish. Mocking or affronting, spreading lies or false reports, are variously punished, and "all immoral and obscene books, prints, pictures, etc., are ordered to be burnt" (here the practice of the Spartans is once more cited). Swearing is fined, plural officeholding forbidden, and all prices fixed by the senate. Prisoners must be set to work and minor offenders placed in "bettering houses," modeled on Dutch "houses of correction." Cards, dice, and (with Rousseau) drama are outlawed; Catholics may not hold public office; voting is by ballot and all men of good behavior over twenty-one, if they are Protestants, may vote. Finally: "Since we are all brethren, and God has given to men a natural right to liberty, we allow of no slavery among us."[11]

There were Dissenters, and later, nineteenth-century Evangelicals, who long continued to make social blueprints on this nastily puritanical plan. In 1787, for instance, Granville Sharp designed a real Utopia for freed Negroes in Sierra Leone. His "temporary regulations (until better shall be proposed)" included a seventy-one-hour work week and a pride and indolence tax on those who did not work. Like Burgh, Sharp had a plan for mutual supervision within families and neighborhoods. Among the imaginary Cessareans, the head of every family was responsible for the behavior of all its members, and "all the families in every town or parish are answerable for the faults or crimes of every person in it." Among the unfortunate settlers of Sierra Leone, "the eye of every neighbour" was upon every other through the institution of the Anglo-Saxon frankpledge system, which Sharp, according to his biographer, believed to have been invented by Moses on the advice of his father-in-law Jethro and introduced into England by King Alfred.[12]

This was a stream of thought which hardly led toward liberty, Lockean or otherwise. A more fruitful initiative, but in response to the same problem which Burgh tried to solve, was Joseph Priestley's *Remarks on a Code of Education, Proposed by Dr. Brown* . . . , published the year after *An Account of the Cessares*, in 1765. Three years later, in 1768, Priestley expanded it into the first Dissenting treatise on political philosophy.

Priestley's 1765 essay on education answered a pamphlet on *Civil Liberty, or Licentiousness, and Faction*, published earlier in that year of the Stamp Act Congress by an Anglican minister named John Brown. Brown was the famous author of *An Estimate of the Manners and Principles of the Times,* published 1757–1758, which had presented an analysis similar to Burgh's of the *vain, luxurious,* and *selfish* EFFEMINACY"[13] in English society. Like Burgh's too was Brown's prescription for the social patient. But unlike Burgh, the more sophisticated Brown articulated the authoritarian remedy he proposed in the language of political philosophy.

Civil liberty, argued Brown in his pamphlet by that title, derives from the "salutary *Restraint*" which society places on natural desires. "Every natural Desire, which might in any respect be inconsistent with the general Weal, is given up as a voluntary Tax, paid for the higher, more lasting, and more important *Benefits,* which we reap from *social Life.*" In this metaphor of the tax Brown well expressed the idea of natural rights as property which can be aliened in exchange for an equivalent return. And at this point in his argument Brown explicitly attacked "Cato's" most radical assertion: "that every Man hath an unalienable Right to worship God in that *Manner* which accords to the Dictates of his own Conscience," as also "to *think what he will,* and *act as he thinks,* provided he *acts not* to the *Prejudice* of another."[14]

Taking his own stand on the environmental psychology which held that culture determined personality and values, Brown rejected the proposition that "natural Conscience" recognized "an *unchangeable* Principle of Right and Wrong, arising universally in the Human Heart." Conscience would and should be guided by whatever religion the state prescribed. A free state was not a state in which men were free, but a state in which virtuous manners and principles predominated. Carefully noting the objection that what he wished was "building civil Liberty on the *Servitude* of the *Mind,* and shackling the infant Soul with *early Prejudice,*" Brown rebutted that to fail to teach a child "salutary Habits and Principles" would be like failing to teach a child to walk erect; that the mind cannot be compelled to receive ideas, therefore offering good ones for its consideration would not coerce it; and that in any case true freedom was to be wise. Hence, then, it appeared "that the private Freedom of the infant Mind is not *violated,* but only *directed* to its *best End,* by early and salutary Instruction."

After extended reference to Sparta, Brown concluded that, besides curbing the licentiousness of the press, the state should introduce "a general and prescribed Improvement of the Laws of Education."[15]

Compulsory public education, as proposed by Brown, posed a challenge direct both to Priestley's libertarian convictions and to (so Priestley said) "all my labours"[16] as a schoolmaster at the Dissenters' Warrington Academy.

Priestley accepted the gist of Burgh's and Brown's critique of existing English society, but in keeping with his faith in man's perfectibility, he thought the way to change it was by more freedom, not less. Education was a young art, and any craft in its beginnings required "experiments" and "a number of awkward attempts." The best plan of education at any given moment became confining as the arts and sciences advanced. Priestley did not fear Brown's favorite term of opprobrium, "licentiousness":

> . . . we can never expect to see human nature . . . brought to perfection, but in consequence of indulging unbounded liberty, and even caprice. . . . The power of nature in producing plants cannot be shown to advantage, but in all possible circumstances of culture. The richest colours, the most fragrant scents, and the most exquisite flavours, which our present gardens and orchards exhibit, would never have been known, if florists and gardeners had been confined in the processes of cultivation; nay if they had not been allowed the utmost licentiousness of fancy in the exercise of their arts.

The "casual experiment," the "undesigned deviation from established rules," the "new, and seemingly irregular methods," the "odd and excentric," had over and over again been fruitful of new truth.[17] (This passage should give pause to those who identify Dissenters in general and Priestley in particular with dry and uniform utilitarianism, with Sabbath gloom and counting-house morality.)

Variety was good for its own sake, Priestley maintained. To seek to create a society with uniform sentiments would be to wish an environment better suited to animals than men. Let us, Priestley cried, "assert the native freedom of our souls," "aspire to the noble privilege of governing ourselves like men," "relax the bonds of authority, rather than bind them faster."[18]

Priestley's refutation of Brown centered on the price Brown had to pay for his accommodation to the psychology of Locke. By insisting on the distinction between vice and virtue while at the same time clinging to the Lockean assumption that our ideas of vice and virtue derive from our environment, Brown sets the stage for a godly totalitarianism: a state which will manipulate the environment and dictate public education to ensure that its citizens are good. The essential difference between Brown and Priestley is that the tradition which passes from Priestley through Paine and Godwin to Garrison and Thoreau insists that men can and must *free themselves*, rather than *be freed* by the external manipulation of educators and planners.

Then Priestley begins the translation of these sentiments into political philosophy. The right to educate one's children is as dear to any parent as the right of conscience, and "if there be any natural rights which ought not to be sacrificed to the ends of civil society," freedom of education is one of them. Priestley states that he would choose to emigrate from a country which required so great a sacrifice, wryly noting that restriction on freedom of travel is necessarily another part of Brown's "scheme." Under Brown's administration, Priestley charges, "a man could enjoy little more than security in the bare possession of his property."[19]

Priestley's 1765 *Remarks on a Code of Education* became Chapter IV of the 1768 *Essay on the First Principles of Government*, written, according to Priestley's preface, to discuss "the subject of Civil and Religious Liberty" without particular reference to Dr. Brown, and to place "the foundation of some of the most valuable interests of mankind on a broader and firmer basis than Mr. Locke and others who had formerly written upon this subject."[20]

Unlike Locke, Priestley begins with freedom of the mind; his first sentence reads: "Man derives two capital advantages from the superiority of his intellectual powers." And this concern leads on to the key distinction in the essay, between "political liberty" and "civil liberty." Here are Priestley's definitions:

> POLITICAL LIBERTY, I would say, *consists in the power which the members of the state reserve to themselves, of arriving at the public offices*, or, at least, *of having votes in the nomination of those who fill them*: and I would choose to call CIVIL LIBERTY, *that power over their own actions, which the members of the state reserve to themselves, and which their officers must not infringe.*

Relating this distinction to the process of social contract as described by Locke, Priestley states that "political liberty" is that which a man receives in exchange for a part of his original "civil liberty." Nevertheless—and this is where Priestley goes beyond Locke—some kinds of civil liberty, complete personal freedom in certain areas of life, remain in full force in the midst of society. Political liberty concerns the form in which the power of the state is exerted; civil liberty is a question of how much power the state, however organized, exerts over individual lives. The task of political liberty is to safeguard civil liberty, but the most democratic state will threaten civil liberty if its power is too great.[21]

With respect to political liberty, natural rights are residually or conditionally inalienable. That is, "no man can be supposed to resign his natural liberty, but on *conditions*," and if the conditions are violated the liberty may be resumed. "Every man retains, and can never be deprived of his natural right . . . of relieving himself from . . . every thing that has been imposed upon him without his own consent; this must be the only true and proper foundation of all the governments subsisting in the world, and that to which the people who compose them have an unalienable right to bring them back." On the other hand, men may by their own consent voluntarily surrender all their political interests, and in that case there is no recourse except to the next generation.[22]

But with respect to civil liberty (here Priestley warmed to his main theme), natural rights are either enjoyed or surrendered, and are in this sense absolute. How much civil liberty exists in a particular state can be measured by "whether a people enjoy more or fewer of their natural rights," or alternatively, by whether the government "leave a man the most valuable of his private rights." Civil liberty has been greatly impaired, says Priestley, by the idea that "the more the cases are in which mankind are governed by this united reason of the whole community, so much the better; whereas, in truth, the greater part of human actions are of such a nature, that more inconvenience would follow from their being fixed by laws, than from their being left to every man's arbitrary will." Men enter society only to procure those things which they cannot procure by their own unaided efforts. In finding out truth, for instance, "individuals are always employed to assist multitudes," not the reverse. Whether public officials be considered in the light of servants or of representatives and deputies, "there are many cases in which it is more convenient for a man to act *in person* than by any deputation whatever."[23]

At this point Priestley might seem to have said that those natural rights which individuals can exercise without assistance, such as religion and education, are absolutely inalienable. He does not quite do so. Such rights are absolute in the sense that unlike those civil rights which can be delegated, they cannot be conditionally relinquished, or merely residually possessed. But Priestley was uncertain whether to articulate this circumstance merely as a fact of nature, or as a right of nature too. At the same time that he wished to widen the area in which individuals might act without government interference, Priestley attempted to make the language of political philosophy more utilitarian: that is, to establish that "the good and happiness of the . . . majority of the members of any state, is the great standard by which every thing relating to that state must finally be determined."[24] But the good of the whole (as Priestley alternatively termed it) is concededly difficult to determine. Only experiments, Priestley concluded, can determine how far the power of the legislature should extend.

The *Essay on the First Principles of Government* thus simultaneously prophesied a laissez-faire society and the pragmatic welfare state. Because it looked both ways it has been forgotten. In its own time, however, the attempt to systematize the Dissenting revision of Locke made the *Essay* an important halfway house, or stepping-stone. As will appear, Price built on it in constructing the definitive statement of Dissenting political philosophy during the first years of the American Revolution. Moreover, the distinction between what Priestley called "political" and "civil" liberty proved lasting. Writing to Jefferson in 1788 and apparently summarizing a series of conversations between them, Tom Paine used different words to separate the rights of man into the same two groups. Paine listed as "natural" rights only those most closely akin to conscience which the individual could exercise unaided: the rights "of thinking, speaking, forming and giving opinions."[25] An alternative formulation was provided by the New Hampshire constitution of 1784: "When men enter into a state of society, they surrender up some of their natural rights to that society, in order to insure the protection of others; and, without such an equivalent, the surrender is void. Among the natural rights, some are in their very nature unalienable, because no equivalent can be given or received for them. Of this kind are the RIGHTS OF CONSCIENCE."

Whatever the terminology, the effect of these new distinctions was to delineate a category of natural rights which "ceased not" when men entered society in the very tangible sense that each individual continued to exercise them personally at all times.

II

The statesmanship of the American Revolution, however, tended to reserve absolute inalienability for the life of the mind (or even more narrowly, for religious conscience), and to leave actions of every kind subject to state regulation. This becomes evident if one examines the bills of rights to the constitutions created by all but two of the thirteen original states. Here one finds the adjective "inalienable" repeatedly applied to two kinds of rights: the right of conscience and the right of revolution.

"All men," said the 1776 constitutions of North Carolina and Pennsylvania, "have a natural and unalienable right to worship Almighty God according to the dictates of their own consciences." But while almost every constitution provided for religious freedom, almost every provision was coupled with a clause protecting the state from disturbance undertaken in the name of religion: ". . . *Provided*, That nothing herein contained shall be construed to exempt preachers of treasonable or seditious discourses, from legal trial and punishment" (North Carolina); ". . . unless, under colour of religion, any man shall disturb the good order, peace or safety of the State, or shall infringe the laws of morality, or injure others, in their natural, civil, or religious rights" (Maryland); ". . . *Provided*, That the liberty of conscience, hereby granted, shall not be so construed as to excuse acts of licentiousness, or justify practices inconsistent with the peace or safety of this State" (New York); ". . . provided it be not repugnant to the peace and safety of the State" (Georgia); ". . . provided he doth not disturb the public peace" (Massachusetts).

The inalienable right to revolution, on the other hand, was available only to majorities. It was "the people" (Maryland and Massachusetts), "the community" (Pennsylvania), more precisely "a majority of the community" (Virginia) which alone could alter, reform, or abolish government. The literature of the Revolution, as Thad Tate has written, "described resistance as a right exercised only by decision of the community, never on the initiative of individuals."[26]

Both definitions of inalienability severely limited the individual's scope of action. For some Dissenting radicals, however, individual self-determination had become the very definition of freedom. Richard Price, in particular, challenged the Lockean assumptions of the state (as later of the federal) constitutions.

Price believed that man was not only capable of intuitively telling good from evil, but that he had free will to choose how to act. Speaking to an audience of children in 1766, Price voiced his doctrine in the simplest terms. "Every one knows," so he told his young audience, that the soul is active. "Every one feels that he has a power of self-motion, that he can begin action or cease from action as he pleases, and that he has an absolute command over his thoughts and determinations."[27]

The principle of what he termed "Spontaneity . . . Self-determination, which constitutes us Agents" became the basis of Price's political thought. In his *Observations on the Nature of Civil Liberty*, the principal English defense of the American Revolution, Price argued that physical, moral, religious, and civil liberty were all aspects of "liberty in general," linked together by "one general idea, that runs through them all; I mean, the idea of *Self-direction . . . Self-government.*" Liberty, "natural and unalienable," was therefore the opposite of slavery, or submission to forces outside oneself:

> Without *Physical Liberty*, man would be a machine acted upon by mechanical springs, having no principle of motion in himself, or command over events; and, therefore, incapable of all merit and demerit.—Without *Moral Liberty*, he is a wicked and detestable being, subject to the tyranny of base lusts, and the sport of every vile appetite.—And without *Religious* and *Civil Liberty* he is a poor and abject animal, without rights, without property, and without a conscience, bending his neck to the yoke, and crouching to the will of every silly creature who has the insolence to pretend to authority over him.[28]

The consequences of this position for Americans were largely reserved for the nineteenth century. Then it turned out to make considerable difference whether one said slavery was wrong because every man has a natural right to the possession of his own body, or because every man has a natural right freely to determine his own destiny. The first kind of right was alienable: thus Locke neatly derived slavery from capture in war, whereby a man forfeited his labor to the conqueror who might lawfully have killed him;[29] and thus Dred Scott was judged permanently to have given up his freedom. But the second kind of right, what Price called "that power of self-determination which all agents, as such, possess,"[30] was inalienable as long as man remained man. Like the mind's quest for religious truth from which it was derived, self-determination was not a claim to ownership which might be both acquired and surrendered, but an inextricable aspect of the activity of being human.

Under heavy attack for his defiant criticism of his own government in time of war, Price insisted that his principles were "the same with those taught by Mr. Locke, and all the writers on Civil Liberty who have been hitherto most admired in this country."[31] But as Anthony Lincoln says, Price differed from Locke "in certain cardinal aspects: in his psychological beliefs and in the purpose of his work"; if in expressing his philosophy "he sometimes fell into the prevailing terminology of property, it was because he felt that moral self-determination was the most precious property a man could possess."[32]

Where Price went beyond Locke most obviously was in his extension of Priestley's concept that the individual retains some natural rights when in society, to the conclusion: "In every free state every man is his own Legislator."[33] This phrase, Price remarked in his subsequent Additional Observations, "has been much exclaimed against, and occasioned no small part of the opposition which has been made to the principles advanced in the Observations on Civil Liberty."[34]

Price responded to this criticism ambiguously. On the one hand, he said what he meant was that "every independent agent in a free state ought to have a share in the government of it." On the other hand, however, Price stated that with certain limitations he accepted the charge that the liberty for which he pleaded was "a right or power in every one to act as he likes without any restraint."[35]

In the characteristic manner of Dissenting thought, Price built his case on an analogy to religion. All men have "the same unalienable right" to religious liberty, he began, provided only that "no one has a right to such a use of it as shall take it from others." This reasoning "is equally applicable to the Liberty of man in his civil capacity," Price continued. Citing Priestley's Essay, Price said that it "may be accommodated to all I have said on this subject, by only giving some less general name to that which Dr. Priestley calls civil Liberty." In fact, however, whereas Priestley still took it for granted that, in joining society, men must "voluntarily resign some part of their natural liberty," in Price's account the idea of the surrender of natural rights has disappeared. It was something more than a change in names that Price no longer spoke of those specific natural liberties (religion and education) which society might not infringe, but referred simply to "liberty" in general: "Just government, therefore, does not *infringe* liberty, but *establish* it.—It does not *take away* the rights of mankind, but *protect* and *confirm* them." In passages such as these Price seemed to be saying that all natural liberty is inalienable. For Price a government constructed on any other plan represented

> the folly of *giving up* liberty in order to *maintain* Liberty; and, in the very act of endeavouring to secure the most valuable rights, to arm a body of enemies with power to destroy them.[36]

In sum, then, Dissenting political philosophy as it culminated in the *Observations* and *Additional Observations* of Richard Price shifted the burden of proof from the individual who sought to preserve control over his own actions to the state which claimed the right to regulate them. As Halévy observes, this amounted to abolishing the social contract:

> . . . it may be held that men formed the original pact in order to guarantee a certain number of pre-existing natural rights. This is the sense in which Price and Cartwright tend to interpret Locke's theory. But, in this case, . . . what is the point of the mediation of the contract? When men have adopted a position of legitimate insurrection, what is the point of saying that they are rising because the contract which should have guaranteed their rights has been violated, instead of saying, more simply, that they are rising because their rights have been violated?[37]

It was this same conception which the Declaration reflected when it made the purpose of government "to secure these rights" and said not one syllable about rights given up. The more restricted, less ambiguous field of vision of the 1787 Constitutional Convention is evident in a comment which occurs in one of the working papers of the Committee of Detail: "we are not working on the natural rights of men not yet gathered into society, but upon those rights, modified by society."[38] In contrast, writing to Francis Gilmer after his retirement from the presidency, Jefferson still declared:

> Our legislators are not sufficiently apprized of the rightful limits of their power; that their true office is to declare and enforce only our natural rights and duties, and to take none of them from us. . . . The idea is quite unfounded, that on entering into society we give up any natural right.[39]

III

The idea of a natural law self-evident to the common man; the idea that liberty was man's inalienable right to self-determination: these were the axioms to which abolitionism added only corollaries. Down to Civil War and Reconstruction abolitionists quoted the same natural law theoreticians cited by the Dissenters in contending, as the Dissenters had, "that an immoral law cannot be valid."[40] Indeed the religious fervor of abolitionism was closer in spirit to Dissenting radicalism than was the cool deistic religiosity of the Founding Fathers. For Garrison and his associates just as for Price or Priestley, the Bible provided an alternative expression of nature's truths. A century after the embroilments of John Wilkes, Thaddeus Stevens and John Bingham quoted, "Ye shall have the same law for the stranger as for one of your own country";[41] just as Granville Sharp had protested a law for the return of fugitive slaves with the words:

> "Thou shalt not deliver unto his master the servant which is escaped from his master unto thee: He shall dwell with thee, even among you, in the place WHICH HE SHALL CHOOSE" (manifestly as a freeman) "in one of thy GATES where IT LIKETH HIM BEST: thou shalt not oppress him."[42]

The natural rights philosophy was championed by Dissenters until the moment abolitionists took it up. During the Missouri Compromise debates in 1819–1820, when Senator Rufus King of New York declared that laws enacting human slavery "are absolutely void, because contrary to the law of nature, which is the law of God, by which he makes his way known to man, and is paramount to all human control," King noted that "the Senate was adjourned under much excitement created by my introduction of what was called original principles."[43] The revival of these far from original principles in the United States presumably was encouraged by the fact that in England as late as those same years the old Dissenting radical John Cartwright still explained in pamphlet upon pamphlet that "human rights . . . have their origin . . . and obligatory force in the immutable Law of God, who created man a moral being," and that a law at variance with this law of God was "void and of no effect."[44]

The transition from eighteenth-century to nineteenth-century radicalism may be illustrated by the case of William Ellery Channing.[45] Born in 1780, Channing grew up in Newport, Rhode Island. His grandfather signed the Declaration of Independence; George Washington once slept at the Channings' home; Channing himself was present at the Rhode Island convention which ratified the United States Constitution. The pastors of the First and Second Congregational Churches which his family attended were Samuel Hopkins, pioneer abolitionist but also the expositor of Calvinist orthodoxy, and William Patten, who in 1795 published *Christianity the True Religion* in reply to Paine's *Appeal to Reason*. At Harvard, according to his classmate Joseph Story, Channing studied Locke's essay on human understanding and Bishop Watson's apology for the Bible, which the Harvard Corporation placed in the hands of every student. As a senior Channing instigated an address supporting President John Adams in his cold war with revolutionary France. In brief, if there was a conservative influence which failed to influence Channing's youth, it is not recorded.

But while at Harvard he chanced on Richard Price's *Review of Morals*. "Price," he wrote two years before his death, "saved me from Locke's philosophy. He gave me the doctrine of ideas, and during my life I have written the words Love, Right, etc., with a capital. That book profoundly moulded my philosophy into the form it has always retained." Then, during two seminal years as a tutor in Richmond, Virginia,

Channing read Rousseau and Godwin. His emergent radicalism, as he expounded it in letters to friends from Virginia, contained three cardinal ideas:

1. "I am convinced that virtue and benevolence are *natural* to man," for the "principle of benevolence, sympathy, or humanity is . . . *strongly impressed on the heart by God himself.*"

2. "You evidently go upon the supposition," Channing wrote to one of his correspondents, "that the circumstances of our lives are decided by Heaven. I believe they are decided by ourselves. Man is the artificer of his own fortune."

3. "I find *avarice* the great bar to all my schemes, and I do not hesitate to assert that the human race will never be happier than at present till the establishment of a community of property."

Having thus enunciated the characteristic Dissenting axioms of the natural goodness of man and of free will, and (in an extreme form) the equally characteristic corollary that human rights come before property rights, the young prophet ended: "My dear Shaw, I fear you will say I am crazy. No, no,——"

NOTES

1. Locke's lack of concern to safeguard the rights of individuals once they have entered society is emphasized by Willmoore Kendall, *John Locke and the Doctrine of Majority-Rule* (Urbana, Ill., 1941) and C. B. Macpherson, *The Political Theory of Possessive Individualism* (Oxford, 1962).

2. Georges Lefebvre, *The Coming of the French Revolution*, tr. Robert R. Palmer (New York, 1947), pp. 177–78, 180, 181.

3. *Declaration of Independence*, preface to the 1942 edition, pp. xiii–xiv.

4. Quoted in J. W. Gough, *Fundamental Law in English Constitutional History* (Oxford, 1955), p. 195.

5. Davis, *Problem of Slavery*, p. 413.

6. Francis Hutcheson, *A System of Moral Philosophy* (London, 1755), I, 257, 295. Hutcheson first distinguished alienable from inalienable rights in *An Inquiry into the Original of Our Ideas of Beauty and Virtue* (London, 1725), p. 261, where the "marks" of an inalienable right are said to be (*a*) that it is not within our natural power to transfer the right, and/or (*b*) that the transfer would serve no "valuable Purpose."

7. James Burgh, *Britain's Remembrancer . . . Being Some Thoughts on . . . the Effects of the Vices Which Now Prevail*, 5th ed. (London, 1746), p. 8 *et passim*.

8. *Political Disquisitions*, III, 2–3, 17, etc.

9. *Account of the Cessares*, p. 10.

10. *Ibid.*, p. 85.

11. *Ibid.*, pp. 9, 25, 33–37, 71 n., 77, 78, 80–83, 86–87. Compare the legislation recommended by Burgh in *Political Disquisitions*, III, 193.

12. *Account of the Cessares*, p. 78; Granville Sharp, *A Short Sketch of the Temporary Regulations (Until Better Shall Be Proposed) for the Intended Settlement . . . near Sierra Leone*, 3d ed. (London, 1788), pp. 1–2, 15–19, 21, 69, 73; E. C. P. Lascelles, *Granville Sharp and the Freedom of the Slaves in England* (London, 1928), pp. 13–14.

13. John Brown, *An Estimate of the Manners and Principles of the Times* (London, 1757, 1758), I, 29.

14. [John Brown], *Thoughts on Civil Liberty, or Licentiousness, and Faction*, 2d ed. (London, 1765), pp. 13, 19.

15. *Ibid.*, pp. 33, 36–41, 153–60.

16. Joseph Priestley, *An Essay on a Course of Liberal Education for Civil and Active Life . . . to Which Are Added, Remarks on a Code of Education, Proposed by Dr. Brown, in a Late Treatise, Intitled, Thoughts on Civil Liberty, Etc.* (London, 1765), p. 138.

17. *Ibid.*, pp. 144, 146–47, 147–48.

18. *Ibid.*, pp. 149–51.

19. *Ibid.*, pp. 154–55, 173.

20. "Essay on Government," *Works*, XXII, 3.

21. *Ibid.*, XXII, 8, 11–12.

22. *Ibid.*, XXII, 27, 12–13.

23. *Ibid.*, XXII, 29–32.

24. *Ibid.*, XXII, 13.

25. Paine to Jefferson, [January or February, 1788], *Papers of Jefferson*, XIII, 4–5.

26. Thad W. Tate, "The Social Contract in America, 1774–1787: Revolutionary Theory as a Conservative Instrument," *William and Mary Quarterly*, 3d ser., XXII (1965), 378.

27. Richard Price, *The Nature and Dignity of the Human Soul* (London, 1766), p. 4. There may be a connection between Priestley's somewhat less absolute insistence on individual liberties and the fact that, in contrast to Price, he was a philosophical determinist; the two friends debated the matter in *A Free Discussion of the Doctrines of Materialism, and Philosophical Necessity, in a Correspondence Between Dr. Price and Dr. Priestley* (London, 1778). It is also of some interest that Anthony Collins (1676–1729), from whom Priestley said that he first learned of philosophical materialism and who inspired the youthful Franklin's *Dissertation on Liberty and Necessity, Pleasure and Pain* (London, 1725), is thought to have been a collaborator of Trenchard and Gordon, who were attacked for their determinism in John Jackson, *A Defense of Human Liberty, in Answer to the Principal Arguments Which Have Been Alleged Against It; and Particularly to Cato's Letters on That Subject . . .* (London, 1725).

28. Richard Price, *Observations on the Nature of Civil Liberty, The*

Principles of Government, and the Justice and Policy of the War with America, 8th ed. (London, 1778), pp. 1–3, 5–6.

29. *Second Treatise,* Sections 22–24. Leslie Stephen comments: "Locke could reconcile slavery to his theories; Rousseau declares that the words 'slavery' and 'right' are contradictory and mutually exclusive" (*History of English Thought in the Eighteenth Century,* 3d ed. of 1902 [reprinted New York, 1949], II, 192).

30. Price, *Additional Observations,* p. 2.

31. Preface to *Observations,* 5th ed.

32. Lincoln, *English Dissent,* pp. 114–15. Price's work, as Lincoln adds, "reveals the extent to which the theories of Locke had become a technique, a political text capable of sustaining any gloss, and yet certain, from its familiarity, to excite attention" (*ibid.,* p. 148).

33. *Observations,* p. 6.

34. *Additional Observations,* p. 10.

35. *Ibid.,* pp. 10, 10–11.

36. *Ibid.,* pp. 11–13, 14 n., 17. The quotation from Priestley is in "Essay on Government," *Works,* XXII, 10; see also *ibid.,* XXII, 12: "It is a man's civil liberty which is originally in its full force, and part of which he sacrifices when he enters into a state of society; and political liberty is that which he may, or may not acquire in the compensation he receives for it."

37. Élie Halévy, *The Growth of Philosophical Radicalism,* tr. Mary Morris (London, 1928), p. 138.

38. *The Records of the Federal Convention of 1787,* ed. Max Farrand (New Haven, London, Oxford, 1911), II, 137.

39. Thomas Jefferson to Francis W. Gilmer, June 7, 1816, *The Writings of Thomas Jefferson,* ed. Paul L. Ford (New York and London, 1899) X, 32.

40. "The Fugitive Slave Law," *The Complete Essays and Other Writings of Ralph Waldo Emerson,* ed. Brooks Atkinson (New York, 1940), p. 866. "Cicero, Grotius, Coke, Blackstone, Burlamaqui, Vattel, Burke, Jefferson, do all affirm this," Emerson stated.

41. Bingham is quoted in *Congressional Globe,* 39th Cong., 1st Sess., p. 1292; Stevens' speech of September 4, 1866, at Bedford, Pennsylvania, is quoted from a manuscript in Stevens' papers in W. R. Brock, *An American Crisis: Congress and Reconstruction, 1865–1867* (London, 1963), p. 150.

42. Granville Sharp, *Extract of a Letter to a Gentleman in Maryland . . . ,* 4th ed. (London, 1806), pp. 3–4.

43. Rufus King to Christopher Gore, February 17, 1820, *The Life and Correspondence of Rufus King,* ed. Charles R. King (New York, 1900), VI, 276–77 and n.

44. Major [John] Cartwright, *New Preamble and Explanatory Table of Contents, of a Bill of Rights and Liberties* (London, 1819), p. 5.

45. John W. Chadwick, *William Ellery Channing: Minister of Religion* (New York and Boston, 1903), pp. 42–43; *Memoirs of William Ellery Channing,* 5th ed. (Boston, 1851), especially I, 102, 109–15.

II

PRAXIS

CHAPTER 3:

THE
EARTH
BELONGS
TO
THE
LIVING

The latent tension within the natural rights philosophy of the Declaration of Independence between an outlook on society based on property and a contrasting perspective built on conscience, or on self-determining human activity, could not long be avoided. It was symbolic that the year of the Declaration also witnessed the publication of *The Wealth of Nations,* which developed the idea of inalienable liberty in the direction of laissez-faire liberalism, and of the Newcastle address of Thomas Spence, which held that "the power of alienating the least morsel [of land], in any manner, from the parish, either at this or any time hereafter, is denied."[1]

The ambiguity of the Declaration reflected the composite character of the Revolution as a social movement. Both capitalist and democratic, the Revolution drew support from many social groups: Southern slaveholders as well as Northern merchants, poor tenant farmers and artisans as well as men of wealth. The Revolution's manifesto had to speak to and for all of them. The Declaration could no more counterpose property rights and human rights than its framers could permit their coalition around the single goal of independence to degenerate into a squabble between North and South. When Jefferson's draft attacked the slave trade as oppressive to the "sacred rights of life and liberty" (not property) of "human nature itself," the passage was excised. But after the Revolution, still more after the adoption of the Constitution, the contradictions within the coalition became visible and the ambiguities in the ideology had to be confronted.

The most precise formulation of the relation between human rights and property rights in the Declaration of Independence was suggested by James Madison. Writing to James Brown of Kentucky in 1788, Madison said that at the beginning of the Revolution "the two classes of rights were so little discriminated, that a provision for the rights of persons was supposed to include of itself those of property; and it was natural to infer, from the tendency of republican laws, that these different interests would be more and more identified." But experience had shown, Madison continued, that "in all populous countries the smaller part only can be interested in preserving the rights of property." He went on to recommend the creation of a separate legislative chamber, elected by property holders only, to protect property rights.[2]

Radical Dissenters, who had done so much to formulate the axioms of the Revolution's natural rights philosophy, helped also to clarify a corollary argument opposed to Madison's. John Adams blamed advocacy of unicameral legislatures on the lamentable fact that

> my countrymen were running wild and into danger from a too ardent and inconsiderate pursuit of erroneous opinions of government which have been propagated among them by some of their ill-informed favorites and by various writings which were very popular among them, such as the pamphlet called *Common Sense*, for one example among many others, particularly Mrs. Macaulay's *History*, Mr. Burgh's *Political Disquisitions*, Mr. Turgot's *Letters*.[3]

From the dialogue alluded to by Adams developed Jefferson's critique of inheritance and Thoreau's attack on alienated labor. These Americans did not carry the economic argument to the conclusions of Karl Marx, but by taking many of the same first steps they opened up new possibilities for the criticism of private property's political companion, the bourgeois nation-state.

I

Despite Bernard Bailyn's assertion that the Dissenters did not advocate "social or economic reforms" and were not concerned "to recast the social order nor with the problems of economic inequality and the injustices of stratified societies,"[4] Dissenting radicalism raised awkward questions about the absolute right of private property from its first pamphlet to its last. James Burgh, for example, protested in 1749 that common opinion does not condemn those who get rich "by grinding the face of the poor," but shames those who are "poor for want of impudence to elbow mankind, or through too much narrowness of conscience, or too much largeness of heart"; held in 1754 that "the general consent of society, or the law of the country, in which a person lives, may, for wise and generally beneficial purposes, render property, otherwise rightful, not tenable; and may make all things common"; and maintained in 1756 that "all above the Conveniencies of Life is absolutely useless."[5]

There were three key Dissenting arguments against the right to unlimited accumulation justified by Locke's *Second Treatise* and taken for granted by the "commonwealthmen" of the early eighteenth century. The first was the ancient conception that the earth was given by God, its ultimate owner, to mankind in common: or as the American Quaker John Woolman put it, that "the Creator of the earth is the owner of it."[6] The second argument, congenial to Nonconformist asceticism, was that a man has a right only to that property which he requires for his subsistence. Thus Franklin observed to (of all people) the financier Robert Morris: "All the Property that is necessary to a Man, for the Conservation of the Individual and the Propagation of the Species, is his natural Right, which none can justly deprive him of: But all

Property superfluous to such purposes is the Property of the Publick. . . ."[7] The third argument exposed the central contradiction in the thought of Locke and was the basis of all Jefferson's comments on this subject. It was that the inheritance of private property is rightfully just as subject to social regulation as the inheritance of political power.

The drift of the Dissenting discussion was to turn upside down Locke's conception that property was the most absolute of rights, and that, therefore, all other rights were a kind of property. For the Dissenters conscience, and the allied intellectual rights, were absolute and inalienable, while economic arrangements were increasingly viewed by them as matters of convenience. An interesting illustration of their feeling for these matters is Granville Sharp's discussion of what rights of the king are inalienable. The king, says Sharp, cannot sell his subjects, for "liber homo" is "quasi res sacra" who "vendi non potest" (the quotations were taken by Sharp from Bracton). Other rights are "inherent in the Crown, for the public good, and cannot therefore be disposed of, or alienated, viz. such as Peace, Justice, etc." Still other rights can be aliened for a time, among them "sea-wrecks, treasures found, great fish, as whales, sturgeons, and other royal fish." But land—mere land—can be aliened absolutely.[8]

Dissenting protest against the outrage of human rights in the name of property rights might take the form either of denying property rights or of insisting that human rights were just as tangible. Thus, on the one hand, Priestley contended in his *Essay on Government* that "the very idea of property . . . is founded upon a regard to the general good of the society under whose protection it is enjoyed; and nothing is properly *a man's own*, but what general rules, which have for their object the good of the whole, give to him." Hence "whenever . . . riches . . . are abused, to the injury of the whole," the citizenry may demand that they be given up.[9] This was also the basis of Franklin's protest at the very end of his life against a plan to change Pennsylvania's unicameral legislature into a conventional bicameral institution. Supposing that the rich (those owning property valued at one thousand pounds) were no more than two percent of the total freemen, Franklin asked why they should be given a negative on the majority's will. Illustrating his argument by the familiar example of an Indian society in which "hunting is free for all," Franklin contended that the accumulation of property in such a society would be the result, not of individual effort only, but of "the Protection afforded to it by the joint Strength of the Society." And therefore, Franklin continued,

> Private Property . . . is a Creature of Society, and is subject to the Calls of that Society, whenever its Necessities shall require it, even to its last Farthing; its Contributions therefore to the public Exigencies are not to be considered as conferring a Benefit on the Publick, entitling the Contributors to the Distinctions of Honour and Power, but as the Return of an Obligation previously received, or the Payment of a just Debt. The Combinations of Civil Society are not like those of a Set of Merchants, who club their Property in different Proportions for Building and Freighting a Ship, and may therefore have some Right to vote in the disposition of the Voyage in a greater or less Degree according to their respective Contributions; but the important ends of Civil Society, and the personal Securities of Life and Liberty, these remain the same in every Member of the society; and the poorest continues to have an equal Claim to them with the most opulent, whatever Difference Time, Chance, or Industry may occasion in their Circumstances.

"On these Considerations," Franklin concluded, he was sorry to see a disposition among some of the people of Pennsylvania "to commence an Aristocracy, by giving the Rich a predominancy in Government."[10]

If Franklin and Priestley turned in a direction Locke had not intended the latter's argument that the security of property requires laws and judges, so, on the other hand, some Dissenters pressed to un-Lockean ends Locke's conception of life and liberty as properties. "Every man," James Burgh contended in those *Political Disquisitions* so widely read in America, "has what may be called property, and unalienable property. Every man has a life, a personal liberty, a character, a right to his earnings, a right to a religious profession and worship according to his conscience, etc. and many men, who are in a state of dependence upon others, and who receive charity, have wives and children in whom they have a right."[11] This line of argument culminated in Shelley's cry, in his *Philosophical View of Reform* almost half a century later, that Malthus was seeking to take from the poor even marriage, "that property which is as strictly their birthright as a gentleman's land is his birthright."[12]

Cartwright's *Legislative Rights of the Commonalty Vindicated* (1776) exemplified the whole battery of Dissenting queries to Locke's teaching on property. Eighteenth-century England was a society in which a ten-year-old girl might be hanged for stealing a pocket handkerchief. Thundered Cartwright: "The greater felons, who are ready at its command to destroy their country, are caressed and rewarded: but little ones, indeed, who take a purse or steal a sheep, are hanged without remorse. . . ." (Just so, in revolutionary France, Brissot argued against capital punishment for theft on the ground that only an infringement of natural rights deserved death.) There were other kinds of property, Cartwright continued, in addition to "what is vulgarly called property." Though a man

> should have neither lands nor gold, nor herds nor flocks; yet he may have parents and kindred, he may possess a wife and an offspring to be solicitous for. He hath also by birthright a property in the English constitution: which, if not unworthy of such a blessing, will be more dear to him than would be many acres of the soil without it.

Further, according to Cartwright, "those valuable members of the state by whose manual labours its very existence is preserved . . . and *on which depend also the affluence, the ease, and all the elegancies of the more fortunate classes of the people*," have a right to the products of their labor. "It is certain that every man who labours with his hands, hath a *property* which is of importance to the state: for Mr. Locke has admirably well observed that, 'every man has a property in his own person; the labour of his body and the work of his hands, we may say are properly his'." Cartwright remarked that the laboring man or mechanic cannot obtain food or clothes or tools without paying sales taxes. Hence, "according to *the received doctrine of property,*" they should vote. After all, Cartwright concluded this portion of his discussion, it is not property which constitutes freedom. "Doubtless it is the immediate gift of God to all the human species, by adding *free-will* to *rationality.*" If political representation were based on "the *accident* of property," then what was represented would be property as much as men. Cartwright agreed with Beccaria that property is the means, not the end, of the social compact. The scavenger had a better right to his vote than the peer to his coronet or the king to his crown: for the latter derived from the laws of men, the former from the laws of God. Anticipating Franklin, Cartwright insisted that society was not a trading company. The one depends on property, the other on *"personality."* The one can make any artificial rule it pleases, the other rests on that civil liberty which "is a natural blessing." Therefore:

> A right of being represented, every man owes to God, who gave him his freedom; but many a man owes his wealth to the devil. It ought, in that case, to give him a rope, rather than a representative.[13]

These ideas, like Cartwright's complementary confidence in the common man's ability to know, developed gradually among Dissenters. It should not be supposed that all Dissenting radicals were equally indignant about poverty, above all not that they were consistently so. Priestley, for instance, expressed opinions on the poor laws as ferocious as those of Locke. For most of his life, too, Priestley's political opinions were "Trinitarian": in a revision of his *Lectures on History and General Policy,* published in Philadelphia in 1803, Priestley favored an electoral college, bicameral legislatures, property and literacy qualifications for voting, and representative rather than direct democracy. Yet for a moment at the height of the French Revolution (we shall find this same phenomenon in Jefferson) Priestley's political opinions were very different from those just enumerated. In a tract published in London in 1791 and entitled *A Political Dialogue on the General Principles of Government,* Priestley argued that just as no system of checks and balances was needed in the government of a parish or township, so a nation needed none. To Madisonian bicameralism he laid the sharpest axe of all: if private property required special protection, then private property should be abolished. In Priestley's words,

> if the majority of the people understand their own interest, there can be no good reason why they should not have the power of promoting it, and that with as little obstruction and delay as possible. If the obstruction and delay arise from orders of men who have interests opposite to that of the majority of the people, such orders ought not to exist, but should be exterminated as a nuisance, necessarily operating to the diminution of public happiness.[14]

The views of Richard Price evolved in roughly similar fashion. His *Review of Morals*, published twenty years before the outbreak of the American Revolution, expressed conventional views toward private property. But his *Observations on the Importance of the American Revolution*, published ten years after it, contains a remarkable passage. The happiest social state, Price wrote (echoing Rousseau and indeed Locke), is the middle state between the savage and refined. There is a danger that as commerce develops it will not endure. With this in mind, Plato, More, and "Mr. Wallis" have

> proposed plans, which, by establishing a community of goods and annihilating property, would make it impossible for any one member of a State to think of enslaving the rest, or to consider himself as having any interest distinct from that of his fellow-citizens. Such theories are in speculation pleasing; nor perhaps are they wholly impracticable. Some approaches to them may hereafter be made; and schemes of government may take place, which shall leave so little, besides personal merit, to be a means of distinction, as to exclude from society most of the causes of evil. But be this as it will; it is out of doubt that there is an equality in society which is essential to liberty, and which every State that would continue virtuous and happy ought as far as possible to maintain.—It is not in my power to describe the best method of doing this.[15]

The most significant exemplar of a progressively more radical attitude toward private property, because of his wide American readership, is Thomas Paine. *Common Sense* explicitly blamed what is wrong with the world on government, not on property. "Oppression is often the *consequence*, but seldom or never the *means* of riches. . . . But there is another and greater distinction for which no truly natural or religious reason can be assigned, and that is the distinction of men into KINGS and SUBJECTS." Male and female, continued Paine in *Common Sense*, "are the distinctions of nature, good and bad the distinctions of heaven; but how a race of men came into the world so exalted above the rest, and distinguished like some new species, is worth inquiring into." When he wrote *Agrarian Justice* twenty years later, Paine viewed the Garden of Eden more in the manner of John Ball ("When Adam delved and Eve span/ Who was then the gentleman?"). "It is wrong to say God made *rich* and *poor*; He made only *male* and *female*; and He gave them the earth for their inheritance." Poverty, Paine now held, "exists not in the natural state." Neither did property. Therefore a landowner properly owns only the improvements he makes on a piece of land, not the land itself, and "owes to the community a *ground-rent* (for I know of no better term to express the idea)."

Paine disclaimed any desire to redivide property by an "agrarian law." For those dispossessed by "the landed monopoly" from their portion in the common inheritance of the earth, Paine asked only an indemnity. Like Jefferson, he sought to find a rectifying instrument in the process of inheritance. A heavy inheritance tax would serve to correct an unjust "system" without disturbing the individual present possessors, whom Paine considered innocent. A "national fund" would distribute fifteen pounds to each person as he reached the age of twenty-one, and ten pounds a year to every person fifty years and over, "as a compensation in part, for the loss of his or her natural inheritance, by the introduction of the system of landed property."

Despite these moderate features, *Agrarian Justice* (taken together, of course, with more sweeping proposals such as those of Spence and William Godwin) signified the end of what has been termed the political theory of possessive individualism. It insisted that because "the earth, in its natural uncultivated state was, and ever would have continued to be,

the *common property of the human race*," society owed every
individual, as a matter not of charity but of justice, a livelihood
no worse than would have been his in a state of nature. It
recognized that "personal property" as well as land derived
most of its value from society. Further, cognizant of the
transition from a handicraft to an industrialized economy,
Paine remarked that "the accumulation of personal property
is, in many instances, the effect of paying too little for the labor
that produced it; the consequence of which is that the working
hand perishes in old age, and the employer abounds in affluence."

What was decisive was Paine's recognition that a civil
society based on the unlimited accumulation of property was
no longer untouchable. He still regarded government as the
basis of society, but "a revolution in the state of civilization
[the economic system] is the necessary companion of revolutions in the system of government." Throughout Europe
there was a new "consciousness" that the prevailing civilization "is as unjust in its principle, as it is horrid in its effects."
The "superstitious awe, the enslaving reverence, that formerly
surrounded affluence, is passing away in all countries."[16] Re-
phrasing Paine's insight in the language of recent historiography, one might say that the French and American revolutions
caused the erosion of "deference," not merely for aristocracy
as a social estate, but for the inherited inequality of wealth
which made gentlemen possible.

The intellectual transition from *Common Sense* to *Agrarian
Justice* may be diagrammatically summed up as follows. In
1776, in keeping with Madison's observation in his letter to
James Brown, Paine made no distinction between property and
the other "natural rights" which the "hereditary right" of monarchy threatened. Paine's 1788 letter to Jefferson expressed a
further distinction between the rights of the mind, "natural
rights" not surrendered by the individual in society, and "civil
rights" such as that "of acquiring and possessing property."
In the second part of *Rights of Man*, Paine in turn divided
the latter, discriminating property which resulted from a
man's own labor from that engendered by unjust and "un-

natural" laws of inheritance. *Agrarian Justice* elaborated this final distinction.

Thus a subsequent controversy about forms of property lay concealed in the Revolutionary controversy about forms of government. Price and Cartwright quarreled with Burke about the nature of representation before Burke condemned Price and Paine for their views on patriotism and aristocracy at the time of the French Revolution; Paine's attack on inherited property in *Rights of Man, Part Second,* began as a response to Burke's advocacy of the inherited political rights of the aristocracy to representation in the House of Lords. Similarly John Adams, alarmed by Paine's support for unicameralism in *Common Sense* and Turgot's support for it in a letter published by Price, wrote his *Thoughts on Government* and *Defense of the Constitutions of America* to recommend the bicameral system. But a straight line led from bicameralism to the concept that private property was an absolute right beyond the reach of government, as from unicameralism to the Rousseauian concept that private property was a social convention at the disposal of a majority of the people. "Property, property! that is the difficulty," Adams noted as he reread *The Social Contract* when President of the United States.[17] It was indeed.

II

The most important American reflection of Dissenting discussion about property was Jefferson's doctrine that the earth belongs to the living. It was in this form that the Revolutionary generation approached most nearly the socialist conception that living labor has claims superior to any property rights.

The origin of Jefferson's idea has been enveloped in considerable mystery. It was, according to Jefferson's editor Julian P. Boyd, "the one great addition to Jefferson's thought that emerged from his years of residence at the center of European intellectual ferment." But Boyd, following Adrienne Koch, thinks the immediate catalyst for Jefferson's articulation of the concept was not a Frenchman but an English physician named Richard Gem. Jefferson expressed the idea

that "the earth belongs in usufruct to the living" in a letter
to Madison written September 6, 1789, during a week's illness in the midst of the great National Assembly debates about
the Declaration of the Rights of Man and the confiscation
of feudal privileges. Gem attended Jefferson in his illness,
Jefferson placed his letter to Madison in Gem's hands, and
undated communications between the two very strongly suggest that Jefferson's letter was preceded and followed by Gem-
Jefferson conversations on the same subject.[18]

Although little is known about him, Gem evidently exemplified the close relationship between English Dissenters and
French *philosophes.* An Englishman with (in the words of
a contemporary) an "openly-avowed penchant to unitarianism," and (so Boyd says) "an ardent devotee of republican
principles," Gem was described by Jefferson as "a pure theorist,
of the sect called the oeconomists, of which Turgot was considered as the head." Boyd notes also that Jefferson possessed
a declaration of rights written by Condorcet and translated
by Gem into English. These references to Turgot and Condorcet take on new meaning when laid beside a passage of
Priestley's hitherto unnoticed. In his *Lectures on History and
General Policy,* first published in 1788, Priestley wrote as follows:

> The safe *transferring,* as well as the secure *possession* of prop-
> erty, is a privilege which we derive from society. But it is a
> question among politicians, how far this privilege should extend.
> That all persons should have the absolute disposal of their prop-
> erty during their own lives, and while they have the use of their
> understanding, was never disputed. But some (and among them
> is M. Turgot) say, there should be no *testament;* a man should
> have no power of disposing of his property after his death, but
> it should be distributed by the law, according to the degrees of
> consanguinity. Whereas in most, if not all the civilized states
> of Europe, every man has an indefinite power over his property,
> so that he can direct the enjoyment of it in all future time.[19]

Immediately after his parenthetical reference to Turgot, Priestley placed the following footnote: "See *Vie de M. Turgot* (by
Condorcet), 1786, p. 234." Condorcet's book seems a very
likely source for the doctrine which, then, would only have

been reinforced in 1789 by the friend of Turgot and Condorcet, Richard Gem.

Once more, however, we are clearly dealing with an idea which was in the air among an international circle of intellectual friends and cannot, without misplaced concreteness, be attributed to any single author, time, or place. More than that: the idea that the earth belongs to the living represented a resolution of a deep-seated contradiction within the thinking of Locke and Locke's followers, and should be seen in the context of earlier responses to the problem by Jefferson himself.

Locke's concern in his too little read *First Treatise* was, of course, to refute the thesis of Sir Robert Filmer that the right of kingship was inherited from Adam. Locke's dilemma was to deny the inheritance of political power without denying the inheritance of property as well. Why, he asks explicitly, when parents die intestate does their property "not return again to the common stock of mankind"? Primogeniture posed a particular problem for him because of its similarity to the inheritance of the throne; and again Locke comments in so many words that

> in Countries where their particular Municipal Laws give the whole Possession of Land entirely to the First Born, and Descent of Power has gone so to Men by this Custom, some have been apt to be deceived into an Opinion, that there was a Natural or Divine Right of Primogeniture, to both *Estate* and *Power;* and that the Inheritance of both *Rule* over Men and *Property* in things, sprang from the some Original, and were to descend by the same Rules.[20]

Thus, just as in the chapter on property in the *Second Treatise,* Locke formulates (in the process of discarding) later radical arguments that God gave the earth to men in common and that no man should own more than he can personally consume, so in his discussion of inheritance in the *First Treatise* Locke put into words (if only to refute) something very close to Jefferson's subsequent idea. For Locke, as Paul Lucas has expressed the matter in a brilliant dissertation, it "had to be shown that property did not fall with the state. Property had to be rendered legally secure while crowns were made legally precarious"; or in another of Lucas'. formulations: "Locke wanted to have the best of two worlds—to bind property by consent to the State to avoid anarchy, and at the same time, by rendering its inheritance a natural right, to allow for revolutions that would not endanger property."[21]

But neither radicals nor conservatives would long permit the two kinds of inheritance to be differently conceptualized. Dissenters saw kingship and primogeniture as aspects of a single "Norman Yoke." Thus Catharine Macaulay maintained that "by the, system of government imposed by William the Norman tyrant, all but the great landholders, who held their estates from father to son, by feudal entail, were in a state of abject and impassable vassalage, excluded from any voice in the legislature, or property in the soil."[22] Similarly Paine, writing in the 1790s, mixed economic and political metaphors together in arguing that "man has no property in man; neither has any generation a property in the generations which are to follow," or again, that "our ancestors, like ourselves, were but tenants for life in the great freehold of rights."[23]

If radicals tended to the conclusion that the dead cannot bind the living either in politics or economics, conservatives drifted toward the inverse proposition that, as Lucas puts it, "the over-mighty subject who challenges a royal heir's right to the Crown questions his own title to his own property."[24] That proposition was axiomatic for Burke, but an earlier and more complex discussion which, in addition, undoubtedly influenced Jefferson, was William Blackstone's.

Blackstone simultaneously affirmed that the inheritance of kingship "in general corresponds with the feodal path of descents, chalked out by the common law on the succession to landed estates," *and* that neither lands nor thrones were "naturally descendible." His account of the origin of private property followed that of Locke and other theorists of the social contract with the all-important exception that Blackstone considered its end product—a "permanent right of property" legitimizing bequests from father to son—"no *natural,* but merely a *civil* right." No more than Hume did Blackstone intend skepticism concerning Locke's natural rights philosophy to undermine the continuance of private property, which all three took for granted. Still, there were the words: "naturally speaking, the instant a man ceases to be, he ceases to have any dominion."[25] Jefferson was forgetting Blackstone's *Commentaries* when, in his 1789 letter to Madison, he characterized "the question Whether one generation of men has a right to bind another" as one which "seems never to have been started either on this or our side of the water."[26]

By the time he wrote the Declaration of Independence Jefferson had long held views on the nature of land tenure which (so he commented later) were shared only by his mentor in the law, George Wythe.[27] These he crisply summarized in his *Summary View of the Rights of British America*, in 1774. According to Jefferson, land grants in the American colonies embodied "the fictitious principle that all lands belong originally to the king" because emigrants from England "were laborers, not lawyers" and misunderstood the situation. In reality, so Jefferson maintained, the fundamental form of landholding in English common law was not feudal but "allodial," that is, held "in absolute dominion, disencumbered with any superior."

Jefferson believed allodial possession to be "the basis or groundwork" of English land law because he believed it to be the oldest form of ownership. "In the earlier ages of the Saxon settlement feudal holdings were certainly altogether unknown," Jefferson wrote in the *Summary View*.[28] His student notebooks show whence he derived that opinion during "law reading which I found alwais strengthened it."[29] "Somner," runs a characteristic entry, "concurs with those who think feudal tenures were introduced by the Conqueror, Somn. *Gavelk. 112*. If the feudal regulations prevailed at all among our Northern ancestors, before their irruption into the Southern countries, it must have been in a very infantine state, for from a passage in Caesar we find the Germans even in his day had no fixed property in lands. . . . *L. 6 c. 20*—and Tacitus . . . *de mor. Germ. 26*." In Robertson's history of the reign of Charles V, Jefferson found the thesis that "property in land seems to have gone through four successive changes among the people who settled in the various provinces of the Roman empire." The stages were: (1) "While the barbarous remained in their own original countries they had no fixed property in land. . . ."; (2) when the barbarians conquered another country their soldiers took land as freemen "in full property," that is, allodially; (3) then land was held under feudal tenures but only for life; (4) finally, feuds became hereditary.[30]

Who then, according to Jefferson, owned the land of America? Not the king, for "America was not conquered by William the Norman, nor it's lands surrendered to him or any of his successors." Individual farmers? This would seem to follow from Jefferson's definition of allodial tenure as "absolute right." But what Jefferson said in the *Summary View* was:

> From the nature and purpose of civil institutions, all the lands within the limits which any particular society has circumscribed around itself, are assumed by that society, and subject to their allotment only. This may be done by themselves assembled collectively, or by their legislature to whom they may have delegated sovereign authority: and, if they are allotted in neither of these ways, each individual of the society may appropriate to himself such lands as he finds vacant, and occupancy will give him title.[31]

In other words, Jefferson counterposed to feudal tenure under the king of England absolute, allodial ownership *either* by a community *or* by an individual. There was therefore no contradiction between these youthful formulations and the later doctrine that the earth belongs to the living. In a letter of August 1776, Jefferson defined feudal tenure as "separation of the property from the perpetual use of lands," and defined perpetual use to mean men holding "their lands as their personal estate in absolute dominion."[32] Absolute property ownership by an individual meant precisely the right to use it during one's own lifetime.

The famous land reforms which Jefferson pushed through the Virginia legislature after independence gave these views practical expression. The abolition of entail made property available for the use of the present generation. The abolition of primogeniture sought to ensure that all the present generation might use property equally. And so did the proposal, which was not adopted by the legislature, to give each landless (white) adult male a fifty-acre freehold from the wild land in the West owned by the state of Virginia.

The continuity between Jefferson's views on land tenure at the time of the American Revolution and his views on it at the time of the French Revolution is demonstrated by his letter to Reverend James Madison in October 1785. The letter begins with an account of a conversation with a poor woman who

> told me she was a day labourer, at 8. sous or 4 d. sterling the day; that she had two children to maintain, and to pay a rent of 30 livres for her house (which would consume the hire of 75 days), that often she could get no emploiment, and of course was without bread.

The incident suggested to Jefferson the necessity of reducing the inequality of property so far as practicable by changing the laws of inheritance and by progressive taxation. Then he went on:

> Whenever there is in any country, uncultivated lands and unemployed poor, it is clear that the laws of property have been so far extended as to violate natural right. The earth is given as a common stock for man to labour and live on. If, for the encouragement of industry we allow it to be appropriated, we must take care that other employment be furnished to those excluded from the appropriation. If we do not the fundamental right to labour the earth returns to the unemployed.[33]

Here, to begin with, was the justification of the homestead law which Jefferson had proposed to the Virginia legislature in 1776. Here were also clearly anticipated elements of the theory of *Agrarian Justice:* the earth was given to mankind in common; those excluded from this inheritance must be indemnified; this is a natural right, as opposed to the merely conventional rights of property. In one respect Jefferson in this letter appeared to go beyond what either he or Paine said later. He seemed to imply that, in the absence of remedial state action, the unemployed might rightly take the land they needed.

According to Vernon Parrington, it was the belief that the human rights of life and liberty were more valuable than the rights of property which led Jefferson in the preamble to the Declaration of Independence to reject the word "property" and speak instead of "the pursuit of happiness."[34] Boyd, on the contrary, argues that "the pursuit of happiness" was a conventional phrase which Locke himself had used "at least three times, though not in a political context."[35] But whether or not there was significance in Jefferson's use of the words "pursuit of happiness," there may still have been significance in his failure to use the word "property." When early in the French Revolution Lafayette submitted to Jefferson a draft of the Declaration of the Rights of Man, Jefferson struck the word "property" from the rights itemized by Lafayette, putting in its place: "the power to dispose of his person and the fruits of his industry, and of all his faculties."[36] These, we may assume Jefferson to have believed, were natural human energies; property itself was a social convention. In a letter written in 1813, Jefferson explicitly denied that property was a natural right.[37]

Nevertheless, Parrington and the Progressive historians in general exaggerate the extent to which the Declaration, or its author, or the Revolution which they rationalized, frontally attacked the rights of property. When Jefferson returned to the United States shortly after writing to Madison in September 1789, the content of his words about the rights of the living generation shrank. In France he clearly meant not only that no legislature should make public debts which its children would have to repay, and not only that every generation can rewrite its political constitution, but also that "it renders the question of reimbursement a question of generosity and not of right." When hereditary rights are abolished, he went on, "the present holders, even where they, or their ancestors, have purchased, are in the case of bonâ fide purchasers of what the seller had no right to convey."[38] There was no more talk about violation of contracts after Jefferson got home. It was left for Lincoln, not Jefferson, to confiscate without compensation two billion dollars' worth of slaves.

Jefferson as an old man retained of the original doctrine only a vague speculative nostalgia for the primitive communism of barbarian societies. Robertson had described the ancient Germans as being under no "formal obligation to serve the community; all their services were purely voluntary; every individual was at liberty to chuse how far he would contribute towards carrying on any military enterprise. If he followed a leader in any expedition, it was from attachment, not from a sense of obligation."[39] Jefferson and Franklin had just such a society near at hand in their own lifetime in the remaining tribes of Indians. Both frequently glanced sidewise at the intriguing alternative of the propertyless savages. Franklin commented at the time of the Revolution that

> all the Indians of North America not under the Dominion of the Spaniards, are in that *Natural State*, being restrain'd by no Laws, having no Courts or Ministers of Justice, no Suits, no Prisons, no Governors vested with any legal Authority. The Persuasion of Men distinguished by Reputation of Wisdom is the only Means by which others are govern'd or rather led.—And the State of the Indians was probably the first State of all Nations.[40]

A half-century later Jefferson gave a very similar description in that same letter to Francis Gilmer which asserted that, upon joining society, men ought to give up none of their natural rights. "Our Indians," he wrote to Gilmer,

> are evidently in that state of nature which has passed the association of a single family; and not yet submitted to the authority of positive laws, or of any acknowledged magistrate. Every man, with them, is perfectly free to follow his own inclinations. But if, in doing this, he violates the rights of another, if the case be slight, he is punished by the disesteem of his society, or, as we say, by public opinion; if serious, he is tomahawked as a dangerous enemy. Their leaders conduct them by the influence of their character only; and they follow, or not, as they please, him of whose character for wisdom or war they have the highest opinion.[41]

But no more than in the case of chattel slavery did Jefferson see how to bring about what he wanted in a society based on private property, and the expansion of commerce and population. Indian society may be best, Jefferson wrote to Madison a few months before the Constitutional Convention of 1787, but it is not possible for large numbers of people.[42] He held that opinion to the end of his life. In 1822 the early American socialist Cornelius Blatchly sent Jefferson his *Essay on Common Wealths,* which argued that property was a social creation and should be in common. Acknowledging the book, the sage of Monticello said again that "communion of property" was possible only in small societies. Two years later he added in a letter to William Ludlow that the attempt to make property common would be "treading back our steps a little way."[43]

Eighteenth-century radicalism did not transcend private property in theory, any more than in practice. Its characteristic economic demand was not that the public administer the means of production or that the good man give all he had to the poor, but that the laborer be fully paid. Woolman, when all is said and done, asked the owner of property to be a faithful steward. Jefferson's economic reforms were confined to the edges of society: to the West, and (by changing the law of inheritance) to succeeding generations. Even in *Agrarian Justice,* Paine held that "nothing could be more unjust than agrarian law [i.e., an equal distribution of property] in a country improved by cultivation."[44]

But if the revolutionary tradition did not destroy private property, either in theory or practice, it demythologized it. Property in the nineteenth century was no longer the ark of the covenant it had been in the eighteenth. It was recognized to be, not a natural right existing before society, but a social convention. The illegitimizing of inherited political rights was understood to qualify inherited economic rights as well. Property in man was denounced, and the old notion that God had given the things of this earth to mankind in common was revived.

III

Both in England and America, eighteenth-century questioning of private property in the name of natural rights evolved continuously into early nineteenth-century questioning from the standpoint of a labor theory of value. Behind this generalization lay the fact that the lower-middle-class Dissenting preacher or schoolmaster who was the characteristic exponent of radicalism before the 1790s shaded off into the self-educated workingman, reared in a Dissenting chapel or (in America) one of the popular evangelical sects, who pioneered the socialist and abolitionist movements. From a sociological standpoint, Tom Paine, son of a Quaker corset maker, and William Lloyd Garrison, son of a sailor who deserted the family and a seamstress who became a Baptist shortly before Garrison's birth, were the same sort of man; appropriately, Garrison was born in Newburyport near the building where the great eighteenth-century evangelist George Whitefield died. Moreover, many of the early nineteenth-century spokesmen for American radicalism were immigrants from England. Of the six men described by David Harris as "American forerunners of Marx"—Cornelius Blatchly, Daniel Raymond, Langdon Byllesby, William Maclure, William Heighton, and Thomas Skidmore—Byllesby was a printer whose father had emigrated from Lincolnshire, Maclure was born in Scotland, and Heighton, a Philadelphia cordwainer, came to America from England soon after his birth in 1800. After each peak of English radicalism—the corresponding societies of the 1790s, the agitation following the Peace of Ghent—leaders fled to the United States.

Without exception the American forerunners of Marx still spoke the language of inalienable natural rights. The *substance* of artisan radicalism differed sharply from Jeffersonian democracy: they condemned slavery whereas he, in old age, increasingly sympathized with Southern sectionalism and indeed said nothing in public against slavery after he became a candidate for president; they welcomed the abundance which industrialization made possible in contrast to his fear of luxury, cities, and urban workingmen themselves; they, while sharing with Jefferson a Utopia modeled on institutions of local self-government, were more open than he to the possibility that strong measures of state power might be necessary to achieve it. Nevertheless, the *form* of early American proposals for communal property was Jeffersonian. Radicals used his authority in much the same way that their predecessors, the radical Dissenters, had used the authority of Locke.

Skidmore's book, for instance, probably the single most comprehensive statement of this pre-Marxian American radicalism, revealed its indebtedness to Jefferson in its title: *The Rights of Man to Property! Being a Proposition to Make It Equal Among the Adults of the Present Generation: and to Provide for Its Equal Transmission to Every Individual of Each Succeeding Generation, on Arriving at the Age of Maturity.* Skidmore himself stated that the Jeffersonian periodical *Aurora* was the decisive influence on his intellectual development. In support of his version of the rights of the present generation, Skidmore quoted not only Blackstone but a passage from a suit prepared by Jefferson in 1812 to protect "the Public Right to the Beach of the Mississippi, adjacent to New Orleans":

> That the lands within the limits assumed by a nation, belong to the nation, as a body, has probably been the law of every people on earth, at some period of their history. A right of property, in moveable things, is admitted before the establishment of government. A separate property, in lands, not till after that establishment. The right to moveables is acknowledged by all the hordes of Indians surrounding us. Yet, by no one of them has a separate property, in lands, been yielded to individuals. He who plants a field, keeps possession till he has gathered the produce; after which one has as good a right as another to occupy it. Government must be established, and laws provided, before lands can be separately appropriated, and the owner protected in his possession. Till then the property is in the body of the nation, and they, or their chief, as trustee, must grant them to individuals, and determine the conditions of the grant.

Skidmore went on to criticize Jefferson as he had criticized Paine for too readily accepting the existing system of private property, but he did so in the language of the preamble to the Declaration of Independence. How *ought* the earth to have been divided? The answer "is engraved on the heart of man, and there is no power, while he lives and has his faculties, that can efface the engraving. That heart tells him, what it tells every man now who has one; that he has an equal right with any and every other man, to an equal share of the common property. . . ."45

In like fashion Blatchly listed among man's inalienable rights "his perfect right to the full fruits of his own honest ingenuity and labour," and, almost in the words of Jefferson's letter to Gilmer, maintained that "no man by entering into civil government should be abridged of any equitable right to nature." Similarly Daniel Raymond believed, as Jefferson came very close to saying, that all private wealth "should be resolved into the general mass, at least once in every generation." Byllesby too took his stand on the Declaration of Independence, insisting however, as did his cothinkers, that to speak of inalienable rights of life and liberty without providing material means to sustain them would be like saying that "an ox has an inalienable right to fly, or a fish to walk."46 In every case the Jeffersonian vocabulary was made to do service for more-than-Jeffersonian ends.

Comparable continuity with the economic thought of Jefferson and Paine is evident in the case of abolitionism. Consider Congressman George W. Julian, whose agitation against land monopoly during the 1850s and 1860s formed a bridge between the homestead campaign of George Henry Evans and the single-tax movement of Henry George. When Julian first spoke in Congress on behalf of a homestead bill, in 1851, he was obliged to disclaim advocacy of "Agrarianism, or Socialism" or any "leveling policy." Taking his stand on "the broad ground of natural right," Julian maintained that in "the first peopling of the earth, it was as free to all its inhabitants as the sunlight and the air; and every man has, by nature, as perfect a right to a reasonable portion of it, upon which to subsist, as he has to inflate his lungs with the atmosphere which surrounds it, or to drink of the waters which pass over its surface. This right is as inalienable, as emphatically God-given, as the right to liberty or life. . . ." Like the early American socialists Julian went on to say that a natural right to land was self-evident because without it the right to life lacked substance. After the Civil War, comparing the American "railway power" to "the power of the old feudal barons over the roads passing through their territory," Julian cited Locke, Vattel, John Stuart Mill, Sismondi, and "our Puritan ancestors" in support of "the scriptural truth that the earth belongs 'to the children of men'."[47]

In the homestead agitation Radical Republicans, like Jefferson before them, sought to make uncultivated public land available to pioneers. The Radical Republicans went beyond Jefferson when, during the Civil War, they pressed for confiscation and division of plantations. Their rhetoric in these debates was astonishingly radical. Julian himself advocated "parceling out the plantations of rebels in small farms for the enjoyment of the freedmen, who have earned their right to the soil by generations of oppression, instead of selling it in large tracts to speculators, and thus laying the foundations of a system of land monopoly in the South scarcely less to be deplored than slavery itself." Failure to do so, Julian said, would mean replacing chattel slavery by "the system of wages-slavery, the child of land monopoly."[48] Julian was only one of many who talked this way.

Senator Trumbull of Illinois asserted that "you cannot draw a contract so strong by which one person shall give his time and services to another, that the paramount authority of the Government cannot abrogate that contract." Senator Morrill of Maine observed that "what we are witnessing and encountering is the old struggle of a class for power and privilege which has so often convulsed the world, repeating itself in our history." Senator Howard of Michigan remarked that Nestor had seized and carried off the herds of the Aeleans to compel them to pay their debts, and Henry VIII had seized the monasteries. But the analogy which dominated the imagination of Howard and others of the group who came to be called "Jacobins" was to the French Revolution. "The revolution of 1789," declared Howard,

> by which the feudal system was destroyed and the French nation regenerated, owed its successes and the final triumph of the great principles which lay at its foundation, to confiscations of the property of the enemies of the republic within the limits of France.

The fashion, Howard continued, is to speak of those confiscations "not as precedents to be followed, but warnings to be heeded." But the French had not been barbarians. "They were struggling for freedom and equal rights." "They drew the sword against *privilege,* and threw away the scabbard." Howard argued that to say the Fifth Amendment protected property in the midst of wartime would require one to say the same of life, and so create "a non-combatant, Quaker Constitution." Trumbull, too, hammered away at the implication of those opposed to confiscation that the Constitution protects property more absolutely than life or liberty. "Somehow or other," he said,

> a distinction seems to be drawn in favor of the property. The great rights of life and liberty used to be considered more sacred than everything else; for the question is asked, "what shall a man give for his life?" It seems, however, that a distinction is now drawn, and property has become much more sacred, and the guarantees of the Constitution protect it much more efficiently than they do the life or liberty of the citizen.

Congressman Gurly of Ohio cited the emancipation of the serfs in Russia and Congressman Owen Lovejoy of Illinois, brother of the martyred Elijah Lovejoy, the peaceful process whereby ex-slaves had acquired farms in the British West Indies. Senator Sumner of Massachusetts, winding up the debate on land confiscation in the Senate, turned again to France. Robespierre's confiscations, Sumner said,

> aroused at the time the eloquent indignation of Burke, and it still causes a sigh among all who think less of principles than of privileges. . . . Cruel as were many of the consequences, this confiscation must be judged as a part of that mighty revolution whose temper it shared; nor will it be easy to condemn anything but its excesses, unless you are ready to say that the safety of France, torn by domestic foes and invaded abroad, was not worth securing, or that equality before the law, which is now the most assured possession of that great nation, was not worth obtaining.[49]

This forthright defense of the French Revolution in all its phases had a significance comparable to the defense of Cromwell in eighteenth-century England, or of the Bolshevik

Revolution in the United States today. Radical Republicans were charged by their legislative colleagues with adventuring "upon the wide sea of revolution," breaking down "the idea of property" which "is the animating spirit of the country."[50]

The most suggestive abolitionist attack upon private property, however, was not the wartime campaign to divide the plantations (which, after all, failed), nor previous assaults upon the "lords of the loom" who manufactured cotton cloth (for just as much was said about the need of the South for "Northern institutions"). It was Henry Thoreau's critique of alienated labor.

Just as Dissenters had criticized priests and kings in the name of living conscience, so that radicalism which grew from Dissent criticized property in the name of living labor. Jefferson, in defending the present generation, Paine, in his sensitivity to the "working hand," expressed in varying forms the idea that he who works should be fed. Thoreau, like Marx, cut beneath analysis of misuse of the *product* of labor to examine the *process* of labor in an industrialized capitalist economy.

For Thoreau as for Marx, political democracy was a step forward but only a partial step. "America," Thoreau wrote in *Life Without Principle,*

> is said to be the arena on which the battle of freedom is to be fought; but surely it cannot be freedom in a merely political sense that is meant. Even if we grant that the American has freed himself from a political tyrant, he is still the slave of an economical and moral tyrant.[51]

Similar was Marx's expression in the early *On the Jewish Question:*

> *Political* emancipation certainly represents a great progress. It is not, indeed, the final form of human emancipation, but it is the final form of human emancipation *within* the framework of the prevailing social order.[52]

Full freedom required that political democracy be extended to the economy as well, that the man absolutely free as a citizen while still economically unfree be set at liberty in what Marx called "his sensuous, individual and *immediate* existence."[53]

This was a radicalism which went beyond the American Revolution, but only in the way that Thoreau himself did. Taking political democracy for granted, Thoreau set about to discover why "the laboring man . . . has no time to be anything but a machine" and "men have become the tools of their tools."[54] He visualized capitalist society as a larger version of the Australian gold fields:

> the numerous valleys, with their streams, all cut up with foul pits, from ten to one hundred feet deep, and half a dozen feet across, as close as they can be dug, and partly filled with water, —the locality to which men furiously rush to probe for their fortunes,—uncertain where they shall break ground,—not knowing but the gold is under their camp itself,—sometimes digging one hundred and sixty feet before they strike the vein, or then missing it by a foot,—turned into demons, and regardless of each others' rights, in their thirst for riches,—whole valleys, for thirty miles, suddenly honeycombed by the pits of the miners, so that even hundreds are drowned in them,—standing in water, and covered with mud and clay, they work night and day, dying of exposure and disease.[55]

Thoreau might speak of pushing down the road of life a barn seventy-five feet by forty, and Marx of the fetishism of commodities, but they meant very much the same thing. Who, for example, wrote these words?

> . . . Captain Hamilton reports that the devout and politically free inhabitant of New England is a kind of Laocoön who makes not the least effort to escape from the serpents which are crushing him. *Mammon* is his idol which he adores not only with his lips but with the whole force of his body and mind. In his view the world is no more than a Stock Exchange, and he is convinced that he has no other destiny here below than to become richer than his neighbour. Trade has seized upon all his thoughts, and he has no other recreation than to exchange objects. When he travels he carries, so to speak, his goods and his counter on his back and talks only of interest and profit. If he loses sight of his own business for an instant it is only to pry into the business of his competitors.[56]

That is not *Walden* but Marx, writing about Thoreau's neighbors very much as Thoreau himself did.

What is alienated, for both Marx and Thoreau, is not only

part of the workingman's product but the human capacities, energies, potentialities which should express themselves in joyful labor. As they saw it the essence of man's oppression in "civilized" society is that man's characteristic activity, productivity, becomes (to use Marx's terms) "self-sacrifice" and "mortification" rather than (to use Thoreau's) a "pastime." Thoreau expressed human subordination to inanimate things as plowing oneself into the soil for compost.[57] Marx put it this way:

> . . . the worker is related to the *product of his labour* as to an *alien* object. For it is clear . . . that the more the worker expends himself in work the more powerful becomes the world of objects which he creates in face of himself, the poorer he becomes in his inner life, and the less he belongs to himself.

Repeatedly Marx insisted that "alienation appears not merely in the result but also in the *process* of *production*, within *productive activity* itself." The following words, in fact by Marx, might just as well have been Thoreau's:

> What constitutes the alienation of labour? First, that the work is *external* to the worker, that it is not part of his nature; and that, consequently, he does not fulfill himself in his work but denies himself, has a feeling of misery rather than well-being, does not develop freely his mental and physical energies but is physically exhausted and mentally debased. The worker, therefore, feels himself at home only during his leisure time, whereas at work he feels homeless. His work is not voluntary but imposed, *forced labour*. It is not the satisfaction of a need, but only a *means* for satisfying other needs. Its alien character is clearly shown by the fact that as soon as there is no physical or other compulsion it is avoided like the plague.[58]

Similar, too, were the two men's visions of an alternative. In the same years (1845–1846) that Marx described in *The German Ideology* a Utopia in which men would do physical labor in the morning and write literary criticism after lunch, Thoreau was doing just that at Walden Pond.

Because Marx and Thoreau shared a literary style which emphasized contradiction and drove conclusions to extremes, at times the parallelism is almost uncanny:

. . . In the large towns and cities, where civilization especially prevails, the number of those who own a shelter is a very small fraction of the whole. The rest pay an annual tax for this outside garment of all, become indispensable summer and winter, which would buy a village of Indian wigwams, but now helps to keep them poor as long as they live. . . . On the one side is the palace, on the other are the almshouse and "silent poor." The myriads who built the pyramids to be the tombs of the Pharaohs were fed on garlic, and it may be were not decently buried themselves. The mason who finishes the cornice of the palace returns at night perchance to a hut not so good as a wigwam. It is a mistake to suppose that, in a country where the usual evidences of civilization exist, the condition of a very large body of the inhabitants may not be as degraded as that of savages.[59]

. . . Man is regressing to the *cave dwelling,* but in an alienated, malignant form. The savage in his cave (a natural element which is freely offered for his use and protection) does not feel himself a stranger; on the contrary he feels as much at home as a *fish* in water. But the cellar dwelling of the poor man is a hostile dwelling, "an alien, constricting power which only surrenders itself to him in exchange for blood and sweat." He cannot regard it as his home, as a place where he might at last say, "here I am at home." Instead, he finds himself in *another person's* house, the house of a *stranger* who lies in wait for him every day and evicts him if he does not pay the rent.[60]

The reader may correctly identify the author of each of these passages, but I suspect it will take him a few moments. Here obviously were the spokesmen, not of two utterly alien traditions with nothing to say to one another, but of two variants of one tradition springing from Rousseau's insight that (as Thoreau expressed it) "just in proportion as some have been placed in outward circumstances above the savage, others have been degraded below him."[61]

This is what matters to us in our own day, when the Marxist and libertarian American traditions are characteristically counterposed as expressions of "revolution" as over against "rebellion," or of an ideological "closed society" in contrast to a pragmatic "open" one. In its own time, and in the context of the unfolding of an American revolutionary tradition, what mattered about the abolitionist questioning of private property was that it weakened respect for the state power by which that property was protected.

They need the state most, observed Thoreau in *Civil Disobedience*, who require it to protect their property.[62] By its guerrilla attacks upon the right of property, the revolutionary tradition prepared the ground for a frontal assault upon the authority of the state.

NOTES

1. Quoted in J. Morrison Davidson, *Concerning Four Precursors of Henry George* (London and Glasgow, [c. 1900]), p. 29.
2. James Madison to John Brown, [October 1788], *Letters and Other Writings of James Madison*, ed. William C. Rives (Philadelphia, 1865), I, 187–88.
3. John Adams to Richard Price, May 20, 1789, *The Works of John Adams*, ed. Charles F. Adams (Boston, 1850–1856), IX, 558–59.
4. Bailyn, *Ideological Origins*, pp. 47, 283. Quite in contrast to his exhaustive treatment of the earlier "commonwealthmen," Bailyn characterizes the Dissenters inaccurately on the basis of a single secondary source which he misinterprets. Thus Bailyn quotes this source to the effect that "the extreme English radicals of the Revolutionary period" (Bailyn's phrase) were "no democrats." But in fact Ian Christie uses the expression "no democrats" about a small group of ideologues "in the years before 1769" including Thomas Hollis, Richard Baron, and Thomas Brand, *not* about Wilkes, Burgh, Priestley, and Cartwright (*Ideological Origins*, p. 283 n.; Ian R. Christie, *Wilkes, Wyvill and Reform: The Parliamentary Reform Movement in British Politics, 1760–1785* [London, 1962], p. 15). Relying exclusively on Christie, Bailyn follows him in the belief that "between 1763 and 1785 discontent among the masses due to widespread social or economic grievances contributed little, if anything, to the agitation for reform" (*Wilkes, Wyvill and Reform*, p. 223), ignoring, for example, the evidence of George Rudé that the "most loyal and vociferous" of Wilkes's early supporters were "the London craftsmen, journeymen and labourers" (*Wilkes and Liberty: A Social Study of 1763 to 1774* [Oxford, 1962], p. 192). What Bailyn does, in effect, is to seek to sustain Miss Robbins' thesis that the Dissenters merely continued the "commonwealth tradition," not as she did by the argument that both groups were radical, but by the contrary argument that both groups were conservative. He writes in this vein: "Christie's description of the radicals of the 1760's holds equally well for most of the commonwealthmen and coffeehouse radicals of the early eighteenth century, whose views became so influential in America. Trenchard and Gordon, for example, refused to

consider any alteration in the property structure of England (*Cato's Letters*, no. 85); objected not to inequality as such but only to artificial inequality (no. 45); were anti-majoritarian (no. 62); and were vehemently opposed to charity schools. . . ." (*Ideological Origins*, p. 283 n.). Not one of these four beliefs was characteristic of the Dissenters.

5. James Burgh, *Thoughts on Education* (Boston, 1749), p. 18; *Dignity of Human Nature*, p. 258; *Youth's Friendly Monitor* . . . (London, 1756), p. 16.

6. "A Plea for the Poor," *Journal and Essays*, ed. Gummere, p. 403.

7. Benjamin Franklin to Robert Morris, December 25, 1783, *Writings*, ed. Smyth, IX, 138.

8. Granville Sharp, *A Short Tract Concerning the Doctrine of "Nullum Tempus occurrit Regi"* . . . (London, 1779), pp. 3–7. In this and other quotations from Sharp I have usually omitted italics, which he employed superabundantly.

9. "Essay on Government," *Works*, XXII, 26. Note the indignation this passage aroused in Josiah Tucker, *A Treatise Concerning Civil Government, in Three Parts* (London, 1781), pp. 16–17.

10. "Queries and Remarks Respecting Alterations in the Constitution of Pennsylvania," *Writings*, X, 58–60.

11. *Political Disquisitions*, I, 37; this passage is quoted by Christie, *Wilkes, Wyvill and Reform*, p. 55.

12. "A Philosophical View of Reform," *Political Tracts of Wordsworth, Coleridge and Shelley*, ed. R. J. White (Cambridge, 1953), p. 239.

13. Cartwright, *Legislative Rights*, pp. xxii, 28–34, 50–51; as to Brissot and French revolutionary thinking about property, see K. D. Toennesson, "The Babouvists: From Utopian to Practical Socialism," *Past and Present* (1962), p. 62.

14. "Lectures on History and General Policy," *Works*, XXIV, 226–27; Lincoln, *English Dissent*, p. 164; *Lectures on History and General Policy* . . . (Philadelphia, 1803), II, lectures 41, 43; "A Political Dialogue on the General Principles of Government," *Works*, XXV, 86–88, 95–96.

15. Price, *Observations on the Importance of the American Revolution* (London, 1784), pp. 70–71.

16. "Common Sense," *Complete Writings*, I, 9; "Agrarian Justice," *ibid.*, I, 609–23.

17. Zoltán Haraszti, *John Adams and the Prophets of Progress* (Cambridge, Mass., 1952), p. 96.

18. *Papers*, ed. Boyd, XV, 384–91.

19. "Lectures on History and General Policy," *Works*, XXIV, 225. An English translation of Condorcet's biography was published in London in 1787; see p. 305: "The right of property in any individual is nothing more than the right of using freely whatever belongs to him. . . . There should . . . be no wills."

20. John Locke, *Two Treatises of Government*, ed. Peter Laslett (Cambridge, 1960), pp. 224, 227.

21. Paul Lucas, "Essays in the Margin of Blackstone's *Commentaries*,"

unpublished Ph.D. dissertation, Princeton University, 1962, pp. 211, 214.

22. *History of England*, V, 360–61.

23. "Rights of Man," *Complete Writings*, I, 251; "Dissertation on First Principles of Government," *ibid.*, II, 575.

24. "Essays," p. 196.

25. William Blackstone, *Commentaries on the Law of England. In Four Books*, ed. Edward Christian (London, 1809), I, 192–193; II, 10–11. See also Blackstone's *A Treatise on the Law of Descents in Fee-Simple* (Oxford, 1759), pp. 16–17: ". . . all rules of succession to estates are creatures of the civil polity, and *juris positivi* merely. The right of property, which is gained by occupancy, extends naturally no farther than the life of the present possessor; after which the land by the law of nature would again become common, and liable to be seised by the next occupant: but society, to prevent the mischiefs that might ensue from a doctrine so productive of contention, has established conveyances, wills, and successions," etc.

26. Jefferson to Madison, September 6, 1789, *Papers*, XV, 392.

27. "Autobiography," *The Works of Thomas Jefferson*, ed. Paul L. Ford (New York, 1904–1905), I, 14.

28. "A Summary View of the Rights of British America," *Papers*, I, 132–33.

29. Jefferson to Edmund Pendleton, August 13, 1776, *ibid.*, I, 491.

30. *The Commonplace Book of Thomas Jefferson: A Repertory of His Ideas on Government*, ed. Gilbert Chinard (Baltimore, 1926), pp. 190, 229–32. These ideas went back to the early seventeenth-century antiquarian Henry Spelman; see Samuel Kliger, *The Goths in England: A Study in Seventeenth and Eighteenth Century Thought* (Cambridge, 1952), especially p. 128, and J. G. A. Pocock, *The Ancient Constitution and the Feudal Law* (Cambridge, 1957), especially p. 119.

31. "Summary View," *Papers*, I, 133.

32. Jefferson to Edmund Pendelton, August 13, 1776, *ibid.*, I, 492.

33. Jefferson to James Madison, October 28, 1785, *ibid.*, VIII, 681–82.

34. Vernon L. Parrington, *Main Currents in American Thought* (New York, 1927), I, 344.

35. Julian P. Boyd, *The Declaration of Independence: The Evolution of the Text* (Princeton, 1945), pp. 3–5, 5 n.

36. Dumas Malone, *Jefferson and the Rights of Man* (Boston, 1951), p. 223; see also *Papers*, XV, 230–33.

37. Jefferson to Isaac McPherson, August 13, 1813, *The Writings of Thomas Jefferson*, ed. Andrew A. Lipscomb and Albert E. Bergh (Washington, 1904), XIII, 333: "It is agreed by those who have seriously considered the subject, that no individual has, of natural right, a separate property in an acre of land, for instance. By an universal law, indeed, whatever, whether fixed or movable, belongs to all men equally and in common, is the property for the moment of him who occupies it, but when he relinquishes the occupation, the property goes with it. Stable ownership is the gift of social law, and is given late in the progress of society."

38. Jefferson to James Madison, September 6, 1789, *Papers*, XV, 396–397.

39. *Commonplace Book*, p. 230.

40. Marginal notes on Allan Ramsay's *Thoughts on the Origin and Nature of Government*, quoted by Paul W. Conner, *Poor Richard's Politicks: Benjamin Franklin and His New American Order* (New York, 1965), p. 118.

41. Jefferson to Francis W. Gilmer, June 7, 1816, *Writings*, ed. Ford, X, 32–33.

42. Jefferson to James Madison, January 30, 1787, *Papers*, XI, 92–93.

43. Jefferson to Cornelius Camden Blatchly, October 21, 1822, *Writings*, ed. Lipscomb and Bergh, XV, 399–400; Jefferson to William Ludlow, September 6, 1824, *ibid.*, XVI, 74–76.

44. "Agrarian Justice," *Complete Writings*, I, 612.

45. Thomas Skidmore, *The Rights of Man to Property* . . . (New York, 1829), pp. 72–73, 243; Harris, *Socialist Origins*, pp. 92, 103. The passage from Jefferson's 1812 brief quoted by Skidmore may be found in *Writings*, ed. Lipscomb and Bergh, XVIII, 45–46.

46. Quoted in Harris, *Socialist Origins*, pp. 17, 18, 33, 38.

47. George W. Julian, *Speeches on Political Questions* (New York, 1872), pp. 51–52, 459, 367–69, 420.

48. *Ibid.*, pp. 210–11, 220.

49. *Congressional Globe*, 37th Cong., 2d Sess., 1862, pp. 944, 1077, 1714–15, 1719, 1817, 2166, 2193–96, Appendix 236.

50. *Ibid.*, pp. 1049, 1803.

51. "Life Without Principle," *The Writings of Henry David Thoreau* (Boston and New York, 1893), IV, 476. Compare the parallel quotations from Marx and Emerson in Herreshoff, *American Disciples of Marx*, pp. 18–25.

52. *Early Writings*, p. 15.

53. *Ibid.*, p. 30.

54. "Walden," *Writings*, II, 6, 41.

55. "Life Without Principle," *ibid.*, IV, 465.

56. "On the Jewish Question," *Early Writings*, p. 35.

57. "Walden," *Writings*, II, 6.

58. "Economic and Philosophical Manuscripts," *Early Writings*, pp. 122, 124–25.

59. "Walden," *Writings*, II, 33, 38.

60. "Economic and Philosophical Manuscripts," *Early Writings*, p. 177.

61. "Walden," *Writings*, II, 37–38.

62. "Civil Disobedience," *ibid.*, IV, 372–74. Note Thoreau's exegesis of "render unto Caesar": "if you use money which has the image of Caesar on it, and which he has made current and valuable, that is, *if you are men of the State*, and gladly enjoy the advantages of Caesar's government, then pay him back some of his own when he demands it."

CHAPTER 4

CAST
YOUR
WHOLE
VOTE

"The philosophers," wrote the youthful Karl Marx in his *Theses on Feuerbach*, "have only interpreted the world; but the thing is, to change it." It was an old Anglo-American idea. The Christian communist Gerrard Winstanley had declared in 1649: "My mind was not at rest because nothing was acted, and thoughts run in me, that words and writings were all nothing, and must die, for action is the life of all, and if thou dost not act, thou dost nothing."[1] The revolutionary American abolitionist was above all an activist in the spirit of this saying. Like Thoreau, he sought to cast his "whole vote, not a strip of paper merely."[2]

Whereas the leaders of the American Revolution conceived conscience as a liberty to think and (with certain limitations) speak, abolitionists insisted on the conscientious freedom to act. A minority, even a minority of one, had the duty of living on the basis of God's law in defiance of all man-made authorities. This proposition underlay Garrison's strategy of immediate emancipation and Thoreau's philosophy of civil disobedience.

Eighteenth- and nineteenth-century American revolutionaries agreed that a political philosophy based on freedom leads to the reconstruction of society as a voluntary association of individuals. But the revolutionaries of 1776, following Locke, made the important qualification that only majorities could renew the social contract. Abolitionism was obliged to discard that restriction so as to justify individual disobedience to laws which sanctioned slavery. For abolitionists the social contract became an association voluntarily re-formed by individuals from day to day. They believed that legitimate government, at any given moment, comprised those laws to which conscientious men could adhere.

To be sure, earlier revolutionaries had had much to say about individual unjust laws, such as the Stamp Act. In 1761 James Otis cited Lord Coke's opinion in Bonham's Case in support of the position that a law against "natural equity" was void.[3] Garrison could and did quote Algernon Sidney, whom he called "the father of modern Abolitionism," to the same effect. *"That which is not just is not Law,"* Sidney had written, *"and that which is not Law, ought not to be Obeyed."* If a lawgiver "be not the Minister of God, he is not a King, at least not such a King as the Apostle commands us to obey."[4]

But the revolutionaries of the abolitionist movement, unlike the revolutionaries of 1776, confronted not an arbitrary king, nor the laws of a Parliament in which they were unrepresented, but unjust laws democratically enacted by a republican government. "All men," Thoreau wrote in *Civil Disobedience*, "recognize the right of revolution."[5] What they did not recognize was minority disobedience to republican government, and to justify this new kind of revolution a new theory was required.

I

Effecting this intellectual transformation was no simple task. One agency was Quakerism. The Friends were undoubtedly the most persistent Anglo-American lawbreakers in the seventeenth and eighteenth centuries, and as time went on their testimony concerning civil disobedience, like their closely related testimony against slavery, began to find its way into more orthodox political discourse. John Woolman prophetically anticipated both Thoreau's action in refusing wartime taxes and the tendency of abolitionist theorizing to link oppression of the Negro to oppression of the Indian and to war.

At the time of the American Revolution the Friends were regarded as advocates of passive obedience and quasi-Tories. Their period of maximum intellectual influence was the early nineteenth century, when the characteristic Quaker doctrine of an "inner light" ("that of God in every man") had the same kind of impact on secular political thought that the similar teachings of the English Dissenters had had in the previous century. Just as the insistence of Dissenters on freedom of conscience proved the key to the thought-world of late eighteenth-century radicalism, so Quakerism most clearly exhibited the constellation of attitudes at the heart of radical abolitionism. Emerson and Bancroft ascribed to George Fox their belief in the common man's capacity to perceive the truth by unaided intuition.[6] Garrison, charged by the churches with irreligion, discovered in Quakerism a religious tradition with which he could identify.[7] Of Lincoln, whose Second Inaugural Address represented the completed fusion of secular and sacred traditions in antislavery thought, Richard Current comments: "Though never quite a Quaker (he assumed that some of his ancestors had been), Lincoln had a strong affinity for the beliefs of the Friends."[8]

The beginnings of the assimilation of Quaker sensibility into the mainstream of American political discourse can be observed in two petitions against slavery submitted to the First Congress in 1790. The petition of the Society of Friends employed religious language, calling for "unfeigned righteousness in public as well as private stations" and "the exercise of a solid uniform virtue." The petition of the Pennsylvania Society for Promoting the Abolition of Slavery used a more secular rhetoric. It appealed to "a regard for the happiness of mankind," and to "a just and acute conception of the true principles of liberty." It made the legalistic argument that the Constitution required the blessings of liberty to be administered "without distinction of color, to all descriptions of people," and the political argument for a "restoration of liberty" to those who, alone in a free land, were "degraded into perpetual bondage" and "groaning in servile subjection." Nevertheless, the two vocabularies overlapped. The Quakers observed that the slave trade "most certainly tends to lay waste the virtue, *and,* of course, the happiness of the people," and that "*both* the true temporal interest of nations, and eternal well-being of individuals, depend on doing justly, loving mercy, and walking humbly before God" (italics added). The Pennsylvania Abolition Society concurred that mankind was "equally designed for the enjoyment of happiness" according to the Christian creed, "and the political creed of Americans fully coincides with the position."[9]

During the "lost generation" of American abolitionism, from 1790 to 1830, a thin grey line of Quakers kept a concern about slavery alive. One of the first writers who appealed to the authority of the Declaration against the authority of the Constitution was the Quaker John Parrish in 1806. Elias Hicks and Benjamin Lundy inspired a group of Friends in the Western Reserve of Ohio who developed in the early 1820s "a synthesis of the Biblical and natural rights arguments" which held slavery not only wrong but unrepublican. These "pioneer antislavery strongholds" voiced the "lay ethical and moral opinions [which] were the matrix of the War Amendments," and sent to Congress representatives such as Joshua Giddings, author of the *Creole* resolutions, and John Bingham, one of the Fourteenth Amendment's founding fathers.[10]

Thomas Clarkson, patriarch of the English antislavery movement, played a considerable part in generalizing Quaker attitudes among other non-Friends. His three-volume *Portraiture of Quakerism,* reprinted in New York in 1806 and in Philadelphia in 1808, and his *Memoirs of William Penn,* which appeared in the same two cities in 1813–1814, were read in the United States together with his *History of the Rise, Progress and Accomplishment of the Abolition of the African Slave-*

Trade. "From the year 1787, when I began to devote my labours to the abolition of the Slave-trade," so Clarkson wrote in introducing the *Portraiture,* "I was thrown frequently into the company of the people called Quakers. . . . Hence I came to a knowledge of their living manners, which no other person, who was not a Quaker, could have easily obtained."[11] The observations of this sympathetic co-worker helped to build bridges between Quaker experience and the traditions of other Protestant Dissenters. Indeed, Clarkson's five volumes about the group which had begun the antislavery struggle before his own involvement and had been his constant companions in it, constitute a kind of Utopia, comparable to Burgh's *Cessares* or Sharp's *Regulations for Sierra Leone.* For the Society of Friends, observed Clarkson, differed "more than even many foreigners do from their own countrymen." Strange dress, unusual forms of written and spoken interchange, the renunciation of music, drama, and the customary national holidays, new names for the very days of the week and months of the year, together with idiosyncratic devotional practices and the advocacy of innumerable reforms, combined to constitute the Friends an internal enclave which more than one contemporary—such as Paine and Jefferson[12]—paused to consider curiously as an alternative to received arrangements.

Clarkson's review of the peculiarities of Quakerism began with the affirmation of what George Fox had termed "that of God in every man," or to use Clarkson's language, "the Divinity [which] resides in him."[13] This inner light is quite distinct from reason. "Man must wait for its inspirations. Like the wind, it bloweth when it listeth."[14] Among the authorities which Clarkson said Friends adduced on behalf of this belief was the author most quoted by Price, Ralph Cudworth:

All the books and writings which we converse with [so Clarkson quoted Cudworth] they can but represent spiritual objects to our understandings, which yet we can never see in their own true figure, colour, and proportion, until we have a divine light within to irradiate and shine upon them. Though there be never such excellent truths concerning Christ and his Gospel set down in words and letters, yet they will be but unknown characters to us, until we have a living Spirit within us, that can decypher them; until the same Spirit, by secret whispers in our hearts, do comment upon them. . . .[15]

This Quaker conception of the inner light grafted neatly onto the older Dissenting belief in active freedom of conscience. Thus Clarkson's prize essay on slavery in 1785 had presented as the gravest of all objections to "commerce of the human species" that the slave, because he was not free to follow his conscience, could not at the Resurrection be fairly judged: "For how can any man be justly called to an account for his actions, whose actions are not *at his own disposal?*"[16]

A second key doctrine shared by Friends and radical abolitionism was perfectibility. That process was conceived to be akin to biological growth, for the "light" was also often called a "seed" which—so Clarkson quoted Isaac Pennington—"consists not in words or notions of the mind, but is an inward thing, an inward spiritual substance in the heart, as real inwardly in its kind as other seeds are outwardly in their kind."[17]

Thirdly, Friends along with radical abolitionists affirmed that this regenerative process was available to all men; and that any man (or woman) might "minister" to a congregation. The subversive implications of this tenet for any kind of authority are apparent. Nor did Clarkson fail to see them. "No servility," he concluded his *Portraiture,*

is allowed either in word or gesture. Neither that which is written, nor that which is uttered, is to please the vanity of the persons addressed, or to imply services never intended to be performed. The knee is not to be bent to any one. It is strengthened, again, and made to shoot, by their own maxims. Is it possible to be in the habit of viewing all men as equal in privileges, and no one as superior to another but by his virtue, and not to feel a disposition that must support it?[18]

In his life of Penn, Clarkson sought to show how these spiritual principles of the Society of Friends might serve as models for society at large. Penn, Clarkson supposed, was a "Christian legislator," which meant among other things "adopting, as it relates to aliens or foreigners, principles of action pure in themselves, founded in justice, of the same tendency with those established for the governed."[19]

Like his panegyricist, Penn was said to have believed that governments "depend upon men rather than men upon governments. . . . Let men be good, and the Government cannot be bad."[20] Clarkson favorably contrasted this emphasis on administrative morality with the faith of his own day in constitution-tinkering. The transition from the outlook of a Madison to that of a Garrison or Thoreau was obviously under way.

Among the particular laws of Penn's Pennsylvania, Clarkson praised "prior to all others" that which protected liberty of conscience. Penn, Clarkson observed, made this law unchangeable. "Here then we see him again under the sublime light of a Christian Legislator, making Liberty of Conscience the grand corner-stone of his civil edifice. What a contrast does this afford to the conduct of those who have legislated in this department on [the basis of] the policy of the world!"[21]

Next Clarkson stressed Penn's penal legislation, which abolished capital punishment except for murder and made all prisons workshops. These ordinances, according to Clarkson, formed the germ of the exemplary prison codes enacted by Pennsylvania at the time of the American Revolution.[22]

Penn's treatment of noncitizens was similarly praised by Clarkson. Naturalization of foreigners was easy. Indian relations exhibited the absolute pacifism which Clarkson himself espoused and which was typically associated with early nineteenth-century abolitionism. Only in Pennsylvania, asserted Penn's admiring biographer, did Europeans plant a colony motivated not by avarice or ambition but by religious concern for the "barbarous nations."[23]

Needless to say, for Clarkson the crowning glory of Penn's "little paradise upon earth" was its treatment of Negroes. Clarkson said that Penn, powerless to prevent the introduction into the colony of this British export among others, nevertheless proposed a law "which should protect the Negroes from personal ill-treatment, by fair trials and limited punishments; and which at the same time, by regulating their marriages, should improve their moral condition." The law failed; but the Minute recorded in the Monthly Meeting Book of Philadelphia at Penn's instance served as precedent for the decision of Philadelphia Friends in 1776 that no member of the Meeting might hold slaves, and for the Pennsylvania abolition law of 1780 which stimulated other Northern legislatures to do likewise.[24]

The plan for legislative melioration leading to gradual emancipation, which Clarkson ascribed to Penn, was that which he himself favored when in 1823 the British antislavery movement began its final push for abolition. The way to help the slaves, Clarkson argued, was first to procure for them "a new and better code of laws" and only then to proceed to the freedom "of which they have been unjustly deprived."[25] This was also the position of the leader of the Parliamentary agitation, Fowell Buxton, who moved on May 15, 1823, that slavery "ought to be gradually abolished throughout the British colonies, with as much expedition as may be found consistent with a due regard to the well-being of the parties concerned."[26] But the failure of the West Indian legislatures to enact significant reforms, together with the persecution of British missionaries to the slaves, doomed the gradualist strategy. The result was a family quarrel among Friends in which Buxton, whose wife and mother were Quakers, was challenged by a left wing which sought to pledge parliamentary candidates to "strenuously promote and vote for the immediate and total abolition of British colonial slavery." The left wing's principal organizer was Quaker Joseph Sturge, its first ideological spokesman the Leicester Friend, Elizabeth Heyrick.[27]

The impact on America of Heyrick's *Immediate, Not Gradual Abolition*, published in England in 1824, is suggested by the fact of its reprinting in Philadelphia in 1824, New York in 1825, Philadelphia in 1836 and 1837, and Boston (by Garrison's associate Isaac Knapp) in 1838. Her immediatism was not yet civil disobedience or insurrection, but drove toward them. When she said, "Why petition Parliament *at all*, to do that for us, which, were they ever so well disposed, we can do more speedily and more effectual [*sic*] for ourselves?"[28] Elizabeth Heyrick meant only to recommend a boycott of the produce of slave labor. But others might give the words other meanings. So indeed might she. As she closed her pamphlet, news arrived of slave insurrections in Demerara and Kingston. The defeated rebels had been punished by hanging, a thousand lashes, or life sentences to a chain gang. What, the white Quakeress wrote five years before David Walker's *Appeal* called for slave insurrection, was the crime being punished? "It was insurrection. But in what cause did they become insurgents? Was it not in that cause, which, of all others, can best *excuse,* if it cannot *justify* insurrection?"[29] Anticipating Frederick Douglass' bitter words of 1848, Elizabeth Heyrick flayed the hypocrisy of those who support white revolutions but condemn black ones:

> How preposterously partial and inconsistent are we in the extension of our sympathy, our approbation and our assistance toward the oppressed and miserable! We extol the resistance of the *Greeks,*—we deem it heroic and meritorious. We deem it an act of virtue,—of *Christian charity,* to supply *them* with *arms and ammunition,* to enable them to *persist in insurrection.* Possibly, in the longest list of munificent subscribers to these *Greek* insurgents, the names of some noble lords and honourable gentlemen may be found—who sanction and approve the visitation of WEST INDIAN SLAVE INSURGENTS, with the GIBBET, and the infliction of ONE THOUSAND LASHES!!"[30]

By the 1830s what might be called philo-Quakerism pervaded the intellectual community of the North, especially in New England. Stanley Elkins states that "our antislavery movement was for practical purposes devoid of intellectual nourishment."[31] It would be more accurate to say that abolitionists turned away from the traditional intellectual menu which featured the works of Locke, and sought sustenance elsewhere: in writers who did not make the sharp distinction between things sacred and things secular of Locke's *Letter Concerning Toleration,* who affirmed the absolute natural rights of individuals in society less ambiguously than did Locke's *Second Treatise,* and above all, who attributed to man's will and conscience more autonomy in determining his actions than did Locke's *Essay Concerning Human Understanding.*

Thus William Ellery Channing, as quoted previously, traced his intellectual awakening to Price's *Review of Morals* which (he said) "saved me from Locke's philosophy." Thus, according to Frederick Hedge, the Transcendentalist discussion group drew together in 1836 on the basis of a common rejection of Locke's environmental psychology.[32] And thus Theodore Parker summed up his intellectual development in the comment that

> the sensational system so ably presented by Locke in his masterly Essay, developed into various forms by Hobbes, Berkeley, Hume, Paley, and the French Materialists, and modified, but not much amended, by Reid and Stewart, gave little help. . . . I found most help in the works of Immanuel Kant.[33]

The Quaker concept of the inner light facilitated the rejection of Locke by offering a homegrown equivalent to the doctrines of Price, Kant, and Coleridge.

The idea of the inner light was closely connected with the idea of immediate emancipation, for to some reformers (David Brion Davis remarks) immediate emancipation "seemed mainly to imply a direct, intuitive consciousness of the sinfulness of slavery, and a sincere personal commitment to work for its abolition."[34] Abolitionists appealed away from texts, whether of the Bible or the Constitution, to the testimony of the heart. As early as the Park Street Church address of July 4, 1829, Garrison declared: "On a question of shame and honor— liberty and oppression—reasoning is sometimes useless, and worse. I feel the decision in my pulse: if it throws no light upon the brain, it kindles a fire at the heart."[35] "As a nation," Angelina Grimké wrote in the next decade, "we have too long educated the *mind*, and left the *heart* a moral waste."[36] It was in this mood that, during the drafting of the Declaration of Sentiments of the American Anti-Slavery Society in 1833, Garrison opposed an amendment which would add Biblical citations to back up one of the statements he had drafted. "It makes the rights of man depend upon a text," he said. "Now, it matters not what the Bible may say, so far as these rights are concerned. They never originated in any parchment, are not dependent upon any parchment, but are in the nature of man himself, written upon the human faculties and powers by the finger of God."[37] A generation later, in the year of Lincoln's election, he continued to maintain that abolitionists did not derive "the rights of man from any book, but from his own nature."[38]

These affirmations of the wisdom of untutored human nature were consistent with the outlook of Dissenters like Priestley who had propounded the "universal maxim, that the more liberty is given to every thing which is in a state of growth, the more perfect it will become."[39] Conversely, such affirmations were inconsistent with the *Weltanschauung* of those who, following Jonathan Edwards, thought that man by nature was totally depraved, or who, with Machiavelli, believed that in making a new government all men should be considered knaves. Persons holding the latter opinions were unlikely to believe that human beings should set their own consciences against law and government: were unlikely, in other words, to develop a theory of civil disobedience.

The point emerges clearly in one of Garrison's first expositions of civil disobedience, in 1835. In the *Liberator* for March 7 of that year he declared, anticipating the provisions of the Fugitive Slave Law of 1850, that if "laws and constituted authorities" required him to assist in the return of fugitive slaves, *"then I will not obey them."*[40] In an address on July 4 Garrison explained himself more fully. God's law, he said, is superior to human law. The question of right or wrong cannot be reduced to the question of lawful or unlawful. Look at the atrocities committed legally: widows burned in India, suppression of the press in Russia, the hanging of men for the slightest offense in England. Quakers and "witches" had been legally executed in the American colonies. To say that the test of right is human law is "atheism and treason against the government of God." Law varied from time to place. Man was not bound to obey national law if it conflicted with allegiance to God.[41]

But who, so Garrison paraphrased Locke's famous question

in the *Second Treatise,* is to judge whether human and divine law are in conflict? His answer—the individual conscience is to judge—expressed his Quakerly confidence in the uneducated common man.

II

Quakerism provided American abolitionists not only with Elizabeth Heyrick's program of "immediate emancipation," but with a systematic discussion of civil disobedience in the works of Jonathan Dymond. Dymond was a Quaker linen draper in southwestern England whose *Essays on the Principles of Morality* were published in America in 1834, six years after his death. Dymond and Algernon Sidney were Garrison's two favorite prose authors, according to Garrison's children; Garrison's sometime opponent James G. Birney also admired Dymond, citing his statement that even "*savages,* to whom the gospel has never been preached" observe the Golden Rule; Charles Sumner, in his speech "War System of the Commonwealth of Nations" in 1849, referred familiarly to Dymond as an exemplar of absolute pacifism.[42]

Dymond's thinking on civil disobedience grew organically from earlier discussions of the theme by the Dissenting radical Granville Sharp and by William Godwin, son and grandson of Dissenting ministers and graduate of a Dissenting academy. All three men went beyond the concept of Christian disobedience characteristic of Dissenters. That traditional conception envisoned quiet resistance to the "offenses which dishonor our country, by declaring our sentiments about them, on all proper occasions, with modesty and humility; by never complying in any instance contrary to our sentiments; and giving, as far as possible, a publick testimony in favour of universal Liberty and the simplicity of the Gospel."[43] The recommended response to bad law was

> to make a remonstrance to the legislature; and if that be not practicable, or be not heard, still, if the complaints be general and loud, a wise prince and ministry will pay regard to them; or they will, at length, be weary of enforcing a penal law which is generally abhorred and disregarded, when they see the people

will run the risk of the punishment, if it cannot be evaded, rather than quietly submit to the injunction. . . .[44]

Good enough for quiet times, this model was abandoned during the American and French revolutions.

For Sharp, we have seen, the laws of God, nature, and England were all one. That had been the basis of Sharp's argument when, in the Sommersett decision of 1772, he extracted from England's leading jurist the judgment that slavery was illegal. To the end of his life in 1813 Sharp quoted Scripture and the law of England interchangeably. The Eleventh Psalm, he wrote in 1797, contains

> exactly the same first principles of right which our ancient English Lawyers very properly deemed "the two first foundations of English Law," viz. 1st, Reason, or the Laws of Natural Right, written, as it were, on the heart of man by his Creator. . . . And, secondly, the revealed laws of God, written in the Holy Scriptures. . . .[45]

In 1807, the year of the abolition of the slave trade in both England and America, Sharp responded to a petition of West Indian planters and merchants which complained that such a bill would "violate the system of colonial laws relative to property," by quoting (once again) the sixteenth-century treatise *Doctor and Student*: "Statutes exist not against REASON, nor against the DIVINE LAW."[46]

Sharp also more than once advised that such illegal laws be broken. In a pamphlet on dueling, published in England in 1773 and in Philadelphia five years later, he argued that even "Gentlemen of the Army" are "Men, as well as Soldiers," and so must "maintain the Natural Privilege of Men, (viz. that of thinking for themselves, and acting agreeable to the Dictates of their own Conscience, as members of the Community)." In words anticipating the Nuremburg Judgments, Sharp continued:

> For the Law will not excuse an unlawful Act by a Soldier, even though he commits it by the express Command of the highest military Authority in the Kingdom. . . .Even in publick military Service, or warlike Expeditions by National authority, the law manifestly requires the Soldier to think for himself; and to

consider, before he acts in any war, whether the same be just; for, if it be otherwise, the Common Law of this Kingdom will impute to him the Guilt of Murder.

And though the Law does not actually punish such general Crimes, as may unfortunately have obtained, at any time, the Sanction of Government, yet the time will certainly come, when all such temporizing military Murderers must be responsible for the innocent blood that is shed in an unjust War, if they have rendered themselves accessaries to it by an implicit, and, therefore, criminal obedience to the promoters of it. "Item fit Homocidium in Bello," (says the learned Bracton) "et tunc videndum utrum Bellum fit justum vel injustum. Si autem injustum, tenebitur occisor: si autem justum, sicut pro defensione patriae, non tenebitur. . . ." [Roughly: Murder also occurs in war, and then it is to be seen whether the war is just or unjust. If unjust, then he who kills will be understood as a murderer; if just, as in the case of the defense of one's fatherland, he will not.]

"Men of true honor, therefore," Sharp concluded,

> at the same time that they are sensible of their duty as Soldiers and Subjects to their King, must be mindful that they are subject also to the empire of reason, and are bound thereby, in common with all mankind, to maintain the dignity and natural freedom of Human Nature: and those Soldiers, who, in addition to their natural reason, have a true sense of Religion, will not only be mindful, that they are Soldiers and Subjects to an earthly King, but that they are also Soldiers and Subjects to the King of Kings; whose Laws and precepts they will, on all occasions, prefer to every other command; and will obey the same with such a steady courage, as may be equal to every adversity, and undeserved suffering that threatens them.[47]

Logically enough, Sharp also contended that the only army appropriate to a free society was a militia made up of citizens in rotation, which elected its officers. A standing army inevitably led to the despicable assertion that "a soldier has no right to judge for himself," indeed to make soldiers "soldiers," that is, mercenaries.[48]

In his pamphlet *A Declaration of the People's Natural Right to a Share in the Legislature*, Sharp noted that even a reviewer in the Dissenting journal *Monthly Review* had taken exception to what the reviewer called the "strange principle" that a soldier might refuse an officer's commands. Sharp replied that this principle would not seem strange to anyone "who admits or believes the divine authority of the holy Scriptures." It was necessary, Sharp argued, to go beyond such authors as Pufendorf who gave no other basis for obedience to law than the power in the hands of the lawgiver. Even the laws of God are "tendered to us under the equitable form of a reciprocal Covenant"; how much the more ought this to hold true of the laws of men. Majority rule is binding on the minority, Sharp declared—and here he went beyond Price, anticipating Thoreau—"only so far as the imposed Obligation is consistent with their superior Covenant and duty to God, which is always to be implied." To say that "every thing whatsoever, that is ordained by Parliament, must be Law, whether it be good or evil, right or wrong [is] a most pernicious and baneful Doctrine . . . a kind of Popery in Politics, (if I may use such an expression)."[49] Here, clearly, Sharp had by 1774 taken precisely the same ground which Garrison was to assume in expounding civil disobedience in 1835.

In 1793 Sharp responded to the passage of the first fugitive slave law by writing to American abolitionists and urging them to break it. He observed that the two bases of English law, reason and Scripture, appeared to him to be both from God, since reason was nothing but that knowledge of good and evil which our first parents acquired at the fall. Citing Fortescue and Fleta, Sharp contended that slavery was "contrary to nature" because liberty was the gift of God, "wherefore when stolen by man, it always earnestly longs to return."[50]

William Godwin was a second important link between eighteenth-century Anglo-American radicalism and the civil disobedience of the radical abolitionists. The basis of Godwin's system consisted of beliefs "common to many branches of Dissenting thought." For him as for other radical Dissenters, liberty of conscience "secularized and transferred to the civil sphere" was the theoretical point of departure.[51] His questions were also the questions of Priestley and Price: "How may the peculiar and independent operation of each individual in the social state most effectually be preserved? How may the security each man ought to possess, as to his life, and the employment of his faculties according to the dictates of his own understanding, be most certainly defended from invasion?"[52]

But Godwin could not accept the characteristic Dissenting view that individual action was autonomously determined except when obstructed by institutions. Confessing his debt to the writing of Holbach and Helvétius on "the nature of man," Godwin was determined to come to terms with the insights of the materialists as to the formative effect of institutions on ideas. From Sidney to Paine, wrote Godwin, English political philosophers had failed to appreciate how society "insinuates itself into our personal dispositions, and insensibly communicates its own spirit to our private transactions."[53]

Godwin asserted, in effect, that what Locke had said about the influence of experience on the mind was true, but that what Price had said about the autonomous role of understanding was true also:

> . . . I shall attempt to prove two things; first, that the actions and dispositions of mankind are the offspring of circumstances and events, and not of any original determination that they bring into the world; and, secondly, that the great stream of our voluntary actions essentially depends, not upon the direct and immediate impulses of sense, but upon the decisions of the understanding.[54]

Man is profoundly influenced by his social environment but is not the helpless victim of climate, or size of population, or luxury, or monarchy, or war.

In the name, then, of that limited freedom which men retain despite the effect of their environment, Godwin went on frontally to attack the traditional distinction between free thought and socially regulated action:

> It is commonly said, "that positive institutions ought to leave me free in matters of conscience, but may properly interfere with my conduct in civil concerns." But . . . what sort of moralist must he be, whose conscience is silent as to what passes in his intercourse with other men?

The distinction between thought and action, Godwin continued, presupposed that "it is of great consequence whether

I bow to the east or the west; whether I call the object of my worship Jehovah or Alla; whether I pay a priest in a surplice or a black coat," but not of great consequence whether, for example, I am a free citizen or a slave. "In reality, by as many instances as I act contrary to the unbiassed dictate of my own judgment, by so much I abdicate the most valuable part of the character of man."[55]

Godwin concluded that established authority has no more right to regulate an individual's actions than to regulate his thoughts. "This immediately follows from the observations of Rousseau": for if a whole people is unable to delegate its will, "neither can any individual delegate his authority." Moreover, Godwin continued, just as one generation cannot bind the next, so an individual should not promise how duty will appear to him at some future point in time.[56]

Obedience, therefore, is a question of expediency. The decision to obey or disobey a law is a matter-of-fact one, involving a calculation of the alternative consequences (not only to oneself but to society as a whole) likely to follow from alternative actions. The act of obedience thus motivated is more likely to preserve the citizen's spiritual independence than a theory which supposes that a conforming action implies total inward consent. As Godwin put it: "Obey; this may be right; but beware of reverence."[57]

Proceeding on the assumption that the internal function of government is vastly more important than the external function associated with war, Godwin demolished the former, too, by a sustained demonstration that punishment—the main internal business of government—is incompatible with reliance on conscience. This of course followed from his refusal to separate the domain of conscience from the domain of overt acts. Perhaps the most common effect of punishment, Godwin argued, is "to alienate the mind of the sufferer, from the individual that punishes, and from the sentiments he entertains."[58] Even if punishment changes a man's behavior, even if it changes his opinions, it "leaves him a slave, devoted to an exclusive self-interest, and actuated by fear, the meanest of the selfish passions." Punishment neither reforms the individual offender, deters his potential imitator, nor improves society as a whole. The last legitimate function of government is seen to be essentially harmful. It is also unnecessary. In a society without government, Godwin argued, local juries would decide each case on its own merits without reference to general laws and without reliance on coercive sanctions.

Dymond referred repeatedly to Godwin and accepted much of his reasoning. But Dymond also attacked the utilitarianism both of Godwin and of William Paley, whose *Principles of Moral and Political Philosophy*, first published in 1785, was the standard early nineteenth-century text on the subject both in England and (at Emerson's Harvard, for instance) in the United States.[59] What Paley had done was to elaborate the hedonistic ethics implicit in Locke's environmental psychology. Following the lead of Coleridge, radical abolitionists rejected Paley along with Locke. Thus in a key early paragraph of *Civil Disobedience*, Thoreau took Paley on explicitly, revealing in the process that—all Transcendentalist protestation to the contrary—his own ethic was in the last analysis Christian. "Paley," Thoreau wrote,

> a common authority with many on moral questions, in his chapter on "The Duty of Submission to Civil Government," resolves all civil obligation into expediency; and he proceeds to say that "so long as the interest of the whole society requires it, that is, so long as the established government cannot be resisted or changed without public inconveniency, it is the will of God . . . that the established government be obeyed—and no longer. This principle being admitted, the justice of every particular case of resistance is reduced to a computation of the quantity of the danger and grievance on the one side, and of the probability and expense of redressing it on the other." Of this, he says, every man shall judge for himself. But Paley appears never to have contemplated those cases to which the rule of expediency does not apply, in which a people, as well as an individual, must do justice, cost what it may. If [Thoreau continued] I have unjustly wrested a plank from a drowning man, I must restore it to him though I drown myself. This, according to Paley, would be inconvenient. But he that would save his life, in such a case, shall lose it.[60]

Paley's great failing, as the abolitionists saw it, was what Lincoln in his 1854 Peoria speech termed the insistence "that there is no right principle of action but self-interest."[61]

Dymond criticized Paley along similar lines. First he addressed himself to Paley's denial of an intuitive, inborn capacity to tell right from wrong. Paley, Dymond quoted him, believed "either that there exists no such instincts as compose what is called the moral sense, or that they are not now to be distinguished from prejudices and habits." In opposition Dymond invoked, among others, Price, Cudworth, Rousseau, and Benjamin Rush. He said that all these authorities agreed that there is "some principle or power existent in the human mind" which "possesses wisdom to direct us aright." Further,

> to say that individuals express their notions of this principle or power by various phraseology, that they attribute to it different degrees of superhuman intelligence, or that they refer for its origin to contradictory causes, does not affect the general argument.[62]

With this existential definition of the inner light as baseline, Dymond went on to question Paley's injunction to obey all law. Paley laid it down, Dymond observed, that "so long as we keep within the design and intention of a law, that law will justify us, *in foro conscientiae* as *in foro humano*, whatever be the equity or expediency of the law itself."[63] But for Dymond, a law permitting slavery was invalid.[64] Although he rejected Godwin's argument "that unless the particular law is enforced by morality, it does not become obligatory by the command of the state [that is, that the burden of proof should be on the state to show why a law should be obeyed, rather than on the objector to show why it should not]," Dymond concurred with Godwin that the authority of the state was, in the last analysis, subordinate to a "higher rule." Said Dymond: "That rule, with him [Godwin], is 'justice,'—with us it is the law of God; but the reasoning is the same. . . ."[65]

Dymond even justified nonviolent revolution. The French Revolution had been an "atrocious course of wickedness." Still, it "was *occasioned* by the abuses of the old government," and a "revolution of *some kind*" awaited every despotic government in Europe. Of what kind? Not "an armed resistance to the civil power," for this would violate Christ's command of nonviolence. But consider what might have happened in the American colonies:

> The Americans thought that it was best for the general welfare that they should be independent; but England persisted in imposing a tax. Imagine, then, America to have acted upon Christian principles, and to have refused to pay it, but without those acts of exasperation and violence which they committed. England might have sent a fleet and an army. To what purpose? Still no one paid the tax. The soldiery perhaps sometimes committed outrages, and they seized goods instead of the impost; still the tax could not be collected, except by a system of universal distraint.—Does any man, who employs his reason, believe that England would have overcome such a people? does he believe that any government or any army would have gone on destroying them? especially does he believe this, if the Americans continually reasoned coolly and honourably with the other party, and manifested, by the unequivocal language of conduct, that they were actuated by reason and by Christian rectitude?

The Reformation, Dymond continued, offered a precedent: it "prospered more by the resolute non-compliance of its supporters, than if all of them had provided themselves with swords and pistols." Nonviolence was not only a defensive means, "when the magistrate commands that which it would be immoral to obey," but also a means for "an alteration of existing institutions." Dymond's argument faithfully anticipated Garrison's call for an antislavery revolution without "jacobinical doctrines" and "carnal weapons."[66]

III

In the mid-1830s in America, abolitionists were perforce concerned less about what shade of revolution to advocate than about whether they could advocate anything at all. With dozens of itinerant lecturers playing John Wilkes's old role, the abolitionist movement first confronted constituted authority on the hallowed battleground of free speech. Events such as the mobbing of Garrison in the heart of Boston, the murder of Elijah Lovejoy in the free state of Illinois, the closing of Southern mails to abolitionist literature, and the refusal of Congress to receive abolitionist petitions, forced Americans to consider whether they could keep slavery without abandoning the First Amendment.

This meant that, quite unintentionally, abolitionism picked up the revolutionary intellectual tradition just at the point where Paine and Jefferson had left it: the affirmation that those freedoms associated with the use of the mind were absolutely inalienable. As Dwight Dumond indicates, this was the first "higher law" on which abolitionists insisted. Against schools, churches, and governmental agencies that were hostile or indifferent to free discussion, abolitionists hurled the theory that free discussion was not "something obtained from human convention and human concession" but a "birthright . . . as old as our being, and a part of the original man."[67]

The freedom sought by the abolitionists, however, was a freedom to act as well as think and speak. Their concern was less to ventilate new opinions than to energize an audience which—like the audience at a temperance lecture[68]—already agreed with them in theory. Will was all-important: that free will which Charles Grandison Finney had defined as "the power of originating and deciding our own choices . . . upon moral questions."[69] In his prospectus for the *Public Liberator* in 1830 Garrison defined liberty as "an independency upon the will of another," and like Price in 1776, asserted his opposition to "bondage, under its every aspect—whether spiritual, civil, political, mental or physical."[70] Freedom thus defined as self-determination required acts as well as words.

The famous Lane Seminary incident of 1834 illustrated the connection between free thought and free action in the microcosm of a campus community. What the Lane faculty deplored was not simply that night after night the seminary students debated the rights and wrongs of slavery and of immediate emancipation, but that, having concluded that slavery was wrong and immediate emancipation right, the students made contact with the free Negroes of Cincinnati, conducting classes and mingling on a basis of social equality. Reminding the students that their activities jeopardized the seminary's endowment for which many sacrifices had been made, the faculty statement went on to assert that on entering a college, as on entering society, "men surrender some of their individual rights." Free inquiry was necessarily subordinate to the interests of the institution, said the faculty statement, which interests the faculty (not the students) were to judge. The faculty declared that it favored associations for free inquiry, but not "associations for social public action" which distract from studies, excite the community, and bear on important national issues.

The students, so the faculty observed, claimed that the faculty had no "discretionary power" to regulate student action prior to an actual abuse. The faculty responded that this was a "new claim . . . in the history of the rights of students in literary and theological institutions." The faculty found the president of the student abolitionist society to be suffering from a "want of early guidance and subordination," and to be "relying with a perilous confidence in . . . [the] sufficiency" of his own mind.[71]

That student president, who happened to be Theodore Weld, declared in a countermanifesto that free discussion was an inherent and inalienable right. On entering a seminary one might give up privileges and advantages, "but this *right* the institution 'could neither give nor take away'." Further, "whereas, the single object of ascertaining truth is to learn *how to act*, we are bound to do at once, whatever truth dictates to be done."[72] In the end, the students withdrew with their favorite teachers and started Oberlin College.

Like the struggle for student power on the campus, the struggle for parishioner power in the church helped abolitionists make the transition from a theory of conscience to a theory of government. In 1837 the Congregational clergy of New England issued three "clerical appeals" protesting, in the manner of the resident clergy during the eighteenth-century Great Awakening, against abolitionist itinerants who sought to address their congregations without ministerial permission. Garrisonians responded with variations on the theme of the equality of man, ministers included. The antislavery newspaper *Friend of Man* was quoted to this effect in the *Liberator*. The "clerical appeals," so the selection ran, claimed that parishioners surrendered to their pastor absolute power over the affairs of the church; that any outsider who addressed the parish without the express consent of the pastor violated the latter's rights; and that the alternatives for the parishioners were only to follow the will of the pastor or to elect a new one.

The heart of the clerical argument, *Friend of Man* insisted, was an analogy between the relation of an employer to his servant and the relation of a church to its pastor. According to this controversialist the "clerical appeals"

> take it for granted that the churches must commit their consciences to the keeping of their ministers just as a merchant commits his accounts to a book-keeper, or his money to a banker! He may, indeed, inspect their labor, and discharge them if he thinks proper. But if he does so, it must only be for the purpose of committing the same trust into other hands! An elective papacy, transferrable, at pleasure, from one individual to another, would remain a papacy still.

Thus *Friend of Man* rejected the idea that the work of the pastor was "to take all their moral responsibilities away from" the parishioners so as to "save them the time and trouble of thinking and acting for themselves."[73]

Ultimately the radical abolitionist critique of representative government in school and church became a critique of political representation, too. Thoreau, who had refused to pay taxes for the established church before he refused them for the established government, made the point in another crucial paragraph of *Civil Disobedience:*

> . . . a government in which the majority rule in all cases cannot be based on justice. . . . Can there not be a government in which majorities do not virtually decide right and wrong, but conscience?—in which majorities decide only those questions to which the rule of expediency is applicable? Must the citizen ever for a moment, or in the least degree, resign his conscience to the legislator? Why has every man a conscience, then? . . . The only obligation which I have a right to assume is to do at any time what I think right.[74]

Government thus conceived became one among many voluntary associations which an individual chose whether or not to join. "Government is only an association of individuals," said Wendell Phillips in 1845, "like any other voluntary association of individuals—a temperance or anti-slavery society, a bank or railroad corporation."[75] Correspondingly, it came to be thought by Garrisonians that one might withdraw from a government just as one resigned from a church. By the early 1840s Garrison was calling on abolitionists to "come out" of the federal union rather than "[to covenant] with slaveholders, to fellowship [with] them as co-partners in government."[76]

Garrison and Phillips argued that abolitionists should submit to taxation, which they conceived as involuntary, but should decline the voluntary acts of voting and holding public office. Did this mean that they endorsed the doctrine of "no-government"? No, Phillips answered, only that they refused to cooperate with this particular government. He justified a strategy of withdrawal by citing British precedent:

> Were O'Connell and his fellow Catholics non-resistants, because for two hundred years they submitted to exclusion from the House of Lords and the House of Commons, rather than qualify themselves for a seat by an oath abjuring the Pope? Were the *nonjuring* Bishops of England non-resistants, when they went down to the grave without taking their seats in the House of Lords, rather than take an oath denying the Stuarts and to support the House of Hanover?[77]

Phillips' case against voting duplicated the old Quaker and Dissenting argument against false oaths. "Sir Thomas More need never have mounted the scaffold," Phillips said, "had he only consented to take the oath of supremacy." And in America:

> All executive, legislative, and judicial officers, both of the several States and of the General Government, before entering on the performance of their official duties, are bound to take an oath or affirmation, *"to support the Constitution of the United States."* This is what every office-holder expressly *promises in so many words.* It is a contract between him and *the whole nation.* The voter, who, by voting, sends his fellow citizen into office as his representative, knowing beforehand that the taking of this

oath is the first duty his agent will have to perform, does by his vote, request and authorize him to take it.[78]

In a government whose fundamental law protected the sin of slavery, therefore, citizens should not vote and officeholders should resign. Phillips found a precedent for the latter in the life of "that Patriarch of the Anti-Slavery enterprise, Granville Sharp," who resigned his position rather than process orders for shipment of munitions to put down the American Revolution.

> As the thoughtful underclerk of the War Office takes his hat down from the peg where it has used to hang [sic] for twenty years, methinks I hear one of our opponents cry out, "Friend Sharp, you are absurdly scrupulous." "You may innocently aid Government in doing wrong," adds another. While Liberty Party yelps at his heels, "My dear sir, you are quite losing your influence!" And indeed it is melancholy to reflect how, from that moment the mighty clerk of the War Office (!) dwindled into the mere Granville Sharp of history! the man of whom Mansfield and Hargrave were content to learn law, and Wilberforce, philanthropy.[79]

The problem, Phillips summarized, was: when government enacts laws contrary to the laws of God, what is the proper remedy? "1st. Old-fashioned patriotism replies, with Algernon Sydney: 'Resistance to tyrants is obedience to God'." "2d. Next comes the Christian rule, that too sanctioned by Locke, and by Plato—the course of the Quakers—the motto of the American Anti-Slavery Society—'SUBMIT to every ordinance of man'—but suffer any penalty rather than JOIN in doing a wrong act; meanwhile, let your loud protest prepare a speedy and quiet revolution."[80] Phillips chose the second course.

Thoreau, like Phillips, disclaimed anarchism: "to speak practically and as a citizen, . . . I ask for, not at once no government, but *at once* a better government." Like Phillips, Thoreau advocated revolution: "I think that it is not too soon for honest men to rebel and revolutionize." But Thoreau was critical of abolitionists who paid taxes and "directly by their allegiance, and . . . indirectly . . . by their money" enabled others to fight a war which they eschewed. When laws are unjust, "men generally, under such a government as this, think that they ought to wait until they have persuaded the majority to alter them." In the case of slavery, however, "the State has provided no way: its very Constitution is the evil." The "definition of a peaceable revolution, if any such is possible," would be for a thousand men not to pay their taxes, and when confronted by the tax gatherer's question, "what shall I do?," answer, "resign."

Thoreau summed up: "When the subject has refused allegiance, and the officer has resigned his office, then the revolution is accomplished."[81]

Thoreau's philosophy of civil disobedience was much less a merely personal production, and much more the manifesto of a movement, than Thoreau himself imagined. Its rationale for individual and state secession reflected the Garrisonian strategy expounded by Phillips in an address at the Concord Lyceum, in the spring of 1845, which Thoreau attended and publicly praised.[82] In asserting (in *Civil Disobedience*) that "we should be men first, and subjects afterwards" or (as he put it in *Slavery in Massachusetts*) "men first, and Americans only at a late and convenient hour,"[83] Thoreau was in accord with Massachusetts Senator Charles Sumner, who declared in response to the Fugitive Slave Law: "I am a *man*, although I am a *Commissioner*."[84] Thoreau spoke for many others, too, when he wrote in *Slavery in Massachusetts*:

> I have lived for the last month . . . with the sense of having suffered a vast and indefinite loss. I did not know at first what ailed me. At last it occurred to me that what I had lost was a country.[85]

NOTES

1. "A Watch-word to the City of London, and the Armie," *Works*, ed. Sabine, p. 315.

2. "Civil Disobedience," *Writings of Thoreau*, IV, 371.

3. *Pamphlets of the Revolution*, ed. Bailyn, pp. 412–13.

4. Algernon Sidney, *Discourses Concerning Government* (London, 1698), pp. 300, 301; for Garrison's appreciation, *Liberator*, March 11, 1837.

5. "Civil Disobedience," *Writings*, IV, 360.

6. The theme of Bancroft's glowing chapter on the Friends (*History of the United States* . . . [Boston, 1838], II, Ch. 16) is that "almost for the first time in the history of the world, a plebeian sect proceeded to the complete enfranchisement of the mind." He also stated that the doctrine of the inner light reappeared in the teaching of Rousseau and Kant (*ibid.*, II, 330, 355). One of Emerson's early lectures on representative men dealt with Fox who, like Swedenborg and Luther, "owes all to the discovery that God must be sought within, not without" (*Journals of Ralph Waldo Emerson*, ed. E. W. Emerson and W. E. Forbes [Boston and New York, 1910], III, 432).

7. See Garrison's letter to Elizabeth Pease, June 1, 1841, which detailed his religious beliefs and concluded: "If this be infidelity, then is Quakerism infidelity." *William Lloyd Garrison, 1805–1879: The Story of His Life Told by His Children* (New York, 1885–1889), III, 10.

8. *The Lincoln Nobody Knows* (New York, Toronto, London, 1958), p. 69.

9. *The Debates and Proceedings in the Congress of the United States* . . . (Washington, 1834), II, 1182–83, 1197–98.

10. Howard Jay Graham, "The Early Antislavery Backgrounds of the Fourteenth Amendment," *Wisconsin Law Review*, XXX (1950), 622, 660.

11. Thomas Clarkson, *A Portraiture of Quakerism* . . . (London, 1806), I, i.

12. Paine stated in his *Age of Reason* that the "only sect that has not persecuted are the Quakers" (*Complete Writings*, I, 597). In successive letters toward the end of his life, Jefferson praised "the Quaker policy" of nonviolence, and remarked "how much wiser are the Quakers" than other religious groups in avoiding doctrinal disputes (to John Adams, June 1, 1822, and to Benjamin Waterhouse, June 26, 1822, *Works*, XII, 240, 243).

13. *Portraiture*, II, 122.

14. *Ibid.*, p. 123.

15. Quoted in *ibid.*, pp. 129–30. See also pp. 205–6.

16. *An Essay on the Slavery and Commerce of the Human Species*, 2d ed. (London, 1788), pp. 162–63.

17. *Portraiture*, II, 204.

18. *Ibid.*, III, 434.

19. *Memoirs of the Private and Public Life of William Penn* (Philadelphia, 1814), II, 309.

20. *Ibid.*, p. 310.

21. *Ibid.*, pp. 318, 323.

22. *Ibid.*, pp. 326–32.

23. *Ibid.*, pp. 344–45.

24. *Ibid.*, p. 362. This was a highly idealized version of the facts, which were "that William Penn bought and owned Negro slaves, that a Quaker-dominated government of Pennsylvania enacted a harsh slave code, . . . that as late as 1730 Quaker merchants in Philadelphia

were importing and selling West Indian Negroes" (Davis, *Problem of Slavery*, p. 304).

25. *Thoughts on the Necessity of Improving the Condition of the Slaves in the British Colonies* . . . (New York, 1823), p. 20.

26. This position represented a step forward from the belief that abolition of the slave trade would automatically bring about "a new system of treatment" (Clarkson, *The History of the . . . Abolition of the African Slave-Trade* . . . [London, 1808], II, 586).

27. Henry Richard, *Memoirs of Joseph Sturge* (London, 1865), Chs. 4, 5.

28. Elizabeth Heyrick, *Immediate, Not Gradual Abolition* . . . (Boston, 1838), pp. 16–17.

29. *Ibid.*, p. 31.

30. *Ibid.*, p. 32.

31. Stanley M. Elkins, *Slavery: A Problem in American Institutional and Intellectual Life* (Chicago, 1959), p. 205.

32. Quoted in James E. Cabot, *A Memoir of Ralph Waldo Emerson* (Boston and New York, 1887), I, 244–45.

33. "Experience as a Minister," *Autobiography, Poems and Prayers*, ed. Rufus Leighton (Boston, 1907), p. 301.

34. Davis, "Emergence of Immediatism," p. 209.

35. Quoted in *Garrison, 1805–1879*, I, p. 132.

36. *Liberator*, November 3, 1837.

37. Quoted in *Garrison, 1805–1879*, I, 407 n.

38. William Lloyd Garrison, *The "Infidelity" of Abolitionism* (New York, 1860), pp. 9–10.

39. "Essay on Government," *Works of Priestley*, XXII, 123.

40. *Liberator*, March 7, 1835.

41. *Ibid.*, July 4, 1835.

42. *Garrison, 1805–1879*, IV, 314; James G. Birney, *Sinfulness of Slaveholding in All Circumstances; Tested by Reason and Scripture* (Detroit, 1846), pp. 5–6; *The Works of Charles Sumner* (Boston, 1875–1883), I, 183. A second printing of Dymond's *Essays* appeared in 1847 in New York. Portions of the work which dealt with war appeared separately as *On the Applicability of the Pacific Principles of the New Testament to the Conduct of States* (Brooklyn, N.Y., 1832) and *An Inquiry into the Accordancy of War with the Principles of Christianity*, ed. Thomas S. Grimké (Philadelphia, 1834, also Hartford, 1836, New York, 1847, etc.).

43. Richard Price, *Britain's Happiness, and the Proper Improvement of It* (London, 1759), p. 20.

44. "Essay on Government," *Works of Priestley*, XXII, 28.

45. *Serious Reflections on the Slave Trade and Slavery* (London, 1805), pp. 10–11.

46. *"The System of Colonial Law" Compared with the Eternal Laws of God; and with the Indispensable Principles of the English Constitution* (London, 1807), pp. 4–5.

47. *Remarks on . . . Manslaughter and Murder* (London, 1773), pp. 67–70. This essay was reprinted, with Beccaria on crime and punish-

ment and a fragment by Rousseau on dueling, in *An Essay on Crimes and Punishments* . . . (Philadelphia, 1778). The copy in the Sterling Library of Yale University belonged to Joseph Hewes, a signer of the Declaration of Independence.

48. *Tracts, Concerning the . . . Free Militia*, 3d ed. (London, 1782), especially pp. 21 n., 47–48, 59 n., 92.

49. *A Declaration of the People's Natural Right to a Share in the Legislature*, pp. xxxv–xxxvi, xiii–xviii, xxii–xxiii, xxix. A second edition of the pamphlet on dueling published in London in 1790 made the same defense of the doctrine that a soldier may disobey orders contrary to the law of God: the doctrine would not seem strange to anyone who took the Bible seriously.

50. *Letter from Granville Sharp, Esq. of London, to the Maryland Society for Promoting the Abolition of Slavery, and the Relief of Free Negroes and Others, Unlawfully Held in Bondage* (Baltimore, 1793), pp. 3–7. See Thomas F. Harwood, "Great Britain and American Antislavery," unpublished Ph.D. dissertation, University of Texas, 1959, pp. 14 ff., 54–55.

51. *Political Justice*, ed. Priestley, III, 79, 55.

52. *Ibid.*, I, 1–2.

53. *Ibid.*, p. 4.

54. *Ibid.*, p. 26.

55. *Ibid.*, pp. 175–76.

56. *Ibid.*, pp. 193, 194–214.

57. *Ibid.*, p. 230.

58. *Ibid.*, II, 374.

59. Wilson Smith, "William Paley's Theological Unitarianism in America," *William and Mary Quarterly*, 3d ser., XI (1954), gives a college-by-college, year-by-year chart of the use of Paley's book and states that the book was as well known as McGuffey's reader or Noah Webster's speller. He also remarks that "Paley's text well represented the gradualist position of many moralists in the early slavery debates" (*ibid.*, p. 421).

60. *Writings*, IV, 361–62. Sumner referred disapprovingly to a similar passage from Paley in his address on "War System of the Commonwealth of Nations" (*Works*, I, 184).

61. See Coleridge's reference in a letter of 1808 to "those who, with Dr Paley in his Chapter on Moral Obligation, annihilate the *Idea* of Virtue by placing it's *essence* in Selfishness" (*Collected Letters of Samuel Taylor Coleridge*, ed. Earl L. Griggs [Oxford, 1956–1959], III, 153).

62. *Essays in the Principles of Morality, and on the Private and Political Rights and Obligations of Mankind* (New York, 1834), pp. 34–35, 60–66, 70–71.

63. *Ibid.*, p. 76.

64. *Ibid.*, pp. 113, 386–90.

65. *Ibid.*, pp. 74, 79.

66. *Ibid.*, pp. 235 n., 255–58; compare "Declaration of Sentiments Adopted by the [American] Peace Convention . . . 1838," *Selections*

from the Writings and Speeches of William Lloyd Garrison (Boston, 1852), p. 75, and *Garrison, 1805–1879*, I, 409.

67. Dwight L. Dumond, *Antislavery: The Crusade for Freedom in America* (Ann Arbor, Mich., 1961), pp. 230–32, 397 n. 11; Jacobus TenBroek, *The Antislavery Origins of the Fourteenth Amendment* (Berkeley and Los Angeles, 1951), p. 107.

68. Abolitionists often compared the immediate change they asked of American supporters of slavery, to the temperance pledge: see, for example, William Lloyd Garrison, *Thoughts on African Colonization* (Boston, 1832), pp. 55–56.

69. Quoted in Anne C. Loveland, "Evangelicalism and 'Immediate Emancipation' in American Antislavery Thought," *Journal of Southern History*, XXXII (1966), 177.

70. *Garrison, 1805–1879*, I, 200, 202. In 1828 Garrison declared that slavery would be ended "by the will, not by the wealth, of the people" (*ibid.*, p. 98).

71. Quoted in the *Liberator*, January 17, 1835.

72. *Statement of the Reasons Which Have Induced the Students of Lane Seminary to Dissolve Their Connection with That Institution* (Cincinnati, 1834), quoted in *ibid.*, January 10, 1835. Compare the statement of six students convicted for conducting a sit-in at the Berkeley campus of the University of California for the right to distribute peace literature next to a table where information about service in the armed forces was being distributed: "The rights of free political expression and association are supposed to be the inalienable rights of all citizens. When we enter the campus of the University of California, we do not surrender our citizenship" (*National Guardian*, January 28, 1967).

73. *Liberator*, November 24, 1837.

74. *Writings*, IV, 358.

75. [Wendell Phillips], *Can Abolitionists Vote or Take Office Under the United States Constitution?* (New York, 1845), pp. 23, 26.

76. *Practical Christian*, June 1844, quoted in the *Liberator*, June 7, 1844.

77. *Can Abolitionists Vote?*, pp. 3–4.

78. *Ibid.*, pp. 5, 9–10.

79. *Ibid.*, p. 6.

80. Wendell Phillips, *Review of Lysander Spooner's Essay on the Unconstitutionality of Slavery* (Boston, 1847), pp. 10–11.

81. *Writings*, IV, 357, 361, 365, 367, 368, 371.

82. "Wendell Phillips Before the Concord Lyceum," *ibid.*, pp. 311–15.

83. *Ibid.*, pp. 358, 401.

84. "Our Immediate Antislavery Duties," *Works*, II, 408.

85. *Writings*, IV, 405.

CHAPTER 5:

MY COUNTRY IS THE WORLD

To an increasing number of American abolitionists it came to seem that their government was systematically oppressing, not only the Negro, but dark-skinned people throughout the Western Hemisphere. Despite the Monroe Doctrine's assertion that it was "our policy . . . to consider the government *de facto* as the legitimate government for us," the United States denied recognition to the black republic of Haiti until 1862. In 1825 the House Committee on Foreign Affairs recommended that the United States not send delegates to the Panama conference of Western Hemisphere republics lest it lend countenance to "five nations, who have at this moment black generals in their armies and mulatto members in their congresses."[1] The Cherokee Indians were expelled from Georgia under a treaty of December 1835, although they had proved their capacity for "civilization" by devising a written alphabet, framing a constitution, and holding slaves. A second war against the Seminole Indians of Florida, a tribe which harbored fugitive slaves, broke out in 1835 and lasted until 1843. Texas independence in 1836, and the war against Mexico for Texas which finally took place in 1846–1848, were the more ironic because Mexico, unlike the United States, had abolished slavery at the time it achieved its independence. Thoreau drew these themes together when he wrote in *Civil Disobedience* that "the fugitive slave, and the Mexican prisoner on parole, and the Indian come to plead the wrongs of his race" should find the free American in jail, "where the State places those who are not *with* her, but *against* her."[2]

Not all abolitionists were prepared to recognize this pattern of oppression. Some believed that slavery was an isolated evil in an American body politic that was otherwise healthy. Thus in 1838 James Birney, then Corresponding Secretary of the American Anti-Slavery Society and two years later presidential candidate for the new Liberty party, wrote in his annual report that "our social system . . . [is] sound in its essential nature—the rottenness has prevailed fearfully in spots, but it does not pervade the mass."[3] To such men the task of abolition was restoration of American society to its original purity.

In contrast revolutionary abolitionists believed, as Garrison said on July 4, 1837, that the foundations of American society had been laid in blood and violence: "in slavery and the slave trade—in a war of extermination with the proprietors of the soil—in cruelty, bigotry, which derided the claims of conscience, and whipped, banished or hanged those whose religious views differed. . . ." How, he asked, anticipating Marx and Lincoln, could a superstructure "remain long, which is not based upon a solid foundation"? "We had enlarged, but not changed this foundation . . . having merely substituted Abolitionists for Quakers and Baptists, upon whom to wreck our intolerance."[4] To Garrisonians, inevitably, the task of abolition could not be to restore; America must be made new.

Historians for whom the American experience is a success story find this view strange, and seek some special explanation for it. Garrison's multi-issue radicalism of the late 1830s has been attributed, for example, to his meeting in March 1837 with the millenarian perfectionist John Humphrey Noyes.[5]

Almost a year earlier, however, Garrison had begun a series of polemics against Reverend Lyman Beecher, in which he attacked Beecher's solicitude for the success of the American "experiment." It was, said Garrison, an experiment "to see how long we can plunder, with impunity, two millions and a half of our population." Garrison rejected the idea that the progress of liberty in the world depended on what happened to the United States:

> As if God had suspended the fate of all nations, and hazarded the fulfilment of his glorious promises, upon the result of a wild and cruel "experiment" by a land-stealing, blood-thirsty, man-slaying and slave-trading people in one corner of the globe! As if God could not easily dash this nation in pieces, as a potter's vessel is broken, and thereby vindicate his eternal justice. . . .[6]

Thoreau, as usual, condensed Garrisonian sentiments into a sentence: "This people must cease to hold slaves, and to make war on Mexico, though it cost them their existence as a people."[7] Seeking to be faithful to the principles of the American Revolution, abolitionists were driven outside the framework of national allegiance and began to understand themselves as citizens of the world.

I

Like so many aspects of the revolutionary tradition, the idea of world citizenship was a late eighteenth-century commonplace to which the nineteenth century gave new life. Men who shared the thought-world of Anglo-American Dissent took it for granted that *ubi libertas, ibi patria* (where liberty is, there is my country).[8] Franklin, for instance, wrote to a correspondent in the last year of his life:

> I hope the fire of liberty, which you mention as spreading itself over Europe, will act upon the inestimable rights of man, as common fire does upon gold; purify without destroying them; so that a lover of liberty may find *a country* in any part of Christendom.[9]

And again, to another:

> God grant, that not only the Love of Liberty, but a thorough Knowledge of the Rights of Man, may pervade all the Nations

of the Earth, so that a Philosopher may set his foot anywhere on its Surface, and say, "This is my country."[10]

This idea was more than rhetoric. It led Price, Priestley, and their friends to support the American Revolution against their own government. Franklin and Jefferson assumed it when, prompted by a proposed act of Parliament to limit emigration from the British Isles, they argued that emigration from one country to another was a natural right which God (in Franklin's words) has given even "to the beasts of the forest, and to the birds of the air." Franklin asked: "shall man be denied a privilege enjoyed by brutes, merely to gratify a few avaricious landlords?"[11] And Jefferson invoked the "right, which nature has given to all men, of departing from the country in which chance, not choice has placed them."[12]

An early example of the term "citizen of the world" in the literature of Dissenting radicalism occurs in Granville Sharp's *The Law of Retribution; or, A Serious Warning to Great Britain and Her Colonies,* published in 1776. This tract was the more interesting because it employed the idea of world citizenship as a weapon against slavery, just as Garrison and his associates did later. "Under the glorious Dispensation of the Gospel," stated Sharp, "we are absolutely bound to consider ourselves as *Citizens of the World.*" By this he meant no detached cosmopolitanism, but a conviction that all men were our *"Brethren of the Universe"* because God had made the nations of one blood and, even in the Old Testament, commanded those who believed in Him to love the stranger.[13] (These passages in *The Law of Retribution* were reprinted in the United States in 1836 as an appendix to a biography of Sharp by Charles Stuart, English abolitionist and close friend of Theodore Weld, whose presence in America was itself an instance of world citizenship.)

It was the concept of world citizenship, defended by Richard Price in his *Discourse on the Love of Our Country* (1789), which provoked Burke's *Reflections* and Paine's answering *Rights of Man.* Love of our country, Price contended on this famous occasion, "does not imply any conviction of the superior value of it to other countries." Were this implied the majority of mankind would be exempt from the duty of loving their country, "for there are few countries that enjoy the advantage of laws and governments which deserve to be preferred."[14]

Franklin had written in 1785: "Justice is as strictly due between neighbour Nations as between neighbour Citizens. A Highwayman is as much a Robber when he plunders in a Gang, as when single; and a Nation that makes an unjust War, is only a *great Gang.* . . ."[15] In his 1789 address Price employed the same logic, suggesting that even the most celebrated patriotism was contemptible if it required the subjugation of others.

> What was the love of their country among the old *Romans?* We have heard much of it; but I cannot hesitate in saying that, however great it appeared in some of its exertions, it was in general no better than a principle holding together a band of robbers in their attempts to crush all liberty but their own.[16]

Why was it, Price continued, that Jesus said nothing about patriotism but recommended "UNIVERSAL BENEVOLENCE"? Surely because Scripture like reason instructs us that we should love our country "ardently, but not exclusively," that "we ought to consider ourselves as citizens of the world."[17]

The phrase "my country is the world," was coined a few years later by Paine,[18] who, harried out of the country of his birth (England), imprisoned and almost executed by one adopted country (France) and left to die neglected by a second (the United States), had good reason to be emancipated from allegiance to nation states. Without (so he maintained) having read Paine, Garrison included in his 1830 prospectus for the *Public Liberator* the words, "My country is the world; my countrymen are mankind"; likewise the first issue of the subsequent *Liberator* carried on its masthead the motto, "Our country is the world, our countrymen are mankind."[19]

Wherever he derived these words, Garrison used them in the same sense Paine had. The eighteenth-century conception of world citizenship involved both the idea of an international fraternity of philosophers and the idea of the unity of all men. The former is illustrated by a letter written by Franklin to Sharp on June 9, 1787, for the Pennsylvania Society for

Promoting the Abolition of Slavery, informing Sharp that he had been enrolled as a corresponding member, "for, in this business, the friends of humanity in every country, are of one nation and religion."[20] The latter is celebrated in Paine's *Rights of Man:* "Every history of the Creation, and every traditionary account, whether from the lettered or unlettered world, however they may vary in their opinion or belief of certain particulars, all agree in establishing one point, *the unity of man;* by which I mean that men are all of *one degree.* . . . ."[21] Garrison shared Paine's burning awareness of the oneness of the human family.

Something of what the *Liberator*'s masthead motto meant to its editor and readers is suggested by verses from a poem reprinted from the *Emancipator* in November 1837:

I love that free, that pure, exalted mind,
Which spurns the bounds of clime and native soil;
And in his fellow men can brethren find;
Whether a prince or child of care and toil!
In *justice* says—by no mean prejudice confined—
"My country is the world, my countrymen mankind!"

All are my brethren. Why should I disdain,
To own that God has made his creatures one?
Or why should I from righteous acts refrain,
To those whose features are unlike my own?
Such thoughts as these should not my conscience blind—
"My country is the world, my countrymen mankind!"

In every land, in every tribe I see,
Each bears the image of a gracious God;
Jews, Greeks, Barbarians, Scythians, bond or free,
Savage or tame, wherever man has trod.
And if I roam from east to west, I find.
"My country is the world, my countrymen mankind!"[22]

II

Practically, the question of the unity of man first confronted abolitionists in the form of the problem: Who should participate in the abolitionist movement?

Garrison insisted that Negroes, workingmen, women, and foreign antislavery agitators should be welcomed by the American abolitionist movement as co-workers. That he did not support militant trade-unionism should not obscure the fact that Garrison, himself the son of a seaman and a lifelong working printer, strongly identified with the poor. When he was nearly lynched by "men of property and standing" in 1835, Garrison assailed the Mayor of Boston for class sympathies:

> He shamefully truckled to wealth and respectability. If it had been a mob of working men assaulting a meeting of merchants, no doubt he would have acted with energy and decision, and they would have been routed by force. But broadcloth and money alter the case: they are above the law, and the imperious masters of poor men.[23]

In 1836, the crux of Garrison's indictment of Beecher was the charge "that Dr. Beecher's sympathies and tears side only with the rich and the powerful." Beecher had said, so Garrison quoted him: "There are demagogues who seek to make our laboring population feel as if they were despised and wronged, and that there is oppression in the fact that others should be richer than they." On which Garrison commented:

> And is it not true that our laboring population are, to an alarming extent, despised and wronged? Is not honest labor becoming more and more servile and despicable in the eyes of a growing aristocracy, *both at the north and at the south*? To say nothing of the treatment of the southern laboring population . . . , our northern working-men have every reason to be alarmed at the prospect before them. There is a conspiracy all over the land against them. There is a proud aristocracy at the north, sympathizing with and publicly approbating a still more haughty aristocracy at the south; and, together, it is their aim, if possible, to degrade and defraud *working-men of all classes, irrespective of color*. The attempt at the north to subjugate the laboring population, may never succeed so far as to make merchandise of their bodies; but, unless this class arises in its might for the extirpation of southern slavery, it will be ground more and more to the dust, its time will be more and more limited, its wages more and more inadequate, its means of intelligence more and more circumscribed. [Italics added.][24]

These passages suggest, not a fundamental hostility toward the agitation of Northern workingmen, but—as in the case of

Du Bois later—concern lest that agitation turn its back on fellow workers in the South.[25]

Garrison believed that abolitionism entrusted the people with "the management of their own cause" more than did other reform movements. "Nearly every other moral and religious enterprise in the land is placed under the control of an almost self-elected, irresponsible body of men, who have little or no sympathy with the 'common people'." Abolitionism, in contrast, had a "*republican* character," because it encouraged the participation of "persons of both sexes, and of all classes and complexions—farmers, mechanics, workingmen, 'niggers,' women, and all."[26] At the World's Anti-Slavery Convention in 1840, Garrison refused to take his seat when American women delegates were excluded.

World citizenship, in short, began at home: in an open door to all kinds of men and women in the abolitionist movement. Was it not the case, queried the *Liberator*, that the great men of history—Columbus (son of a weaver and a weaver himself), Molière, Cervantes, Homer, Oliver Cromwell, Shakespeare ("son of a wool stapler"), Robert Burns, Cardinal Wolsey ("son of a butcher")—were often of humble origin?[27] In the same vein the *Liberator* printed the anecdote of a man who resisted abolitionism because Garrison was "nothing but a printer." The victim of this disaparagement responded:

> The grand difficulty seemed to be that many of the anti-slavery men were not liberally educated, as the phrase is; they had not been to college, and were not, of course, adorned with the diplomas of A.B. A.M. D.D. or L.L.D., or other mystical characters that are appended to the names of the college-learned.[28]

Here was an internationalism different from the genteel cosmopolitanism of a Jefferson or even of a Franklin: an internationalism of men who had not been to college and were still poor.

The "outside agitators" in the American abolitionist movement were English antislavery veterans like Charles Stuart and George Thompson who, after the success of English abolitionism in 1833, came to the United States to lend a hand. Thompson, whose appearance in Boston in 1835 was the occasion for the assault on Garrison, rejected the charge that a citizen of one country should not criticize the institutions of another. In Edinburgh before he left for the United States, and again in an address to the second annual meeting of the American Anti-Slavery Society, Thompson insisted that "the cause of liberty knows no bounds—no color." He quoted, in both talks, the words of Terence: *"Homo sum, nil humani a me alienum puto"* (I am a man, nothing human is alien to me).[29] These were also the words with which, in 1777, John Wilkes had closed his protest against the suspension of habeas corpus in the American colonies; and which, according to his children, comprised the "favorite maxim" of Karl Marx.[30]

Abolitionism, in fact, created something not unlike Marx's First International. As early as 1833 English abolitionist Joseph Sturge proposed the formation of a society for the abolition of slavery throughout the world. Organized in 1839 as the British and Foreign Anti-Slavery Society, this was the body which sponsored the World's Anti-Slavery Convention of 1840. Sturge again, together with American abolitionist Elihu Burritt, sponsored a series of international peace conventions just before and after 1850; and for a time during the 1850s the latter published a journal appropriately entitled *Burritt's Citizen of the World*.[31]

The kinship with all human beings demonstrated by radical abolitionists in their attitude toward membership in their own movement stood them in good stead when they were obliged to formulate an attitude toward the government of the United States.

III

Introducing the eighth volume of the *Liberator* in December 1837, Garrison announced that henceforth it would concern itself with peace as well as abolitionism. The mottoes of "Our Country Is the World" and "Universal Emancipation" would be used in their "widest latitude." The paper set its face against "government of brute force," whether in the form of national wars, or in the domestic form of capital punishment and the suppression of slave insurrections.[32] In September 1838, Garrison joined in forming the New England Non-Resistance Society, which pledged its members to nonparticipation in all wars, to voluntary self-exclusion from all political offices which might oblige the officeholder to use violence, and to abstention from voting for others "to act as our substitutes." These policies were justified by a millennialist rhetoric similar to that "of the pacifist sects of the Anabaptist-Mennonite tradition."[33]

But this recourse to the world view of the Radical Reformation proved, as so often in the development of the revolutionary tradition, to be a prelude to new political departures. In 1843 Garrison added to the masthead of the *Liberator* a new motto, "No Union with Slaveholders," and in 1844 the American Anti-Slavery Society endorsed a secession strategy. Indeed that strategy won support from a surprisingly broad spectrum of New England opinion on the eve of Texas annexation in 1845.

The Texas issue catalyzed a widespread disposition among reformers to be suspicious of war and patriotism because of their connection with slavery. All branches of the antislavery movement, to begin with, linked slavery and violence. Birney, so often contrasted with Garrison, regularly made his first complaint against slavery that it rested on force: that—as he put it in his letter to the Presbyterian Church of Kentucky in 1834—"it originated, has always been, and is at this day, maintained by a violence that is utterly at variance with the mild spirit of the gospel."[34] Theodore Parker felt precisely the same way. "The relation of master and slave begins in violence; it must be sustained by violence—the systematic violence of general laws, or the irregular violence of individual caprice. There is no other mode of conquering and subjugating a man."[35] From that perception it was an easy step to the thesis that war and slavery were interchangeable modes whereby men sought to coerce other men against their will, and that the soldier, in Thoreau's language, was a "small movable fort" at the disposal of another's orders. Thus John

Quincy Adams, in a famous address in 1837, declared that the "ills of war and slavery" were man's creation and that man should seek not only the abolition of slavery but also the "total abolition of war upon earth."[36] Thus Frederick Douglass condemned capital punishment, flogging in the navy and "the whole naval system," as well as "the Florida bloodhound war, and the still more glorious one waged against Mexico."[37]

It was in the 1830s, as one expression of this intellectual atmosphere, that there began the custom of making anti-patriotic speeches on the Fourth of July. Andrew Jackson wanted Texas to "extend the area of freedom," but many Jacksonian Democrats did not accept the creed of Manifest Destiny. "Patriotism," said one in a Fourth of July oration to the trade-unionists of Boston in 1834, "consists in nothing but a brotherly affection, an extensive love toward the whole human family."[38] Talk of national glory, Seth Luther said in his *Address to the Working Men of New England* in 1833, often covered over human suffering; and in a Fourth of July speech to mechanics and workingmen in 1836, Luther bitterly rebuked those who condemned striking workers because there were foreigners among them. Did not the Bible say that God had made the nations of one blood, a truth confirmed by the Declaration of Independence? Lafayette, Pulaski, Steuben, and others had helped in the Revolution. "It is *this* damnable principle [of nationalism] which has desolated the earth for centuries," Luther declared, "and made our beautiful earth one vast slaughter house."[39] The next year, 1837, William Leggett noted that abolitionists had hung out the flag on the Fourth of July with a placard saying, "Slavery's Cloak." He would, he said, see his right arm cut off before rallying around the "glorious emblem" to crush a slave rebellion. "The obligations of citizenship are strong," said Leggett, "but those of justice, humanity and religion stronger."[40] Later would come other Fourth of July heresies: Sumner denouncing war on Boston Common in 1845; Douglass' 1852 address on "The Meaning of July Fourth for the Negro"; Garrison burning the Constitution at Framingham in 1854.

The political development of William Ellery Channing illustrates the process by which the Texas question pushed men initially hostile to Garrison to espouse Garrison's position. Channing was a very moderate sort of radical: according to Arthur Schlesinger, Jr., "the work of Channing in sabotaging the liberal impulses of his day by his theory of 'internal' reform, with its indifference to external social change, has never been properly appreciated."[41] All the more striking, then, was Channing's transformation after 1835.

In that year Channing proposed, in his pamphlet Slavery, a program of gradual emancipation very much like that which Buxton had urged on Parliament in 1823. Freedom was to be preceded by piecemeal reforms which citizens of the free states would recommend quietly and reasonably to their Southern brethren. Channing's 1837 letter to Henry Clay upon the possible annexation of Texas revealed a hardened spirit. For to Channing as to other opponents of slavery, annexation of Texas and (what he had no doubt would follow) war with Mexico meant that the South was asking that slavery become "the predominant interest of the state."[42] If in defiance of the public conscience the South took Texas anyway, Channing urged Northern secession. Was the United States to make war to extend slavery? "Sooner perish!" cried Channing with Garrison and Thoreau. "Sooner be our name blotted out from the record of nations!" Or more soberly: "I do not desire to share the responsibility, or to live under the laws of a government adopting such a policy, and swayed by such a spirit, as would be expressed by the incorporation of Texas with our country."[43]

Implicit in Channing's "Letter to Clay" was an analogy between intersectional and international relations. The United States should have assisted its "less civilized" sister republics in Latin America by example and exhortation, but not by force;[44] just so the duty of the North was to intervene, but only nonviolently.

> We are told that the slave-holding States [Channing wrote in his "Remarks on the Slavery Question"] . . . stand on the same ground with foreign countries, and are consequently to be treated with equal delicacy and reserve. . . . The position is false, that

nation has no right to interfere morally with nation. . . . I claim
the right of pleading the cause of the oppressed, whether he
suffer in this country or another. I utterly deny that a people can
screen themselves behind their nationality from the moral judgment of the world.

Channing placed his trust in the "grand moral tribunal" of
world public opinion.[45]

But the South (Channing continued) asked active support
from the North in, for example, returning fugitive slaves.
"Slavery more than touches us," said Channing. "We feel its
grasp."[46] The doctrine of nonintervention, accordingly, revealed its double edge. In "Emancipation" (1840), Channing
stated that the political duties of the North "may be reduced
to two heads, both of them negative": *not* to use coercion
against slavery where it existed, but also *not* to use the powers
of the state or national governments to support slavery where
it existed.[47] "This is not a question of abolitionism," Channing
said. "It has nothing to do with putting down slavery. We
are

> simply called, as communities, to withhold support from it, to
> stand aloof, to break off all connection with this criminal institu-
> tion. The free states ought to say to the South, "Slavery is yours,
> not ours, and on you the whole responsibility of it must fall.
> We wash our hands of it wholly. We shall exert no power against
> it; but do not call on us to put forth the least power on its
> behalf. We cannot, directly or indirectly, become accessories
> to this wrong. We cannot become jailers, or a patrol, or a watch,
> to keep your slaves under the yoke. You must guard them your-
> selves. If they escape, we cannot send them back. . . . In case
> of insurrection, we cannot come to you. . . . Neither in our sep-
> arate legislatures, nor in the national legislature, can we touch
> slavery to sustain it. On this point you are foreign communi-
> ties. . . ."[48]

Peaceful persuasion if possible, peaceful secession if necessary,
remained Channing's program until his death in October 1842.
In August of that year he said: "I deprecate all political action
on slavery except for one end, and this end is to release the
free States from all connection with this oppressive institution. . . ."[49]

In the years between Channing's death and Texas annexation, abolitionists in and out of Congress treated Northern secession as a live option. Wendell Phillips' resolutions at the May 1844 meeting of the American Anti-Slavery Society declared that the impending annexation of Texas would be "null and void," and require the free states of the North to call a new constitutional convention to "form a real Union."[50] This language was hardly stronger than that used seven years earlier by John Quincy Adams, the ex-President in the House of Representatives: "any attempt by act of Congress or by treaty to annex the Republic of Texas to this Union would be a usurpation of power, unlawful and void, and which it would be the right and the duty of the free People of the Union to resist and annul."[51] In March 1843 Adams' famous "disunion letter," signed by twelve other northern Whig congressmen, stated that annexation would be "IDENTICAL WITH DISSOLUTION" and that the people of the free states "WOULD NOT SUBMIT TO IT."[52] In March 1845 William Jay, son of the former Chief Justice of the Supreme Court, likewise called "for an amicable dissolution of the Union."[53] The Massachusetts legislature declared that Texas annexation "would have no binding force whatever on the people of Massachusetts," the Maine legislature termed it "tantamount to dissolution."[54]

When Texas was annexed the Northern states did not secede, but the decade of struggle against what Channing called this "prostitution" of the national government had a long-lasting impact on the strategy of American abolitionism. The petition campaign of the 1830s had asked Congress to *use* its constitutional powers to abolish slavery in the District of Columbia. From the early 1840s down to the late 1850s, however, antislavery men in politics sought to *obstruct* the use of federal power, because they believed with Channing that "the federal government has been, and is, the friend of the slaveholder, and the enemy of the slave."[55]

This negative strategy is exemplified by the congressional career of Joshua Giddings. Elected in 1838, Giddings' first approach to the slavery question occurred in 1839 when he presented a petition for abolition in the District. By 1841, in contrast, Giddings was contending that "the federal government had no right, no constitutional power" to wage a war "for slavery" against the Seminole Indians.⁵⁶ The same year there took place the mutiny of slaves upon the *Creole*, sailing from Richmond to New Orleans, who took over the ship, killed one of the crew, and piloted the vessel to Nassau in the British West Indies, where the authorities refused to hand them over to the United States. In support of the British authorities Giddings introduced congressional resolutions, one of which maintained "that slavery, being an abridgment of the natural rights of man, can exist only by force of positive municipal law, and is necessarily confined to the jurisdiction of the power creating it."⁵⁷ God's writ not man's, in other words, ran in international waters. Once on the high seas the slaveholder was a pirate, according to Giddings, and the President who used federal power to protect him was transcending "his constitutional obligations . . . [by involving] our nation in the support of this piracy."⁵⁸

What was true of God's ocean held for His Western territories, too. Senator William H. Seward supplied the key phrase. As a New York lawyer in the late 1830s, Seward had demanded that fugitive slaves receive trial by jury, that all distinctions in constitutional rights based on complexion be abolished, and that a law permitting the importation of slaves into the state of New York be replaced. In 1839, writing to the Governor of Virginia concerning three free Negro sailors who had helped a slave to flee, Seward appealed to the "moral sense of men" which must be obtained "not from the sentiment of one state or people, but from the universal sentiment of mankind." In 1841 he told another correspondent that it was as absurd to speak of property in "immortal beings" as "of a division of property in the common atmosphere." Then in 1850, during the debate on the admission of California, Seward declared: "it is true, indeed, that the national domain is ours; . . . but we hold, nevertheless, no arbitrary power over it." Americans were "God's stewards," charged to enact a "democratic revolution." And so, finally: "There is a higher law than the Constitution which regulates our authority over the domain."[59]

Congressman John Quincy Adams had always believed in higher law. As a young Federalist, responding to the majoritarian doctrine of Paine, Adams wrote: "The eternal and immutable laws of justice and of morality are paramount to all human legislation."[60] This same stance now transformed Adams into an abolitionist hero. He gave only qualified support to Giddings' *Creole* resolutions of 1842, but the contemporary case of the *Amistad* led Adams even beyond Giddings' position. The *Amistad* was a Spanish slaver on which the slaves had rebelled and directed two of their owners to sail them to Africa. The two Spaniards, however, took the vessel westward until finally a ship of the United States Navy apprehended the *Amistad* and imprisoned its briefly liberated Negroes. Adams, consenting under abolitionist pressure to plead for the prisoners' freedom, had to deal with the fact that the *Amistad* was within the territorial waters of the United States when seized. Pointing repeatedly to copies of the Declaration of Independence which hung in the Supreme Court chambers where he spoke, Adams insisted that only the Declaration, only the "law of Nature and of Nature's God," was applicable. Slavery, said Adams, could be justified by "the doctrine of Hobbes, that *War* is the natural state of man." But if the rights to life and liberty "are inalienable, they are incompatible with the rights of the victor to take the life of his enemy in war, or to spare his life and make him a slave." Nature's law of love must take precedence over slavery derived from war, which is "utterly incompatible" with the inalienable right to life.[61]

The *Amistad* case underlines the fact that the higher law variously characterized by Seward as "the Law of Nations," "the Law of Nature, written on the hearts and consciences of freemen," and "the Laws of God,"[62] could be understood either (a) to govern in the absence of positive law, or (b) to supersede positive law when the two were in conflict. Abolitionists in politics naturally tended to the first view. "We propose," wrote Salmon Chase on behalf of the Southern and

Western Liberty Convention in 1845, "to effect this [abolition] by repealing all legislation, and discontinuing all action, in favour of slavery, at home and abroad." It was unnecessary to hold that the Constitution rightly interpreted prohibited slavery everywhere; or that the preamble to the Declaration of Independence should be "regarded as the common law of America, antecedent to, and unimpaired by, the Constitution"; or that slaveholding was contrary to "the supreme law of the Supreme Ruler." It was only necessary to affirm that slavery can "subsist nowhere without the sanction and aid of positive legislation."[63]

But Texas annexation, the war with Mexico, and the Fugitive Slave Law were the work of a federal government doing more to help slavery, not less. "I might stand here till the rising of the morrow's sun," Giddings told the New Hampshire legislature in 1847, "repeating instances in which the Federal Government has lent its aid to the institution of slavery."[64] This chain of events pulled even political abolitionists toward civil disobedience.

The Fugitive Slave Law brought matters to a head. By arming federal marshals with summary powers—much the same powers, incidentally, which civil rights workers in the 1960s sought for federal marshals in the South—and by stipulating that all citizens were bound to assist the marshals on demand, the act forced Northern abolitionists to make a practical as well as theoretical decision. Senator Charles Sumner declared in 1852: "By the Supreme Law, which commands me to do no injustice; by the comprehensive Christian Law of Brotherhood; *by the Constitution, which I have sworn to support;* I AM BOUND TO DISOBEY THIS ACT." He was, he said, "encouraged by the example of our Revolutionary Fathers," who resisted the Stamp Act just as "the Slave Act" should be resisted. The grounds of disobedience were the same in both cases: that the enacting authority had exceeded its proper bounds, and that the law itself circumvented trial by jury. Parallel, too, were the means of resistance. "The country was rallied in peaceful phalanx *against the execution of the Act.*" John Adams had recorded in his diary: "In every Colony, from Georgia to New Hampshire inclusively, the stamp distributors and inspectors have been compelled by the unconquerable rage of the people to renounce their offices." So now, Sumner declared, should the officers under the Fugitive Slave Law be compelled by an aroused public to resign; and so should Congress now, as had Parliament then, repeal a law which had become "a dead letter" through the resistance of the people.[65]

As political abolitionism, which shared the Garrisonian premise that the federal government should cease its aid to slavery, was forced toward the Thoreauvian conclusion that this meant breaking federal laws, it found waiting for it the concept of world citizenship: the belief that "man as man" had duties superior to his duties as citizen of a particular nation.

Perhaps the most eloquent statement of what he called that "grand principle" was by William Ellery Channing in connection with the case of the *Creole:*

This principle is, that a man, as a man, has rights, has claims on his race, which are in no degree touched or impaired on account of the manner in which he may be regarded or treated by a particular clan, tribe, or nation of his fellow-creatures. A man, by his very nature, as an intelligent, moral creature of God, has claims to aid and kind regard from all other men. There is a grand law of humanity, more comprehensive than all others, and under which every man should find shelter. He has not only a right, but is bound to use freely and improve the powers which God has given him; and other men, instead of obstructing, are bound to assist their development and exertion. These claims a man does not derive from the family or tribe in which he began his being. They are not the growth of a particular soil; they are not ripened under a peculiar sky; they are not written on a particular complexion; they belong to human nature. The ground on which one man asserts them, all men stand on, nor can they be denied to one without being denied to all. We have here a common interest. We must all stand or fall together. We all have claims on our race, claims of kindness and justice, claims grounded on our relation to our common Father and on the inheritance of a common nature.

Because a number of men invade the rights of a fellow-creature, and pronounce him destitute of rights, his claims are not a whit touched by this. He is as much a man as before. Not a single gift of God, on which his rights rest, is taken away. His relations to the rest of his race are in no measure affected. He is as truly their brother as if his tribe had not pronounced him a brute. If indeed any change takes place, his claims are enhanced, on the ground that the suffering and injured are entitled to peculiar regard. If any rights should be singularly sacred in our sight, they are those which are denied and trodden in the dust.

It seems to be thought by some, that a man derives all his rights from the nation to which he belongs. They are gifts of the state, and the state may take them away if it will. A man, it is thought, has claims on other men not as a man, but as an Englishman, an American or a subject of some other state. He must produce his parchment of citizenship, before he binds other men to protect him, to respect his free agency, to leave him the use of his powers according to his own will. Local, municipal law is thus made the fountain and measure of rights. The stranger must tell us where he was born, what privileges he enjoyed at home, or no tie links us to one another.

In conformity to these views, it is thought that when one community declares a man to be a slave, other communities must respect this decree; that the duties of a foreign nation to an individual are to be determined by a brand set on him on his own shores; that his relations to the whole race may be affected by the local act of a community, no matter how small or how unjust.

This is a terrible doctrine. It strikes a blow at all the rights of human nature. It enables the political body to which we belong, no matter how wicked or weak, to make each of us an outcast from his race. It makes a man nothing in himself. As a man, he has no significance. He is sacred only as far as some state has taken him under its care. Stripped of his nationality, he is at the mercy of all who may incline to lay hold of him. He may be seized, imprisoned, sent to work in galleys or mines, unless some foreign state spreads its shield over him as one of its citizens.

This doctrine is as false as it is terrible. Man is not the mere creature of the state. Man is older than nations and he is to survive nations. There is a law of humanity more primitive and divine than the law of the land. He has higher claims than those of a citizen. He has rights which date before all charters and communities; not conventional, not repealable, but as eternal as the powers and laws of his being.[66]

IV

But the question, What is to be done? remained in all its urgency. The Kansas-Nebraska Act of 1854, the Dred Scott decision in 1857, only reinforced the trend toward greater federal aid to slavery. The acquisition of Cuba appeared in every national Democratic party platform of the 1850s and there was even talk of reopening the slave trade.

Under this pressure, abolitionists at length abandoned non-violence and discovered in the presidential war power the key to emancipation.[67] One after another the leading abolitionists gave up their pacifism and, when the war came, supported the Northern cause with enthusiasm. In the process, the internationalist ideology summed up in the phrase "My country is the world" was transformed into the creed of holy war.

Sumner was a principal facilitator of the change. An outspoken pacifist as late as his assumption of a Senate seat in 1851, Sumner became, during the Civil War, chairman of the Senate Committee on Foreign Relations. It fell to him to justify what he had previously pronounced unjustifiable. Additional irony lay in the fact that Sumner had been an ardent disciple of Channing's, even assisting in the preparation of Channing's pamphlet on the case of the *Creole*.[68]

In the manner of all converts, the ex-pacifist approached the rationalization of violence with the same earnestness which he had brought to the earlier task. Sumner as much as Channing believed that God's law should prevail in politics. "My great aim," Channing had stated in the *Creole* pamphlet, ". . . is to re-unite politics and morality; to bring into harmony the law of the land and the law of God."[69] Sumner, likewise, placed at the head of his "freedom national" speech in 1852 this quotation from Cromwell: "If any man thinks that the interest of these Nations and the interest of Christianity are two separate and distinct things, I wish my soul may never enter into his secret."

Sumner gave up his pacifism step by eloquent step. In his first great peace address, "The True Grandeur of Nations" (1845), Sumner had mocked at the concept of "defensive

war." Its absurdity, Sumner said, "is apparent in the equal
pretensions of the two belligerents, each claiming to act on
the defensive."[70] His 1849 speech, "War System of the Commonwealth of Nations," was more circumspect. Carefully dis-
tinguishing his condemnation of war as a means of settling
international disputes from the doctrine of nonresistance and
from disparagement of the right to internal revolution, Sumner
went on to say, a little equivocally, about war preparations,

> that, if these preparations are needed at any time, according to
> the aggressive martial interpretation of self-defence in its exi-
> gencies, there is much reason to believe it is because the un-
> christian spirit in which they have their birth, lowering and
> scowling in the very names of the ships, provokes the danger,—
> as the presence of a bravo might challenge the attack he was
> hired to resist.[71]

Amid so much else in this speech that brilliantly expounded
a pacifist position, for example the calculation of how many
colleges and libraries the money spent on armaments would
buy, these distinctions foreshadowed the later position of
Sumner, chairman of the Senate Committee on Foreign Relations.

Commenting in his "War System" speech on Immanuel
Kant's treatise *On Perpetual Peace*, Sumner also carefully
pointed out that Kant's philosophy "contemplated not only
Universal Peace, but Universal Liberty. The first article of
the great treaty would be, that every nation is free."[72] What,
however, if a nation were not free? Would another nation be
justified in intervening, to free it so that peace might be
established? Sumner in 1849 had not yet assembled into a new
theory the thoughts which he would use to justify the Civil
War, but all the essential elements were present in his mind.
Defensive war might be justified; intervention might be a
duty; peace was possible only between free partners.

Elected to the Senate just after the unsuccessful 1848 revolutions in Europe, Sumner urged in his first speech that Congress
extend a welcome to the exiled Hungarian patriot Kossuth.
"I inculcate no frigid isolation," Sumner announced. One had
to remember that the United States was becoming more

powerful: a welcome to Kossuth would be "a precedent, whose importance will grow, in the thick-coming events of the future, with the growing might of the Republic."[73] Sumner struck the same note in a letter to a Faneuil Hall meeting in 1851:

> In reaching across the sea as far as distant Turkey, to plead for the freedom of the fugitive Kossuth, our Republic has done well. . . . The step we have thus taken cannot be the last. With increasing power are increasing duties. The influence we now wield is a sacred trust, to be exercised firmly and discreetly, in conformity with the Laws of Nations, and with an anxious eye to the peace of the world, but always so as most to promote Human Rights. Our example can do much. The magnetism of our national flag will be felt wherever it floats; individual citizens may labor faithfully; but all these will be quickened incalculably by a system of conduct, on the part of our Government, at home and abroad, which, while avoiding all improper interference with other countries, and teaching the beauty of honesty, shall show a prompt and benevolent sympathy with those vital principles without which our Republic is but a name.[74]

Southerners well knew where this kind of talk could lead. Senator Berrien of Georgia moved a resolution against congressional action on Kossuth, which said: ". . . it is due to candor to declare that it is not the purpose of Congress to depart from the settled policy of this Government, which forbids all interference with the domestic concerns of other nations."[75] For if intervention in the domestic affairs of other nations could be sanctioned, why not in the domestic affairs of America south of the Potomac?

In 1856 Sumner was caned on the Senate floor by Congressman Brooks, and did not return to the Senate until December 1859. In his first speech after his return, Sumner saw the establishment of freedom in Kansas as contributing to peace and to the United States' mission of "teaching the nations how to live." On the eve of Lincoln's election Sumner again invoked the idea of a mission for the United States. "We shall have not only a new President," he said, "but a new government. A new order of things will begin, and our history will proceed on a grander scale, in harmony with those sublime principles in which it commenced."[76] Then, after Sumter,

Charles Sumner fashioned a new vision of an American foreign policy. He had played with the key ideas—self-defense; selfless intervention; peace possible only between free partners—in 1849. Now he combined them into an apologia for democratic imperialism which later generations would use at need.

On September 10, 1863, Sumner delivered at Cooper Institute a speech on "Our Foreign Relations" which, studded with scholarship as was Sumner's wont, ran to almost 140 printed pages. It at once attracted international attention as a definitive statement of America's wartime foreign policy.

Sumner began by considering intervention. His task was to deny the legitimacy of French and English intervention on behalf of the South; he chose, not the easy way of rejecting intervention in general, but the more difficult method of defining a type of intervention which was legitimate and then showing that Anglo-French support for the South could not be of this type. Sumner said that intervention was justified *"where one side is obviously fighting for Barbarism."* By this criterion a nation could consistently reject intervention in one case and adhere to it in another; thus Cromwell, rightly rejecting intervention by France in the English Civil War, gloriously insisted on intervening on behalf of God's "slaughtered saints" (as Milton called them) in the Piedmont. "Believing, as I do most profoundly," Sumner continued, "that war can never be a game, but must always be a crime when it ceases to be a duty," it followed that intervention was only permissible if *"obviously on the side of Human Rights,"* of "civilization endangered or human nature wronged."

Moving on to the problem of diplomatic recognition, Sumner again chose the high road which avoided easy answers. Sumner could have argued that since the South was not yet clearly in control of its own territory, American doctrine prohibited French and English recognition. Instead, he proclaimed the idea, which Woodrow Wilson would later apply, that to achieve recognition a government must be "fit." Even were the South to establish *de facto* independence, it should not be recognized, for a slaveholding government could not be a fit member of an international community of free nations.

For the same reasons that European intervention to assist the South was wrong, Northern intervention to destroy the South was right. The war was a Holy War of liberation to defend the Rule of Morality and the law of God. "Thus do I, who formerly pleaded so often for Peace, now insist upon Liberty as its indispensable condition." "There can be no consolidation of Peace without the overthrow of Slavery." "There can be no peace founded on injustice." It was a war to make the world safe for liberty.

"Now, at last," Sumner concluded,

> will the Republic begin to live. . . . It will be more than con-querer. . . . It will know the majesty of Right and the beauty of Peace, prepared always to uphold the one and to cultivate the other. . . . It will confess that no dominion is of value that does not contribute to human happiness. . . . It will stand forth to assert the dignity of man, and wherever any member of the human Family can be succored, there its voice will reach,—as the voice of Cromwell reached across France, even to the per-secuted mountaineers of the Alps. . . . Comforter and helper . . . it can know no bounds to its empire over a willing world.[77]

In this way was the idea of holy intervention, hammered out on the anvil of domestic conflict, transferred to application overseas. Willing or unwilling, the world would have a hard time resisting this benevolent imperialism which insisted, as it bombed and strafed, that it had only come to help.

V

Thus at its very moment of success the American revolu-tionary tradition threatened to become its opposite: a means of oppression and a hindrance to further growth.

The Civil War had brought into the open a latent confusion in the tradition about the causes of war. Most exponents of the revolutionary tradition, like Tom Paine, believed the root of war to be monarchy. Commerce, far from engendering conflict, was understood to be a reconciling agent. If "monar-chial sovereignty" were abolished, Paine argued in *Rights of Man*, "the cause of wars would be taken away"; and added in *Rights of Man, Part Second* that commerce "is a pacific system, operating to unite mankind."[78] From this point of view a society characterized by capitalism and republican government would inherently tend toward peace.

There was another view of war within the revolutionary tradition which traced it to economic causes. John Woolman believed "our Treasures" to be "the seeds of war."[79] William Godwin argued that war was "the growth of unequal property."[80] For those who took this position a republican government, so long as it coexisted with a competitive economy, was as much or more prone to war as any other. With this in mind the Abbé Gabriel de Mably had prophetically warned the new nation in 1785: "You will become a kind of Carthage, at once warlike and commercial; and your ambition, grafted upon covetousness, will strive to play the tyrant over all the neighboring states. . . ."[81]

Charles Sumner's apologia for Northern victory was indeed the argument of a republican government in a "warlike and commercial" society. But Sumner's ideological course was not yet run. In several remarkable speeches in 1870–1871 he partially anticipated the anti-imperialist socialism of the twentieth century.

Sumner characterized the Grant administration's plan to annex Santo Domingo in terms still applicable to many an American intervention. The annexation was proposed under color of agreements with one Buenaventura Baez, who, Sumner said, was "sustained in power by the Government of the United States that he may betray his country." Since three vessels of the United States Navy lay immediately off the island,

> it is not astonishing that there is on the seaboard, immediately within their influence, a certain sentiment in favor of annexation. But when you penetrate the interior, beyond the sight of their smoke, at least beyond the influence of their money, it is otherwise.

Further, an American naval officer had gone ashore in the neighboring republic of Haiti (the western half of the island of which Santo Domingo was the eastern half) saying that

if Haiti interfered in any way with Santo Domingo, "he would
blow the town down." "In my judgment," Sumner said, "rather
than carry out such instructions, he ought to have thrown his
sword into the sea."[82]

Returning to the doctrine of nonintervention he had abandoned in 1863, and condemning in President Grant the free
use of the war power which he had urged on President Lincoln,
Sumner identified the "selfish speculators" involved in the
annexation proceedings; and urged that, rather than molest-
ing the black republic which might become "a successful example of self-government for the redemption of the race,
not only on the Caribbean islands, but on the continent of
Africa," President Grant should turn his energy to protecting
Negroes within the United States from the Ku Klux Klan.[83]

Even more surprising were Sumner's comments on the
Franco-Prussian War. One of the reasons that the war was
wrong, he said, was that "nobody suffers in war as the workingman." There was an "uprising of working-men" afoot in the
world which was a strong force for peace. To illustrate this,
Sumner quoted from the statement on the war issued by the
London headquarters of the First International (which Marx
had written) and from addresses by the International's Paris
and Berlin branches, by workingmen's groups in Chemnitz
and Brunswick, and by the "Workmen's Peace Committee"
of Great Britain, all appealing to their fellow workers in other
nations not to fight.[84]

But this was still the same Sumner who, as a young man,
had condemned Comte, Saint-Simon, and Fourier and asserted that progress must not "shake *property*," who during
the revolution of 1848 had argued for disarmament as a means
"of meeting *socialism*."[85] Individual speculators might be at
fault in the case of Santo Domingo, but nowhere in his writings did Sumner's condemnations reach capitalism as a system.
What was necessary for peace was still republicanism: "To
the people alone can mankind look for the repose of nations;
but the Republic is the embodied people. All hail to the
Republic, equal guardian of all, and angel of peace!"[86]

Accordingly, the vision of "my country is the world" passed into the hands of men and movements prepared to oppose not only monarchy and slavery, but capitalism too.

NOTES

1. Quoted in Henry Wilson, *History of the Rise and Fall of the Slave Power in America* (Boston, 1872), I, 116. The Committee also made clear why Haiti should not be recognized: "the peace of eleven states in this Union will not permit the fruits of a successful slave insurrection to be exhibited amongst them. It will not permit black consuls and ambassadors to establish themselves in our cities, and to parade through our country, and to give their fellow-blacks in the United States proof in hand of the honors that await them in a like successful effort on their part."

2. *Writings*, IV, 370–71.

3. *Fifth Annual Report of the Executive Committee of the American Anti-Slavery Society* (New York, 1838), p. 96.

4. *Liberator*, July 28, 1837.

5. It seems quite as likely that Garrison radicalized Noyes; see Truman Nelson's comment that Garrison "went far beyond Noyes in the frontal attack he made on American society" (*Documents of Upheaval: Selections from . . . The Liberator, 1831–1865* [New York, 1966], p. 119).

6. *Liberator*, July 23, 1836.

7. "Civil Disobedience," *Writings*, IV, 362.

8. Paine, according to an apocryphal story, is supposed to have responded to Franklin's use of this phrase: "Where liberty is not, there is mine" (Alfred O. Aldridge, *Man of Reason: The Life of Thomas Paine* [Philadelphia and New York, 1959], pp. 169, 334).

9. Franklin to Samuel Moore, November 5, 1789, *Writings*, ed. Smyth, X, 63.

10. Franklin to David Hartley, December 4, 1789, *ibid.*, X, 72.

11. "A Friend to the Poor," *ibid.*, VI, 298.

12. "A Summary View of the Rights of British America," *Papers*, ed. Boyd, I, 121.

13. Granville Sharp, *The Law of Retribution; or, a Serious Warning to Great Britain and Her Colonies, Founded on Unquestionable Examples of God's Temporal Vengeance Against Tyrants, Slaveholders, and Oppressors* (London, 1776), p. 6.

14. Richard Price, *A Discourse on the Love of Our Country*, 4th ed. (London, 1790), p. 3.

15. Franklin to Benjamin Vaughan, March 14, 1785, *Writings*, IX, 296. The insistence that international relations should be judged by the same standard as interpersonal relations, as opposed to any theory which treats international relations as a separate realm of *Realpolitik* discourse, is a continuing strain in the radical tradition. Thus Sumner in 1870: "War . . . between two organized nations, is in all respects

a duel . . . differing from that between two individuals only in the number of combatants" ("The Duel Between France and Germany," *Works*, XIV, 9).

16. *Discourse*, p. 6.
17. *Ibid.*, pp. 8, 10.
18. "Rights of Man, Part Second," *Complete Writings*, I, 414.
19. *Garrison, 1805–1879*, I, 202, 219 n.; III, 145.
20. Quoted in Charles Stuart, *A Memoir of Granville Sharp* (New York, 1836), pp. 32–33. Price also became a member; see his letter to Franklin, September 26, 1787 (*The Works of Benjamin Franklin*, ed. John Bigelow [New York and London, 1904], XI, 358–59).
21. *Complete Writings*, I, 274.
22. *Liberator*, November 10, 1837.
23. *Ibid.*, December 12, 1835.
24. *Ibid.*, July 30, 1836.
25. In the same spirit Garrison bitterly criticized the Hungarian nationalist leader Kossuth for failing to speak out against slavery. But commenting in the 1850s on England, where the working class was more sympathetic to abolition than in America, Garrison said that the friends of the slave were "those who sympathise with the starving poor at home . . . those who are interested in the various reforms in England —who are arrayed against the Government and the Government against them" (*West India Emancipation. A Speech by William Lloyd Garrison, Delivered at Abingdon, Mass., on the First Day of August, 1854* [Boston, 1854], p. 4).
26. *Liberator*, June 21, 1839. See also the comment in the prospectus for the *Public Liberator* in 1830: "I go for the people—the whole people—whatever be their bodily dimensions, temporal conditions, or shades of color" (*Garrison, 1805–1879*, I, 201).
27. *Emancipator*, quoted in the *Liberator*, December 10, 1836.
28. *Ibid.*, September 8, 1837.
29. *Ibid.*, April 12, 1834; May 23, 1835.
30. *Speeches of Wilkes*, I, 175; Edmund Wilson, *To the Finland Station* (New York, 1940), p. 215.
31. *Memoirs of Joseph Sturge*, Chs. 10, 20.
32. *Liberator*, December 15, 1837. Peace and temperance were "equally dear to my heart" as the abolition of slavery, Garrison had said in introducing the *Public Liberator* in 1830 (*Garrison, 1805–1879*, I, 201); but in the years 1831–1836 antislavery had monopolized his concern.
33. This quotation is from a chapter entitled, "The Ideology of the New England Non-Resistance Society," in a forthcoming study of American pacifism before World War I by Peter Brock.
34. *Mr. Birney's Letter to the Churches* [1834], p. 1.
35. *A Letter to the People of the United States Touching the Matter of Slavery* (Boston, 1848), p. 29.
36. *An Oration Delivered . . . on . . . July 4, 1837* (Newburyport, Mass., 1837), p. 57.

37. *The Life and Writings of Frederick Douglass,* ed. Philip Foner (New York, 1950), II, 13, 159.

38. Frederick Robinson, "An Oration Delivered Before the Trades' Union of Boston and Vicinity, July 4, 1834," *Social Theories of Jacksonian Democracy,* ed. Joseph L. Blau (New York, 1947), p. 325.

39. Seth Luther, *An Address to the Working Men of New England . . . Delivered in Boston, Charlestown, Cambridgeport, Waltham, Dorchester, Mass., Portland, Saco, Me., and Dover, N.H.* (New York, 1833), p. 9; *An Address Delivered Before the Mechanics and Working-Men . . . July 4, 1836* (Brooklyn, N.Y., 1836), pp. 23–24.

40. *A Collection of the Political Writings of William Leggett,* ed. Theodore Sedgwick, Jr. (New York, 1840), II, 328–30.

41. Arthur M. Schlesinger, Jr., *The Age of Jackson* (Boston, 1946), p. 146.

42. "A Letter to the Hon. Henry Clay on the Annexation of Texas to the United States," *The Works of William E. Channing, D.D.* (Boston, 1880), p. 769.

43. *Ibid.,* pp. 766, 773.

44. As to this idea, see Felix Gilbert, *To the Farewell Address: Ideas of Early American Foreign Policy* (Princeton, 1961); Frederick Merk, *Manifest Destiny and Mission in American History: A Reinterpretation* (New York, 1963).

45. *Works,* pp. 784–85.

46. *Ibid.,* p. 791.

47. *Ibid.,* p. 844.

48. *Ibid.,* p. 847.

49. "Address on the Anniversary of Emancipation in the British West Indies," *ibid.,* p. 921.

50. *Liberator,* May 24, 1844.

51. *Speech of John Quincy Adams, of Massachusetts, upon the Right of the People, Men and Women, To Petition . . .* (Washington, 1838), p. 14.

52. *Niles' National Register,* LXIV (March–August, 1843), p. 175.

53. William Jay to H. I. Bowditch, March 19, 1845, reprinted in the *Liberator,* April 11, 1845.

54. See on this whole subject, Norman Trusty, "Massachusetts Public Opinion and the Annexation of Texas, 1843–1845," unpublished Ph.D. dissertation, Boston University, 1964.

55. Channing, "Emancipation," *Works,* 847.

56. Joshua R. Giddings, *Speeches in Congress* (Boston, 1853), pp. 6, 14.

57. George W. Julian, *The Life of Joshua R. Giddings* (Chicago, 1892), p. 119. This was also Lord Mansfield's doctrine in the Sommersett case. Theodore Weld, who helped Giddings draft the resolutions, had used the Sommersett doctrine as early as the mid-1830s (Gilbert H. Barnes, *The Antislavery Impulse 1830–1844* [Gloucester, Mass., 1957], pp. 137–38). Sumner stressed the same precedent in his "freedom national" speech (*Works,* III, 132, 168). See, in general, James Nadelhaft, "The Sommersett Case and Slavery," *Journal of Negro History,* LI (1966), 193–208.

58. *Speeches in Congress*, p. 39.

59. Jane H. Pease, "The Road to the Higher Law," *New York History*, XL (1959), 119, 121–22, 132–33.

60. *An Answer to Pain's [sic] Rights of Man* (London, 1793), p. 11.

61. *Argument of John Quincy Adams Before the Supreme Court of the United States . . .* (New York, 1841), pp. 8–9, 88–89.

62. *Speech of the Hon. Wm. H. Seward, in the Senate of the United States, on the Admission of California* (New York, 1850), pp. 6–7.

63. [Salmon P. Chase], *The Address of the Southern and Western Liberty Convention . . .* (Philadelphia, 1845), p. 8.

64. *Speech of the Hon. Joshua R. Giddings . . . June 29, 1847* (Concord, Mass., 1847), p. 5.

65. "Freedom National, Slavery Sectional," *Works*, III, 194, 169–76.

66. *The Duty of the Free States, or Remarks Suggested by the Case of the Creole* (Boston, 1842), pp. 14–17.

67. For a compendium of apologias, see [William Lloyd Garrison], *The Abolition of Slavery the Right of the Government Under the War Power* (Boston, 1861).

68. David Donald, *Charles Sumner and the Coming of the Civil War* (New York, 1960), pp. 99 ff.

69. *Case of the Creole*, part II, p. 3.

70. *Works*, I, 16.

71. *Ibid.*, II, 217; see Donald, *Sumner*, pp. 119–20.

72. *Works*, II, 243.

73. *Ibid.*, III, 873.

74. *Ibid.*, II, 445–46.

75. *Ibid.*, III, 2.

76. *Ibid.*, V, 124, 339.

77. *Ibid.*, VII, 376, 410–12, 441, 470–71.

78. *Complete Writings*, I, 342, 400. See also John Quincy Adams, *An Oration Delivered . . . on . . . July 4, 1837*, p. 58.

79. "A Plea for the Poor," *Journal and Essays*, p. 419.

80. *Political Justice*, II, 466.

81. Abbé [Gabriel Bonnot] de Mably, *Remarks Concerning the Government and the Laws of the United States of America . . .* (London, 1784), p. 260.

82. *Works*, XIV, 104, 108–9.

83. *Ibid.*, pp. 188–90, 245–49.

84. *Ibid.*, pp. 68–73.

85. Donald, *Sumner*, pp. 106, 120.

86. *Works*, XIV, 85.

BICAMERALISM FROM BELOW

These chapters have described an American intellectual tradition which began with a concept of freedom shared with Rousseau, and culminated in a critique of alienated labor and nationalism shared with Marx. Like Rousseau and Marx, exponents of this American tradition believed that existing society oppressed its members by alienating human powers which nature intended men to reclaim. Like their European counterparts also, twice in the century 1760–1860 they concluded that deliberate lawbreaking and violent resistance to constituted authority were required to put an end to oppression. From all these points of view the ideas we have been considering are properly termed revolutionary.

Two general patterns emerge from the development of American revolutionary ideas. The first is a dialectical process of ideological response to changing social conditions, such that each sharpening of social conflict calls forth a clarification of ideas previously ambiguous. The second is the vision of a

surprisingly consistent Utopia, a decentralized communal
society not unlike that implicit in the rhetoric of the post-
World War II New Left.

Consider the first of these two patterns. The more diverse
the social coalition supporting revolutionary action, the more
ambiguous was the ideology by which that action was justified. When the action succeeded and the erstwhile partners
in the coalition began to quarrel about next steps, tendencies
latent in the coalition ideology were articulated, set one against
another, and developed to their logical conclusions. Around
one of these tendencies, reflecting the leadership of a particular social group, a new ideology justifying a new coalition
would develop and then in its turn fragment into contradictory
world views as the underlying social movement itself divided.

Thus the coalition which won independence from England
failed to make itself clear as to whether natural rights were
retained undiminished in society, because to have done so
would have forced into the open the question of slavery and
so split the coalition. When that coalition disintegrated into
its Northern and Southern components, it became possible to
describe more explicitly the contradiction between the rights
of man and chattel slavery; moreover the nature of the external situation, which was such that for decades a Northern
majority in both houses of Congress seemed unlikely, prompted
the exposition of a theory of civil disobedience to particular
laws of a republican government. Yet abolitionism too had
its silences, particularly concerning the kind of economic
system which the North intended to transplant southward,
and the economic motives behind the war by means of which
the transplantation was effected. These tensions within the
ideology of the second, abolitionist coalition could be exposed
only by the spokesmen of a third revolutionary movement
prepared to be critical, not just of property in man, but of
private property in all its forms.

Precisely because it spoke for the broadest assemblage of
interests and hence had to be articulated in the most generalized form, the Declaration of Independence could remain the
manifesto of each successive revolutionary movement.

All this is true, or appears so to me. But at the same time, detached analysis of the sort exhibited in the previous few pages will not fully satisfy the reader to whom this volume is addressed: the "critic of the American present." Because he is (or should be) an actor as well as an onlooker, that reader will ask from a historical discussion of ideas the identification of ideas which he can trust. To be dialectically conscious of the ongoing many-sidedness of every historical phenomenon does not altogether speak to his condition. Like Thoreau, he wants firm bottom and rocks in place; he wants visions on which he can lean his whole weight; he wants history to do something more than caution against complete commitment: he wants it to help him commit himself with more precision and effect. Fortunately, the story told in this book exhibits a second pattern responsive to this second kind of need.

I

American radicals in the century preceding the Civil War adhered to an essentially unchanging vision of a decentralized good society. They were prepared to use centralized *means:* Paine and the Revolutionary artisans supported strong national government from the first meeting of the Continental Congress (1774) till the adoption of the United States Constitution (1788);[1] Garrison and Thoreau welcomed the use of the presidential war power for emancipation. Strong national government which might be directly influenced by popular pressure always seemed preferable to local "self-government" by a self-perpetuating clique of gentlemen. Nevertheless the *goal* of the revolutionary tradition was not the aggrandizement of power by a socially concerned federal government. "Society in every state is a blessing," Paine wrote in the first paragraph of *Common Sense,* "but government, even in its best state, is but a necessary evil." That government is best, Thoreau concurred at the outset of *Civil Disobedience,* which governs not at all. Like Marx, American revolutionaries sought a society in which the state would wither away.

In contrast to laissez-faire liberalism, however, the revolutionary tradition did not view freedom and fraternity as mutually exclusive. What American radicals wanted was something more than freedom from government restraint. The government rejected was national. Communal decision-making at a local level was regarded, even by Godwin and Thoreau, as the condition for other freedoms. The revolutionary tradition, moreover, took as its point of departure not property but conscience; and readily imagined that free men might manage their economic affairs in the manner of a family rather than on the model of a market.

The difference between this dream and the worldly wisdom of John Locke will stand out more clearly in illustrations drawn from other times and countries. Few groups have been more devoted to personal freedom than the sixteenth-century Anabaptists, who "when asked their trade and location and station in life in court actions . . . replied, 'No master!' (*kein vorsteer*), for in the New Age only Christ was Master."[2] Yet "from the Sacramentist fellowships, through the peasant camp meetings and parliaments, and the great and small synodal deliberations, . . . the Radical Reformation in its main drive was at once individualistic [and] conventicular. . . ."[3] Long before Dr. Martin Luther King used the term, Rufus Jones wrote of the Anabaptists that "they felt themselves to be 'blessed communities'."[4]

Or consider the spokesman of another tradition for which the peasant community, not the market, was the institutional base. Kwame Nkrumah says in *Consciencism*:

> The traditional face of Africa includes an attitude towards man which can only be described, in its social manifestation, as being socialist. *This arises from the fact* [italics added] that man is regarded in Africa as primarily a spiritual being, a being endowed originally with a certain inward dignity, integrity and value.[5]

Nkrumah continues: "This idea of the original value of man imposes duties of a socialist kind upon us. Herein lies the theoretical basis of African communalism. This theoretical basis expressed itself on the social level in terms of institutions such as the clan, underlining the initial equality of all and the responsibility of many for one."[6]

Vinoba Bhave, the Gandhian land reformer, offers another Third World variant of the vision of a decentralized communal society:

> Sarvodaya does not mean good government or majority rule, it means freedom from government, it means decentralization of power. We want to do away with government and politicians and replace it by a government of the people, based on love, compassion and equality. Decisions should be taken, not by a majority, but by unanimous consent; and they should be carried out by the united strength of the ordinary people of the village. . . . There is a false notion abroad in the world that governments are our saviors and that without them we should be lost. People imagine that they cannot do without government. Now I can understand that people cannot do without agriculture, or industries; that they cannot do without love and religion. I can also understand that they cannot do without institutions like marriage and the family. But governments do not come into this category. The fact is that people really do not need a government at all. Governments grow up as a result of certain particular conditions in society. Men have not succeeded in creating a feeling of unity and avoiding divisions; we have not learned fully the art of working together without conflict, so we try to get things done by the power of the state instead; we try to do by punishment what can only be done by educating the community.[7]

Some contemporary communist societies also relate to this vision by utilizing the heritage of village self-government in building socialism.[8]

In the American tradition, too, rebellion against inherited authorities was not mere "anti-institutionalism." Implicit, sometimes explicit in the American revolutionary tradition was a dream of the good society as a voluntary federation of local communal institutions, perpetually re-created from below by what Paul Goodman calls "a continuous series of existential constitutional acts."[9]

The models for radical American imaginings of a good society were English and American local institutions combining sacred and secular functions: the parish, the congregation, the town meeting. Anglo-American utopianism from the seventeenth to the nineteenth century consistently gravitated to these homely exemplars. Gerrard Winstanley, with his belief that "there cannot be a universal libertie, til . . . universal communitie be established," desired "that the People in . . . a Parish may generally meet together to see one anothers faces, and beget or preserve fellowship in friendly love."[10] Winstanley's Buckinghamshire followers accordingly demanded "the government to be by Judges, called Elders, men fearing God and hating covetousnesse; Those to be chosen by the people, and to end all controversies in every Town and Hamlet, without any other or further trouble or charge."[11] The Levellers, similarly, proposed "to erect a court of justice in every hundred in the nation, for the ending of all differences arising in that hundred, by twelve men of the same hundred annually chosen by freemen of that hundred," and the popular election of "mayors, sheriffs, justices of the peace, deputy lieutenants, etc. . . . in case there be any need, after the erection of hundred courts."[12] An attenuated echo of this custom of neighborhood arbitration was heard at the Constitutional Convention of 1787, when Franklin described how members of the Society of Friends settled their differences through committees of their Meetings without going to court.[13]

It was still of parishes that Paine and Godwin spoke when they put forth their plans for a better England in the 1790s. Proposing as one part of his elaborate scenario for welfare spending in *Rights of Man* that every poor family receive a supplement to assist in the education of its children, Paine suggested that "the ministers of every parish, of every denomination" administer the fund. Sketching the outlines of a still more radical scheme for French land reform in *Agrarian Justice*, Paine advised that "each canton shall elect in its primary assemblies, three persons, as commissioners for that canton, who shall take cognizance, and keep a register of all matters happening in that canton," and administer property inheritance.[14] Godwin, too, proceeded on the assumption that "neighbours are best informed of each other's concerns, and are perfectly equal to their adjustment." It followed that government should be decentralized to the district or parish. The districts should "make laws for themselves, without intervention of the national assembly" so that "political power is brought home to the citizens, and simplified into something of the nature of a parish regulation." General laws would not be needed for these small-scale governments, since "the inhabitants of a small parish, living with some degree of that simplicity which best corresponds to the real nature and wants of a human being, would soon be led to suspect that general laws were unnecessary."[15]

American radicals more often invoked the town meeting, lineal descendant of the English parish. Jefferson urged his native state to subdivide its counties into townships or "wards" similar to the towns of New England. These new bodies would administer the laying out of highways, public elementary education, poor relief, and other matters "relating to themselves exclusively." Supplanting the oligarchical authority of justices of the peace, the townships would give "every citizen, personally, a part in the administration of the public affairs."[16]

Abolitionists, as they built the mighty engine of "self-constituted" abolition societies, expressed similar confidence in the town-meeting prototype. Even Thoreau declared himself ready to pay the local highway tax, "because I am as desirous of being a good neighbor as I am of being a bad subject," and maintained that "when, in some obscure country town, the farmers come together to a special town meeting, to express their opinion on some subject which is vexing the land, that, I think, is the true Congress, and the most respectable one that is ever assembled in the United States." He delivered his celebrated defense of John Brown to just such a special town meeting.[17] One of the most systematic presentations of the town meeting as Utopia came from the New England nonresistant Adin Ballou. "When we get beyond our common Town and Municipal officials, who for the most part render much useful service for small pecuniary compensation," Ballou wrote, government was hardly necessary. It might "triumphantly dispense with its army, navy, militia, capital

punishment," and make room for "reconstructed neighborhood society by voluntary association." Echoing Winstanley
and Godwin, and anticipating Lenin's *State and Revolution*,
Ballou affirmed that if in such a social state an occasional individual "broke over the bounds of decency, the whole force
of renovated public sentiment would surround and press in
upon him like the waters of the ocean."[18]

The vision of a decentralized network of self-governing
communities continued to dominate the speculations of late
nineteenth-century American radicals. Laurence Gronlund, for
instance, proposed a "co-operative commonwealth" which rejected "the whole system of representation." Political parties,
appointments from above, and checks and balances would be
abolished. State and society would become synonymous. All
laws would be passed by referendum, as first proposed by
Robespierre. All public functionaries would be elected (letter
carriers would elect postmasters) and hold office during good
behavior. "Anybody can now construct a Socialist administration in his imagination as well as we can," Gronlund remarked,

> if he will only bear in mind that all appointments are to be
> made from below; that the directors are to stay in office as long
> as they give satisfaction and not longer; and that all laws and
> regulations of a general nature must be ratified by those im-
> mediately interested.[19]

Edward Bellamy, his reputation as a planophile notwithstanding, imagined in his book *Equality* a new society which
"greatly diminished the amount of governing." The representative government of late nineteenth-century America was
a "negative democracy," a "pseudo-republic," a "sham democracy": "the period may be compared to the minority of a
king, during which the royal power is abused by wicked
stewards." The new society would institutionalize initiative,
referendum, and recall. Representative bodies would function
like congressional committees, responsible to the people at
large. Citizens would vote perhaps a hundred times in a year.
Recurring to the famous image in *Looking Backward* of capitalist society as a coach groaning upward in which the rich
man sat at ease, Bellamy said that the government of the

future would operate in the spirit of a wealthy man who liked to drive the coach himself.[20]

There was a resurgence of such thinking in the generation just before the First World War, when a current of speculation about postcapitalist society swept through America and Western Europe. During those years thinkers as different as Rosa Luxemburg and Robert La Follette shared a concern to promote what has since been called "participatory democracy." Between those extremes, men and movements such as G. D. H. Cole, the young Harold Laski, the Industrial Workers of the World, French Syndicalism, and English Guild Socialism sought to envision a modern industrial society which would simultaneously enable the people to control their economy yet decentralize the operations of the bureaucratic state.

That intellectual moment is of particular importance because Marxists and "bourgeois democrats" shared a concern to make politics more democratic, whether through workers' councils—the "soviet," originally, was simply a central trade-union of all workingmen in a locality—or through initiative, referendum, and recall. Marx's idealization of the union of legislative and executive powers in the Paris Commune inspired one strand of this thought, paralleling the persistent reversion of American radicals to the town meeting prototype.

The American thinkers who sought most creatively to develop the traditions which Marxism and native American radicalism share were, in my opinion, Thorstein Veblen and W. E. B. Du Bois. Both these great outsiders—the son of Norwegian immigrants who did not speak English well until he reached college, the Negro who ended his life as a citizen of Ghana—studied philosophy before they became social scientists. Both interested themselves particularly in Kant, the philosopher who had systematized the insights of Price and Rousseau. Veblen's doctoral dissertation on Kant's theory of retribution, Du Bois reading *Kritik der reinen Vernunft* in an attic room of Cambridge with Santayana, are just two more illustrations of the fact that in a surprisingly strict and techni-

cal sense the American radical tradition has been based on a
philosophy of free will. Consistently, its standpoint has been
the self-determining human protagonist rather than the impinging environment. For all his awareness of social condi-
tioning, Veblen followed James and Dewey in insisting that
man was an active agent. Similarly Du Bois, although he died
a Communist, never abandoned the philosophical idealism of
his teachers James and Royce.[21]

Neither man saw community as a threat to freedom. Du
Bois hoped that Afro-Americans could transfer to this country
"the communalism of the African clan."[22] Veblen shared
Marx's affection for primitive communism, as in his description
of those peaceable "savage" communities characterized by
"a certain amiable inefficiency when confronted with force or
fraud."[23] Characteristically, he reserved his most passionate
advocacy of that way of life for an appendix to a book on another subject. Here he praised the old Scandinavian "small-
scale, half-anarchistic, neighborhood plan of society," a "con-
ventionally systematized anarchy regulated by common sense"
in which justice meant a readiness to "live and let live" and
"no public authority and no legally concerted action ordinarily is called in to redress grievances." These little Utopias
had been destroyed by technological advance. But ever since
men

> passed the technological limit of tolerance of that archaic scheme
> of use and wont they have been restlessly casting back for some
> workable compromise that would permit their ideal of "local
> self-government" by neighborly common sense to live somehow
> in the shadow of the large-scale coercive rule that killed it.[24]

II

A natural question arises as to whether the good society
envisioned by Winstanley and Lilburne, Paine and Godwin,
Ballou and Thoreau, Gronlund and Veblen—a league of self-
governing fraternities, a national association of congregations
concerned not only (if at all) with religion but with all the
affairs of life—is hopelessly utopian and irrelevant.

The American Revolution provides a working model for

an answer.[25] In 1775–1776 Americans dismembered and overthrew their government. Whether the American War for Independence was also an American revolution is debatable if one looks to the war's effect on American economy or society: slavery, for example, was left essentially undisturbed. But if revolution is defined in its simplest sense, as the overthrow of constituted authority, a revolution obviously occurred. Not only was the jurisdiction of the British government rejected, but in one colony after another the old political institutions lost their authority and new ones—committees of safety and correspondence, provincial conventions—took power.

It was the work of these committees that convinced Tom Paine that most of what central governments did could better be done by autonomous local bodies. "For upward of two years from the commencement of the American War, and to a longer period in several of the American states," Paine wrote, "there were no established forms of government. The old governments had been abolished, and the country was too much occupied in defense, to employ its attention in establishing new governments; yet during this interval, order and harmony were preserved as inviolate as in any country in Europe."[26]

The American Revolution suggests that the kind of decentralized, self-governing institutions idealized by American revolutionaries of the past (and present) tend to emerge spontaneously in revolutionary situations. When masses of people are drawn into resistance to authorities which oppress them, institutions more accessible to those masses will arise of their own accord. They will arise not because someone envisions them beforehand or desires their appearance on grounds of abstract principle; but because they are necessary. "Common interest," as Paine said, "produces common security."[27] Characteristically, such institutions will be open to anyone who wants to come, not merely authorized representatives, and will in fact take their tone from the physical presence of "the mob." So it was with the French National Assembly, when the common people of the Paris "sections" invaded the galleries; or with the Petrograd Soviet, where (according to John Reed) workingmen debated until exhausted, slept in the halls, then returned to the continuous process of decision-making; or with the Boston Town Meeting, in which, so British officials complained, men voted who had no legal right to.

The democratic movement in the American Revolution has usually been associated with the demand for single-chamber legislatures. What the *ad hoc* bodies of the Revolution signified, however, was the additional insistence that the best of legislatures be continually checked and guided by "the people out of doors," acting through new institutions of their own devising. This was a demand not simply for an end to conventional bicameralism, but for what might perhaps be termed "bicameralism from below."

This process is not inconsistent with the recognition, emphasized by recent scholarship, that the character of the Revolution was defensive. In fact most revolutions, including the French Revolution of 1789, are at the outset not aggressive attempts to achieve something new but efforts to defend what already exists.[28] But in our revolution as in so many others, the mob called onto the stage as puppets remained as protagonists, the institutions devised to transmit orders from above began to send up orders from below, old families found themselves thrust out of places of leadership in favor of "new men," and the words of the revolution's manifesto began to quiver with new meanings.

The process of revolution begins when, by demonstrations or strikes or electoral victories in the context of supplementary direct action, the way a society makes its decisions is forced to change. This is something very real even when the beginnings are small. It means, not just that a given decision is different in substance, but that the process of decision-making becomes more responsive to the ordinarily inarticulate. New faces appear in the group that makes the decision, alternatives are publicly discussed in advance, more bodies have to be consulted. As the revolutionary situation deepens, the broadening of the decision-making process becomes institutionalized. Alongside the customary structure of authority, parallel bodies—organs of "dual power," as Trotsky called them[29]—arise. All that had been closed and mysterious in the procedure of the parent institution becomes open and visible in the workings of its counterpart. Decision-makers, appointed to the former, are elected to the latter. Parallel bodies in different places begin to communicate, to devise means of coordination: a new structure of representation develops out of direct democracy and controlled by it. Suddenly, in whole parts of the country and in entire areas of daily life, it becomes apparent that people are obeying the new organs of authority rather than the old ones. Finally, an act or a series of acts of legitimation occur: *ad hoc* committees lay down their powers, submit to re-election, are given new names. The task becomes building into the new society something of that sense of shared purpose and tangibly shaping a common destiny which characterized the revolution at its most intense.

Of course, such institutional improvisation is made easier if there are pre-existing organizations of the poor. Thus in England, when Elizabethan Puritans abandoned their first hope of reorganizing the national church immediately, they were nevertheless able to go a "longer way round" to revolution by organizing on the basis of "household discussion and education" and "congregational independency."[30] When in the 1640s the revolution came, the Baptist congregations of London ratified the Leveller manifestos and the soldiers of the New Model Army drew on their experience of religious organization to throw up a network of "agitators" to enforce their demands.[31] Similarly E. P. Thompson observes of the apparent quiescence of early eighteenth-century Dissenters: "the resolution of the sects to 'patiently suffer from the world' while abstaining from the hope of attaining to its 'Rule and Government' enabled them to combine political quietism with a kind of slumbering Radicalism—preserved in the imagery of sermons and tracts and in democratic forms of organisation— which might, in any more hopeful context, break into fire once more."[32] And in the industrial revolution, according to the Hammonds, Methodist congregations served English workingmen as improvised schools where they might learn the skills of chairmanship and public speaking required to build trade-unions.[33] In our own time, Negro Baptist congregations in the American South served in the same way as organizational nuclei for the civil rights revolt.

III

What, therefore, calls for final emphasis is the fact that "bicameralism from below" is not simply a utopian vision but a means of struggle toward that vision.

The intellectual origins of the American radical tradition were rooted in men's effort to make a way of life at once free and communal. What held together these dissenters from the capitalist consensus was more than ideology: it was also the daily practice of libertarian and fraternal attitudes in institutions of their own making. The clubs, the unorthodox congregations, the fledgling trade-unions were the tangible means, in theological language the "works," by which revolutionaries kept alive their faith that men could live together in a radically different way. In times of crisis resistance turned into revolution; the underground congregation burst forth as a model for the Kingdom of God on earth, and an organ of secular "dual power."

The revolutionary tradition is more than words and more than isolated acts. Men create, maintain, and rediscover a tradition of struggle by the crystallization of ideas and actions into organizations which they make for themselves. Parallel to Leviathan, the Kingdom is dreamed, discussed, in minuscule form established. Within the womb of the old society—it is Marx's metaphor—the new society is born.

NOTES

1. See, on the democratic *and* centralist ideology of the Revolutionary artisans, my *Class Conflict, Slavery, and the United States Constitution*, essays 3 and 4.
2. Franklin H. Littell, *The Origins of Sectarian Protestantism* (New York and London, 1964), p. 59.
3. Williams, *Radical Reformation*, p. 864.
4. Rufus M. Jones, *Mysticism and Democracy in the English Commonwealth* (Cambridge, 1932), p. 26.
5. Kwame Nkrumah, *Consciencism; Philosophy and Ideology for De-*

colonisation and Development with Particular Reference to the African Revolution (London, 1964), p. 68.

6. Ibid., p. 69.

7. Quoted in the Catholic Worker, October 1964.

8. See, for example, Staughton Lynd and Thomas Hayden, The Other Side (New York, 1967), p. 93. Marx's ambivalence as to the possibility of a direct transition from village communalism to socialism is described in Eric Hobsbawm's introduction to Karl Marx, Pre-Capitalist Economic Formations (New York, 1964), pp. 49 ff.; see also Martin Buber, Paths in Utopia (London, 1949), Ch. 8.

9. "The Empty Society," Commentary, November 1966, p. 58.

10. "The Law of Freedom in a Platform," Works, ed. Sabine, pp. 199, 562.

11. "Light Shining in Buckinghamshire," ibid., pp. 615–16; also "More Light Shining in Buckinghamshire" and "A Declaration of the Well-affected in the County of Buckinghamshire," ibid., pp. 638, 646.

12. "An Agreement of the People of England for a Firm and Present Peace upon Grounds of Common Right and Freedom," quoted in Woodhouse, Puritanism and Liberty, pp. 366–67.

13. Records of the Federal Convention, I, 84.

14. Complete Writings, I, 425, 622.

15. Political Justice, II, 195, 292–94.

16. See especially Jefferson to Samuel Kercheval, July 12, 1816, Works, ed. Ford, XII, 3–15, from which these phrases were taken.

17. "Civil Disobedience," Writings, IV, 380; "Slavery in Massachusetts," ibid., p. 397.

18. Adin Ballou, Christian Non-Resistance . . . (Philadelphia, 1846), p. 232, and Practical Christian Socialism . . . (New York, 1854), p. 425.

19. Laurence Gronlund, The Co-operative Commonwealth: An Exposition of Modern Socialism, 5th ed. (London, n.d.), pp. 120–31.

20. Edward Bellamy, Equality (New York, 1897), pp. 18, 21, 106, 274–275.

21. I make this statement on the authority of Du Bois's close friend and literary executor, Dr. Herbert Aptheker.

22. Dusk of Dawn: An Essay Toward an Autobiography of a Race Concept (New York, 1940), p. 219; see also ibid., pp. 304, 321, for Du Bois's advice to Afro-Americans to "evolve and support your own social institutions" and to build "a co-operative Negro industrial system . . . in the midst of and in conjunction with the surrounding national industrial organization."

23. The Theory of the Leisure Class (New York, 1899), p. 7.

24. Imperial Germany and the Industrial Revolution (New York, 1915), pp. 291–315.

25. If it be objected that the American Revolution is an irrelevant model because it took place in a preindustrial society. I answer that under revolutionary circumstances partly and highly industrialized societies create decentralized institutions comparable to the ad hoc bodies of

the American Revolution. Witness the Russian soviets and the underground organization of the European resistance movements.

26. "Rights of Man, Part Second," *Complete Writings*, I, 358.

27. *Idem.*

28. Thus J. H. Hexter writes of John Pym and the Long Parliament at the outset of the seventeenth-century English Revolution that the Parliament had "more likeness to a shield than to a sword" and "every effort to define the new goal that Pym was working toward fails" (*The Reign of King Pym* [Cambridge, Mass., 1941], pp. 199, 205); and Georges Lefebvre states that the first act of the French Revolution was the attempt by the aristocracy "to reassert itself and win back the political authority of which the Capetian dynasty had despoiled it" (*Coming of the French Revolution*, p. 3).

29. *The History of the Russian Revolution*, tr. Max Eastman (New York, 1932), I, Ch. 11.

30. Christopher Hill, *Society and Puritanism in Pre-Revolutionary England* (New York, 1964), pp. 502–3.

31. Richard Baxter recorded that plowmen and artisans in the New Model Army, "being usually dispersed in their quarters," devoured the Leveller pamphlets and hung on the sermons of army chaplains "that had been in London, hatched up among the old Separatists" (*Reliquiae Baxterianae*, quoted in Woodhouse, *Puritanism and Liberty*, p. 389).

32. *The Making of the English Working Class* (New York, 1964), p. 30.

33. J. L. and Barbara Hammond, *The Town Labourer, 1760–1832: The New Civilization* (London, 1917), pp. 271, 287.

INDEX

Made in the USA
Middletown, DE
05 February 2017